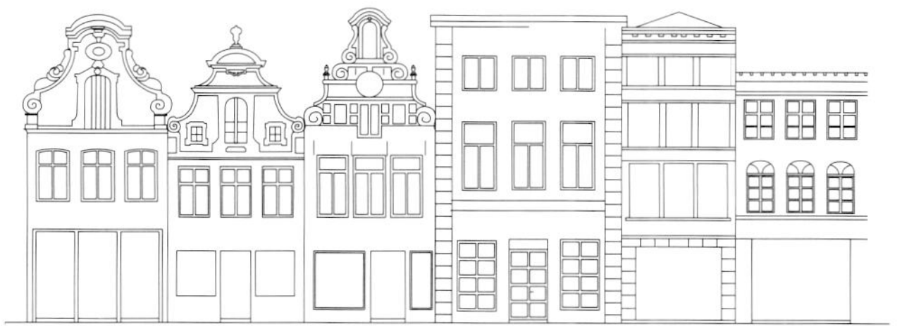

Editorial project:
2020 © **booq** publishing, S.L.
c/ Domènech, 7-9, 2º 1ª
08012 Barcelona, Spain
T: +34 93 268 80 88
www.booqpublishing.com

ISBN 978-84-9936-091-1 [EN]
ISBN 978-84-9936-875-7 [DE]

© Editions du Layeur
Dépôt Légal : 2020
ISBN : 978-2-915126-69-3
Espagne, en mai, 2020

monsa
publications
© 2020 Instituto Monsa de ediciones, S.L.
c/ Gravina, 43
08930 Sant Adrià de Besós, Barcelona, Spain
T: +34 93 381 00 50
www.monsa.com
monsa@monsa.com
ISBN 978-84-17557-22-5

Editorial coordinator:
Claudia Martínez Alonso

Art director:
Mireia Casanovas Soley

Editor:
Lola Gómez Mercader

Layout:
Cristina Simó Perales

Printing in Spain

A HOUSE IN THE CITY

«All the world's a stage,
and all the men and women merely players»

As You Like It (1599)
William Shakespeare

Amsterdam, Dallas, Bangkok, Bari, Dublin, Beijing, Orsay, Mechelen, Mérignac-Bordeaux, Osaka, Kobe, Stuttgart, Anzegem, Ghent, London, Caserta, Melbourne, Nantes, Cavriago, Tokyo, Utrecht, Dublin, Aveiro, Sydney, Victoria, Takatsuki-Osaka, Nishinomiya, São Paulo, Ontario, Toulouse, Kanagawa, Feldberg, Shenzhen... Enter the houses published in this book and you will go around the world.

City Houses travels around several continents collecting samples of single-family homes that reflect the diversity, contrasts and demands of urban life. Residences in America, Europe, Asia and Australia; in cities created in different times and from different cultures. We publish an outstanding selection of works by international architects that project bold and creative designs, which address environmental and territorial, social and economic issues. Projects based on the principles of density, efficiency and flexibility (concepts developed by the architect and professor Christian Gasparini in the epilogue of this book) to meet the needs of the modern city's inhabitants.

The city is a complex construction, conditioned by environmental factors and as a result of diverse planning strategies over time. In the mid-15th century, Leon Battista Alberti wrote in his treatise *De re aedificatoria* that the city was a big house, just as the house was a small city.

In the Middle Ages, the poor had very bad housing. In the cities, their houses were so small that family life was endangered in tiny one-room shacks, with no running water or sanitation, almost no furniture and very few possessions. But there was a different class of people living in the cities who did share in the medieval prosperity: the bourgeois, who would create a new urban civilization. The free city, separated from the predominantly feudal countryside, was something exclusively European. Unlike the aristocrat, who lived in a fortified castle, or the clergyman, who lived in a monastery, or the serf, who lived in a hut, the bourgeois lived in a house.

The typical bourgeois urban house of the 14th century combined residence with work. And the residential part did not consist, precisely, of a series of rooms; on the contrary, there was only a great chamber that ascended to the ceiling, where people cooked, ate, received and slept. These different functions were performed by moving the furniture around as needed. That explains why so much medieval furniture is portable or removable. Something that might seem to be of current interest now. Even in the 16th Century it was rare for anyone to enjoy a room of their own. It took more than a hundred years for these rooms to be designed so that they could be removed from public view. The houses were full of people and one was not yet aware of intimacy. Until the 18th Century, the interior was conceived as a single piece. Individualism would not come until the Enlightenment, the beginning of a radical transformation of the room and the territory. These new spaces in the house were called "private rooms."

In her article *Houses of Great Men* for *Good Housekeeping magazine* (1931) on various aspects of London life, architecture, people and history, the writer Virginia Woolf highlights the ability of some writers to accommodate themselves appropriately: the gift of creating the table, the chair, the curtain, the carpet in their own image. And referring to the London residence of the writer Thomas Carlyle (1795-1881), she comments: "Take the Carlyles, for example. The hour-long stay in house number five on Cheyne Row will reveal more about them and their lives than we will ever know from their biographies. [...] they had no running water. Every drop of water the Carlyles used had to be drawn, by a hand pump, from the well in the kitchen [...] And there is also the wide old stove, with its excessive consumption, where all the containers had to be brought to a boil if one wanted to take a hot bath [...] This tall old house without water, without electric light, without gas heating, full of books, with the air dense with coal smoke, with large beds and with mahogany sideboards [...] During the whole intermediate period of the Victorian era, this house necessarily had to be a battlefield where every day, summer and winter, mistress and maid fought against dust and cold, in search of cleanliness and warmth [...] Of course, thanks to pumping and scrubbing, days of triumph were achieved, evenings of peace and splendour [...] Both husband and wife had talent, they loved each other, but what can love do against woodworm, tin baths and hand pumps on the ground floor ? [...] we thought that Carlyle with a hot water system would not have been Carlyle. And that Mrs. Carlyle without having to kill bugs would have been a different woman than the one we know."

From the Modern Age to Modernity, the idea of an efficient house is being formulated with the incorporation of electricity in homes, important devices like the steam engine and other technologies. Meanwhile, the cities grow in a disorderly and scandalous way, and new types of settlements and urban centres, suburban... with the consequent and everlasting disruption of infrastructure.

Let us hope that, in the merits of a brilliant move, architecture and territory will be combined in a healthy way in our era. Although in my opinion, domestic welfare is something too important to leave to the experts; it is, as it has always been, a matter for families and individuals.

Lola Gómez Mercader

EIN HAUS IN DER STADT

**„Die ganze Welt ist eine Bühne,
und alle Männer und Frauen sind nur Spieler“**

Wie es Ihnen gefällt (1599)
William Shakespeare

Amsterdam, Dallas, Bangkok, Bari, Dublin, Beijing, Orsay, Mechelen, Mérignac-Bordeaux, Osaka, Kobe, Stuttgart, Anzegem, Ghent, London, Caserta, Melbourne, Nantes, Cavriago, Tokyo, Utrecht, Dublin, Aveiro, Sydney, Victoria, Takatsuki-Osaka, Nishinomiya, São Paulo, Ontario, Toulouse, Kanagawa, Feldberg, Shenzhen... Betreten sie die in diesem buch vorgestellten häuser und reisen sie um die welt.

Private Stadthäuser reist durch mehrere Kontinente und sammelt eine Auswahl von Einfamilienhäusern, die die Vielfalt, die Kontraste und die Anforderungen des städtischen Lebens widerspiegeln. Residenzen in Amerika, Europa, Asien, Australien; in Städten, die zu unterschiedlichen Zeiten und aus unterschiedlichen Kulturen entstanden sind. Wir stellen eine herausragende Auswahl von Werken internationaler Architekten vor, die mutige und kreative Entwürfe schaffen, die sich mit ökologischen und territorialen, sozialen und wirtschaftlichen Fragen befassen. Projekte, die auf den Prinzipien der Dichte, Effizienz und Flexibilität basieren – Konzepte, die der Architekt und Professor Christian Gasparini im Nachwort dieses Buches entwickelt hat –, um den Bedürfnissen der Bewohner der modernen Stadt gerecht zu werden.

Eine Stadt ist ein komplexes Bauwerk, das durch Umweltfaktoren und als Ergebnis unterschiedlicher Planungsstrategien im Laufe der Zeit bedingt ist. Mitte des 15. Jahrhunderts schrieb Leon Battista Alberti in seinem Traktat *De re aedificatoria*, dass die Stadt ein großes Haus sei, so wie das Haus eine kleine Stadt sei.

Im Mittelalter hatten die Armen sehr schlechte Wohnverhältnisse. In den Städten waren ihre Häuser so klein, dass das Familienleben in winzigen Einraumhütten ohne fließendes Wasser und sanitäre Einrichtungen, fast ohne Möbel und mit sehr wenig Besitz, gefährdet war. Aber es gab eine andere Klasse von Menschen, die in den Städten lebten und am mittelalterlichen Wohlstand teilhatten: die Bourgeoisie, die eine neue städtische Zivilisation schaffen würde. Die freie Stadt, abgetrennt von der überwiegend feudalen Landschaft, war etwas ausschließlich Europäisches. Im Gegensatz zur Aristokratie, die in befestigten Burgen wohnte, oder zur Geistlichkeit, die in einem Kloster lebte, oder zum Leibeigenen, der in einer Hütte hauste, lebte das Bürgertum in Häusern.

Das typische bürgerliche Stadthaus des 14. Jahrhunderts kombinierte Wohnen und Arbeiten. Und der Wohnteil bestand nicht aus einer Reihe von Räumen; im Gegenteil, es gab nur einen großen Raum, der bis zur Decke aufstieg, in dem gekocht, gegessen, empfangen und geschlafen wurde. Diese verschiedenen Funktionen wurden durch das Verschieben der Möbel nach Bedarf erfüllt. Das erklärt, warum so viele mittelalterliche Möbel tragbar oder abnehmbar sind. Etwas, das jetzt von aktuellem Interesse zu sein scheint. Selbst im 16. Jahrhundert war es selten, dass jemand ein eigenes Zimmer hatte. Es dauerte mehr als hundert Jahre, bis diese Räume so gestaltet wurden, dass sie der Öffentlichkeit nicht mehr zugänglich waren. Die Häuser waren voll von Menschen, und man kannte noch wenig Intimität. Bis ins 18. Jahrhundert war das Interieur als ein einziges Stück konzipiert. Der Individualismus würde erst mit der Aufklärung kommen, dem Beginn einer radikalen Veränderung des Raumes und des Territoriums. Diese neuen Räume im Haus wurden „Privaträume“ genannt.

In ihrem Artikel *Houses of Great Men* für die Zeitschrift *Good Housekeeping* (1931) über verschiedene Aspekte des Londoner Lebens, der Architektur, der Menschen und der Geschichte hebt die Schriftstellerin Virginia Woolf die Fähigkeit einiger Schriftsteller hervor, sich angemessen zu beherbergen: die Gabe, den Tisch, den Stuhl, den Vorhang, den Teppich nach ihrem eigenen Bild zu gestalten. Und mit Bezug auf die Londoner Residenz des Schriftstellers Thomas Carlyle (1795-1881) konstatiert sie: „Nehmen Sie zum Beispiel die Carlyles. Der einstündige Aufenthalt in Haus Nummer fünf in der Cheyne Row wird mehr über sie und ihr Leben verraten, als wir aus ihren Biografien jemals wissen werden. [...] sie hatten kein fließendes Wasser. Jeder Tropfen des Wassers, das die Carlyles benutzten, musste mit einer Handpumpe aus dem Brunnen in der Küche entnommen werden [...] Und da ist auch der breite alte Herd mit seinem übermäßigen Verbrauch, zu dem alle Gefäße zum Kochen gebracht werden mussten, wenn man ein heißes Bad nehmen wollte [...] Dieses große alte Haus ohne Wasser, ohne elektrisches Licht, ohne Gasheizung, voller Bücher, mit Luft dicht vom Kohlenrauch, mit großen Betten und mit Mahagoni-Anrichten [...] während der ganzen Zwischenzeit der viktorianischen Ära, dieses Haus musste zwangsläufig ein Schlachtfeld sein, auf dem jeden Tag, Sommer wie Winter, Herrin und Magd gegen Staub und Kälte kämpften, auf der Suche nach Sauberkeit und Wärme [...] Natürlich wurden dank des Pumpens und Schrubbens Tage des Triumphes erreicht, Abende des Friedens und der Pracht [...] Beide, Mann und Frau, hatten Talent, sie liebten einander, aber was kann Liebe gegen Holzwurm, Zinnbäder und Handpumpen im Erdgeschoss ausrichten? [...] wir dachten, dass Carlyle mit einem Warmwassersystem nicht Carlyle gewesen wäre. Und dass Mrs Carlyle ohne die Notwendigkeit, Wanzen zu töten, eine andere Frau gewesen wäre, als die, die wir kennen.“

Von der Neuzeit bis zur Moderne wird die Idee eines effizienten Hauses unter Einbeziehung der Elektrizität, von wichtigen Geräten wie der Dampfmaschine und anderen Technologien formuliert. Währenddessen wachsen die Städte in einer ungeordneten und skandalösen Weise, und neue Arten von Siedlungen und Stadtkernen, vorstädtisch... mit der daraus folgenden und immerwährenden Störung der Infrastruktur.

Hoffen wir, dass Architektur und Territorium in unserer Ära in den Verdiensten eines brillanten Umzugs auf gesunde Weise miteinander verbunden werden. Obwohl das häusliche Wohlergehen meiner Meinung nach etwas zu wichtig ist, um sie den Experten zu überlassen, ist sie, wie immer, eine Angelegenheit der Familien und Einzelpersonen.

Lola Gómez Mercader

UNE MAISON EN VILLE

« Le monde entier est un théâtre, et tous,
hommes et femmes, n'en sont que les acteurs »

Comme il vous plaira (1599)
William Shakespeare

Amsterdam, Dallas, Bangkok, Bari, Dublin, Pékin, Orsay, Mechelen, Mérignac-Bordeaux, Osaka, Kobe, Stuttgart, Anzegem, Gand, Londres, Caserta, Melbourne, Nantes, Cavriago, Tokyo, Utrecht, Dublin, Aveiro, Sydney, Victoria, Takatsuki-Osaka, Nishinomiya, São Paulo, Ontario, Toulouse, Kanagawa, Feldberg, Shenzhen... Entrez dans les maisons publiées dans ce livre et vous ferez le tour du monde.

Maisons de ville parcourt plusieurs continents pour collecter un échantillon de maisons unifamiliales qui reflètent la diversité, les contrastes et les exigences de la vie urbaine. Résidences en Amérique, en Europe, en Asie, en Australie ; dans des villes créées à des époques différentes et de cultures différentes. Nous publions une sélection exceptionnelle d'œuvres d'architectes internationaux qui proposent des conceptions audacieuses et créatives et qui abordent des questions environnementales et territoriales, sociales et économiques. Des projets basés sur les principes de densité, d'efficacité et de flexibilité - concepts développés par l'architecte et professeur Christian Gasparini dans l'épilogue de ce livre - pour répondre aux besoins des habitants de la ville moderne.

La ville est une construction complexe, conditionnée par des facteurs environnementaux et résultant de diverses stratégies de planification au fil du temps. Au milieu du XVe siècle, Leon Battista Alberti a écrit dans son traité « De re aedificatoria » que la ville était une grande maison, tout comme la maison était une petite ville.

Au Moyen Âge, les pauvres avaient de très mauvais logements. Dans les villes, leurs maisons étaient si petites que la vie de famille était menacée dans de minuscules cabanes d'une pièce, sans eau courante ni sanitaires, presque sans meubles et avec très peu de biens. Mais, il y avait une autre classe de personnes vivant dans les villes qui partageait la prospérité médiévale : les bourgeois. Ils allaient créer une nouvelle civilisation urbaine. La ville libre, séparée de la campagne à prédominance féodale, était quelque chose d'exclusivement européen. Contrairement à l'aristocrate qui vivait dans un château fort, au clergé qui vivait dans un monastère, ou au serf qui vivait dans une hutte ; le bourgeois vivait dans une maison.

La maison urbaine bourgeoise typique du XIVe siècle combinait résidence et travail. La partie résidentielle n'était pas consistuée d'une série de pièces. Au contraire, il n'y avait qu'une grande chambre qui montait jusqu'au plafond, où l'on cuisinait, mangeait, recevait et dormait. Ces différentes fonctions étaient assurées en déplaçant le mobilier selon les besoins. Cela explique pourquoi tant de meubles médiévaux sont portables ou amovibles ; quelque chose qui pourrait sembler être d'actualité maintenant. Même au XVIe siècle, il était rare que quelqu'un puisse profiter d'une chambre à lui. Il a fallu plus de cent ans pour que ces salles soient conçues de manière à pouvoir être retirées de la vue du public. Les maisons étaient pleines de monde et on n'était pas encore conscient de l'intimité. Jusqu'au XVIIIe siècle, l'intérieur était conçu comme une seule pièce. L'individualisme ne viendra qu'au siècle des Lumières, début d'une transformation radicale de la salle et du territoire. Ces nouveaux espaces dans la maison ont été appelés "chambres privées".

Dans son article intitulé « Houses of Great Men » for *Good Housekeeping* (1931), magazine consacré à divers aspects de la vie, de l'architecture, des gens et de l'histoire de Londres, l'écrivain Virginia Woolf souligne la capacité de certains écrivains à s'adapter de manière adéquate : le don de créer la table, la chaise, le rideau, le tapis à leur propre image. Et se référant à la résidence londonienne de l'écrivain Thomas Carlyle (1795-1881), elle commente : « Prenez les Carlyle, par exemple. Le séjour d'une heure dans la maison numéro cinq de Cheyne Row nous en dira plus sur eux et sur leur vie que nous n'en saurons jamais en lisant leur biographie. [...] ils n'avaient pas l'eau courante. Chaque goutte d'eau que les Carlyle utilisaient devait être tirée, par une pompe à main, du puits de la cuisine [...] Et il y a aussi le vieux et large poêle, avec sa consommation excessive, où tous les récipients devaient être portés à ébullition si l'on voulait prendre un bain chaud [...] Cette grande et vieille maison sans eau, sans lumière électrique, sans chauffage au gaz, pleine de livres, avec un air dense de fumée de charbon, avec de grands lits et des buffets en acajou [...] Pendant toute la période intermédiaire de l'ère victorienne, cette maison devait nécessairement être un champ de bataille où chaque jour, été comme hiver, maîtresse et servante luttaient contre la poussière et le froid, en quête de propreté et de chaleur [...] Bien sûr, grâce au pompage et au frottage, des jours de triomphe étaient accomplis, des soirées de paix et de splendeur [...] Le mari et la femme avaient du talent, ils s'aimaient, mais que peut faire l'amour contre les vers du bois, les bains d'étain et les pompes à main du rez-de-chaussée ? [...] nous pensions que Carlyle avec un système d'eau chaude n'aurait pas été Carlyle. Et que Mme Carlyle, sans avoir à tuer des insectes, aurait été une femme différente de celle que nous connaissons ».

De l'ère moderne à la modernité, l'idée d'une maison efficace est formulée avec l'incorporation de l'électricité dans les maisons, d'appareils importants comme la machine à vapeur et d'autres technologies. Pendant ce temps, les villes se développent de manière désordonnée et scandaleuse et de nouveaux types d'établissements et de noyaux urbains, suburbains, suburbain... avec pour conséquence une perturbation permanente des infrastructures.

Espérons que, dans les mérites d'un coup de génie, l'architecture et le territoire seront combinés de manière saine à notre époque. Bien qu'à mon avis, le bien-être domestique soit quelque chose de trop important pour le laisser aux experts, il s'agit, comme cela a toujours été le cas, d'une question qui concerne les familles et les individus.

Lola Gómez Mercader

UNA CASA EN LA CIUDAD

«El mundo entero es un teatro,
y todos los hombres y mujeres meros actores»

Como gustéis (1599)
William Shakespeare

Ámsterdam, Dallas, Bangkok, Bari, Dublín, Pekín, Orsay, Mechelen, Mérignac-Burdeos, Osaka, Kobe, Stuttgart, Anzegem, Gante, Londres, Caserta, Melbourne, Nantes, Cavriago, Tokio, Utrecht, Dublín, Aveiro, Sídney, Victoria, Takatsuki-Osaka, Nishinomiya, São Paulo, Ontario, Toulouse, Kanagawa, Feldberg, Shenzhen... entrad en las casas publicadas en este libro y daréis la vuelta al mundo.

The New Townhouse recorre varios continentes recogiendo un muestrario de viviendas unifamiliares que son el reflejo de la diversidad, de los contrastes y de las exigencias de la vida urbana. Residencias en América, Europa, Asia, Australia; en ciudades creadas en diferentes épocas y de diversas culturas. Publicamos una selección destacada de obras de arquitectos internacionales que proyectan diseños audaces y creativos, que abordan cuestiones ambientales y del territorio, sociales y económicas. Proyectos basados en los principios de densidad, eficiencia y flexibilidad —conceptos que desarrolla el arquitecto y profesor Christian Gasparini en el epílogo de este libro—, para satisfacer las necesidades de los habitantes de la ciudad moderna.

La ciudad es una construcción compleja, condicionada por factores ambientales y como resultado de diversas estrategias de planeamiento en el tiempo. A mediados del siglo XV, Leon Battista Alberti plasmaba en su tratado *De re aedificatoria* que la ciudad era una casa grande, lo mismo que la casa era una ciudad pequeña.

En la Edad Media los pobres tenían unas viviendas malísimas. En las ciudades, sus casas eran tan pequeñas que la vida familiar corría peligro en diminutas zahúrdas de una sola habitación, sin agua corriente ni saneamiento, casi ningún mueble y muy pocas posesiones. Pero había una clase diferente de personas que vivían en las ciudades que sí compartían la prosperidad medieval: los burgueses, que crearían una nueva civilización urbana. La ciudad libre, separada del campo predominantemente feudal, era algo exclusivamente europeo. Al contrario que el aristócrata, que vivía en un castillo fortificado, o el clérigo, que vivía en un monasterio, o el siervo, que vivía en una choza, el burgués vivía en una casa.

La casa urbana burguesa típica del siglo XIV combinaba la residencia con el trabajo. Y la parte residencial no consistía, precisamente, en una serie de habitaciones; por el contrario, no había más que una gran cámara que ascendía hasta el cielo raso, donde la gente cocinaba, comía, recibía y dormía. Esas diferentes funciones se realizaban mediante el cambio de sitio de los muebles según las necesidades. Eso explica por qué tantos muebles medievales son portátiles o desmontables. Algo que podría parecer ahora de plena actualidad. Todavía en el siglo XVI era raro que alguien disfrutara de una habitación propia. Tuvieron que pasar más de cien años hasta que se concibieron estas estancias a las que se podía uno retirar para desaparecer de la vista del público.

Las casas estaban llenas de gente y no se tenía, aún, conciencia de la intimidad. Hasta el siglo XVIII, el interior se concebía como una sola pieza. El individualismo no llegará hasta la Ilustración, inicio de una transformación radical de la habitación y el territorio. A esos nuevos espacios de la casa se les llamó «habitaciones privadas».

En su artículo *Casas de grandes hombres* para la revista *Good Housekeeping* (1931) sobre distintos aspectos de la vida, la arquitectura, las gentes y la historia de Londres, la escritora Virginia Woolf destaca la facultad de alojarse adecuadamente de algunos escritores: el don de crear la mesa, la silla, la cortina, la alfombra a su propia imagen. Y refiriéndose a la residencia en Londres del matrimonio del escritor Thomas Carlyle (1795-1881), comenta: «Fijémonos en los Carlyle, por ejemplo. La estancia, durante una hora, en la casa número cinco de Cheyne Row nos revelará más acerca de ellos y de su vida de lo que jamás podamos llegar a saber mediante sus biografías. [...] no tenían agua corriente. Cada gota de agua que los Carlyle usaban tenía que ser extraída, mediante una bomba de mano, del pozo situado en la cocina [...] Y allí está también el ancho y viejo fogón, con su excesivo consumo, en el que era preciso poner a hervir todos los recipientes si se quería tomar un baño caliente [...] Esta alta y vieja casa sin agua, sin luz eléctrica, sin calefacción de gas, repleta de libros, con el aire denso de humo de carbón, con grandes camas y con aparadores de caoba [...] Durante todo el periodo intermedio de la época victoriana, esta casa forzosamente tuvo que ser un campo de batalla en el que todos los días, verano e invierno, ama y criada lucharon contra el polvo y el frío, en busca de la limpieza y del calor [...] Desde luego, gracias al bombeo y al fregoteo se consiguieron días de triunfo, veladas de paz y esplendor [...] Los dos, marido y mujer, tenían talento, se amaban, pero ¿qué puede el amor contra el carcoma, las bañeras de hojalata y las bombas manuales en la planta baja? [...] pensamos que Carlyle con instalación de agua caliente no hubiera sido Carlyle. Y que la señora Carlyle sin tener que matar bichitos hubiera sido una mujer diferente de la que conocemos».

De la Edad Moderna a la Modernidad se va formulando la idea de casa eficiente con la incorporación de la electricidad en las viviendas, importantes ingenios como la máquina de vapor y otras tecnologías. Mientras tanto, las ciudades crecen de forma desordenada y escandalosa, y se configuran nuevos tipos de asentamientos y núcleos urbanos, suburbanos, de extrarradio... con el consecuente y sempiterno desajuste de las infraestructuras.

Esperemos que, en méritos de una genial jugada, arquitectura y territorio se combinen sanamente en nuestra Era. Aunque a mi juicio, el bienestar doméstico es algo demasiado importante para dejárselo a los expertos; es, igual que ha sido siempre, asunto de las familias y las personas.

Lola Gómez Mercader

STAHL HOUSE. CASE STUDY HOUSE # 22
Los Angeles, California, United States. 1960

The work of architect Pierre Koenig is a mythical reference to the Californian residential architecture of the mid-20th century, which exemplifies the American dream of living in the suburbs.

HAUS STAHL. FALLSTUDIE HAUS # 22
Los Angeles, Kalifornien, Vereinigte Staaten. 1960

Das Werk des Architekten Pierre Koenig ist eine mythische Referenz an die kalifornische Wohnarchitektur der Mitte des 20. Jahrhunderts, die den amerikanischen Traum vom Leben in den Vorstädten veranschaulicht.

MAISON STAHL. CASE STUDY HOUSE # 22
Los Angeles, Californie, États-Unis. 1960

L'œuvre de l'architecte Pierre Koenig est une référence mythique à l'architecture résidentielle californienne du milieu du XXe siècle, qui illustre le rêve américain de vivre en banlieue.

CASA STAHL. CASE STUDY HOUSE # 22
Los Ángeles, California, Estados Unidos. 1960

La obra del arquitecto Pierre Koenig es una referencia mítica de la arquitectura residencial californiana de mitad del siglo XX, que ejemplifica el sueño americano de vida en los suburbios.

70F

BAS TEN BRINKE

Bas ten Brinke (1972) studied architecture and urban development at Eindhoven University of Technology. His very distinctive signature was quick to make an impression; 'Spartan hypermodernism', is how one colleague dubbed it. With top marks for his graduation project, he was immediately recruited by a leading architectural office. At the age of 27 he established *70F architecture,* so that he could build according to his own aesthetic vision. After all, the simpler the design, the more time it takes to get it right.
Now, twenty years on, his passion for architecture remains as strong as ever.

http://70f.com
info@70f.com

Bas ten Brinke (*1972) studierte Architektur und Stadtentwicklung an der Technischen Universität Eindhoven. Seine sehr ausgeprägte Handschrift hinterließ schnell einen bleibenden Eindruck; „spartanische Hypermodernität", wie ein Kollege es nannte. Mit Bestnoten für sein Abschlussprojekt wurde er sofort von einem führenden Architekturbüro eingestellt. Im Alter von 27 Jahren etablierte er die 70F-Architektur, um nach seiner eigenen ästhetischen Vision bauen zu können. Denn je einfacher der Entwurf, desto mehr Zeit braucht man, um ihn richtig hinzubekommen.
Heute, siebzehn Jahre später, ist seine Leidenschaft für die Architektur so stark wie eh und je.

Bas ten Brinke (1972) a étudié l'architecture et le développement urbain à l'université de technologie d'Eindhoven. Sa signature très particulière a rapidement fait impression ; un collègue l'a surnommée «l'hypermodernisme spartiate». Ayant obtenu les meilleures notes pour son projet de fin d'études, il a immédiatement été recruté par un grand bureau d'architectes. À l'âge de 27 ans, il crée 70F architecture, afin de pouvoir construire selon sa propre vision esthétique. Après tout, plus la conception est simple, plus il faut de temps pour la réaliser.
Aujourd'hui, dix-sept ans plus tard, sa passion pour l'architecture reste plus forte que jamais.

Bas ten Brinke (1972) estudió arquitectura y desarrollo urbano en la Universidad Tecnológica de Eindhoven. Su estilo, muy distintivo, no tardó en causar impresión; «hipermodernismo espartano», es como lo denominó un colega. Con las mejores notas por su proyecto de graduación, fue inmediatamente reclutado por una importante oficina de arquitectura. A la edad de 27 años se estableció por su cuenta, abriendo 70F, para poder construir según su propia visión estética. Después de todo, cuanto más simple es el diseño, más tiempo se necesita para conseguirlo.
Ahora, veinte años después, su pasión por la arquitectura sigue siendo tan fuerte como siempre.

HOME2.0

HOME 2.0 includes two terraced houses to modern families with children and puts the concept of 'home' in time, place and society. HOME 2.0 is an ode to family life, but also provides space to relax. Each floor has a different focus. On the ground floor 'living' is the central theme. Here are the living room and kitchen. The first floor is the domain of the children. They have their own bathroom and plenty of storage space on the spacious landing. On the second floor, the parent-floor, are the master bedroom with working space, an en-suite bathroom and a lounge area. Anyone can easily switch between 'being together' and 'being by yourself'.

HOME 2.0 umfasst zwei Reihenhäuser für moderne Familien mit Kindern und setzt das Konzept des „Zuhauses" in Zeit, Ort und Gesellschaft um. HOME 2.0 ist eine Ode an das Familienleben, bietet aber auch Raum für den Rückzug. Jede Etage hat einen anderen Schwerpunkt. Im Erdgeschoss ist „Wohnen" das zentrale Thema. Hier befinden sich das Wohnzimmer und die Küche. Das erste Stockwerk ist die Domäne der Kinder. Sie haben ein eigenes Bad und viel Stauraum auf dem geräumigen Treppenabsatz. Im zweiten Stock, dem Elterngeschoss, befinden sich das Hauptschlafzimmer mit Arbeitsplätzen, ein eigenes Bad und ein Aufenthaltsbereich. Jeder kann leicht zwischen „Zusammensein" und „Alleinsein" wechseln.

HOME 2.0 comprend deux maisons mitoyennes pour les familles modernes avec enfants et place le concept de «maison» dans le temps, l'espace et la société. HOME 2.0 est une ode à la vie de famille, mais elle offre également un espace de retraite. Chaque étage a un objectif différent. Au rez-de-chaussée, le thème central est «la vie». C'est là que se trouvent le salon et la cuisine. Le premier étage est le domaine des enfants. Ils ont leur propre salle de bain et de nombreux espaces de rangement sur le vaste palier. Au deuxième étage, celui des parents, se trouve la chambre principale avec des postes de travail, une salle de bain privative et un coin salon. Tout le monde peut facilement alterner entre «être ensemble» et «être seul».

El proyecto HOME 2.0 incluye dos casas adosadas para dos familias modernas con niños, colocando el concepto de «hogar» en el tiempo, el lugar y la sociedad. HOME 2.0 es una oda a la vida familiar, pero también proporciona espacio para el descanso. Cada piso tiene un enfoque diferente. En la planta baja, el concepto «vivir» es el tema central. Aquí se encuentran la sala de estar y la cocina. El primer piso es el dominio de los niños. Tienen su propio baño y mucho espacio de almacenamiento. En la segunda planta, la planta de los padres, se encuentra el dormitorio principal con una zona de trabajo, un baño completo y una sala de estar. Se trata de un proyecto en el que cualquiera puede pasar fácilmente del «estar juntos» al «estar solo».

LOCATION
Almere, Netherlands

PHOTOS
© Luuk Kramer

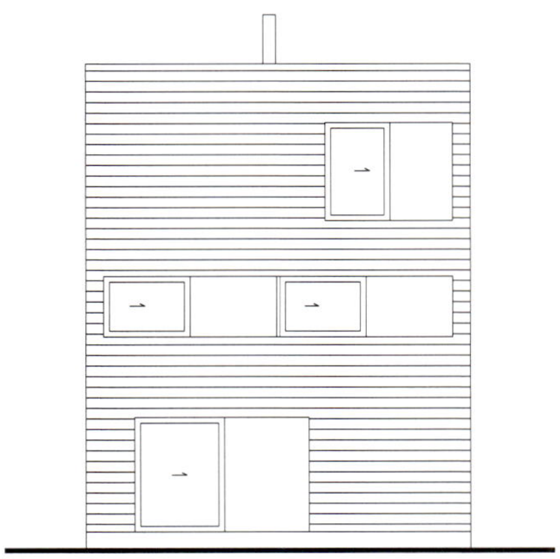

Back elevation

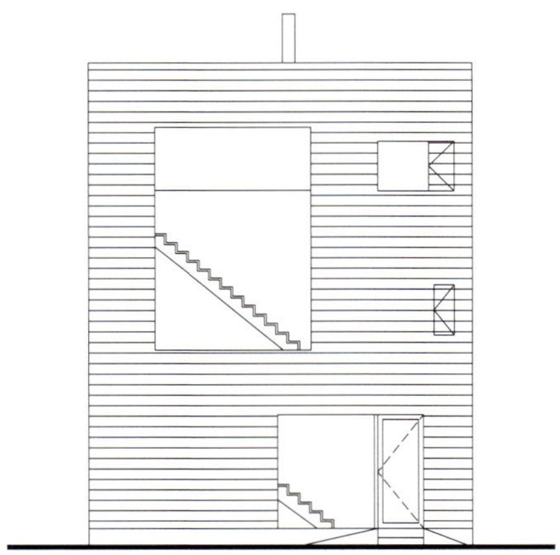

Front elevation

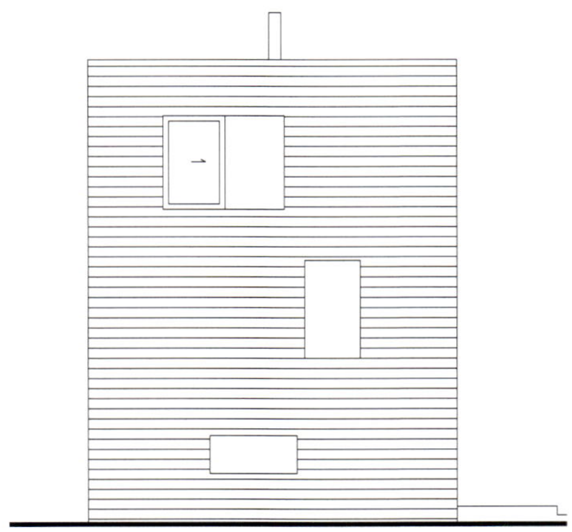

Side elevation

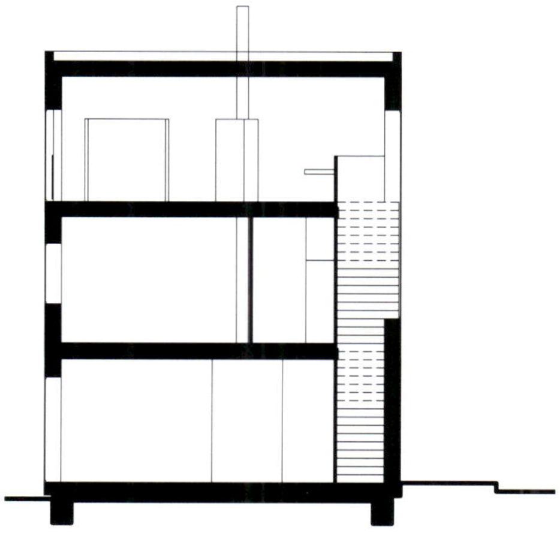

A-A′ section

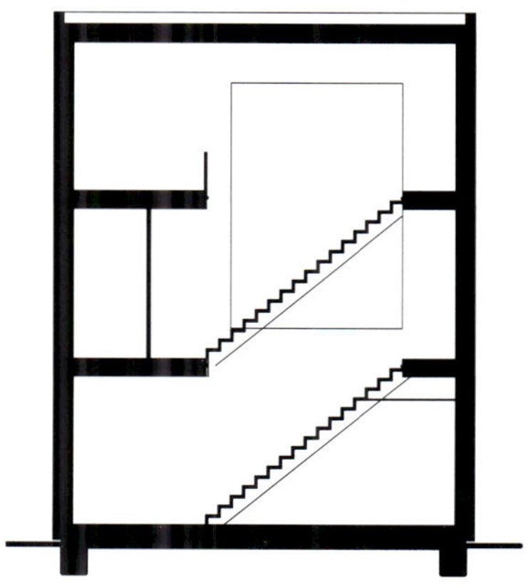

B-B′ section

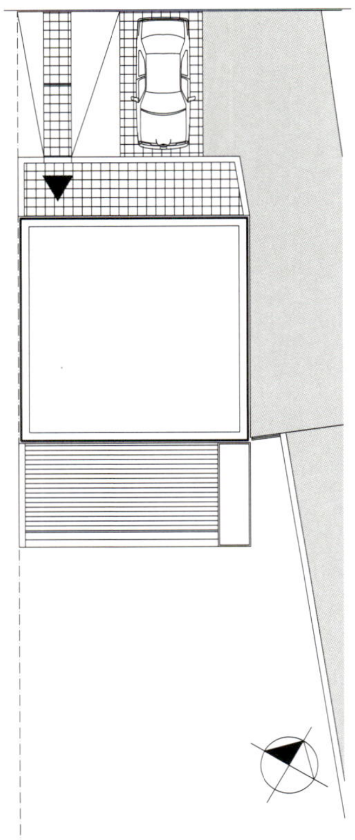

Site plan

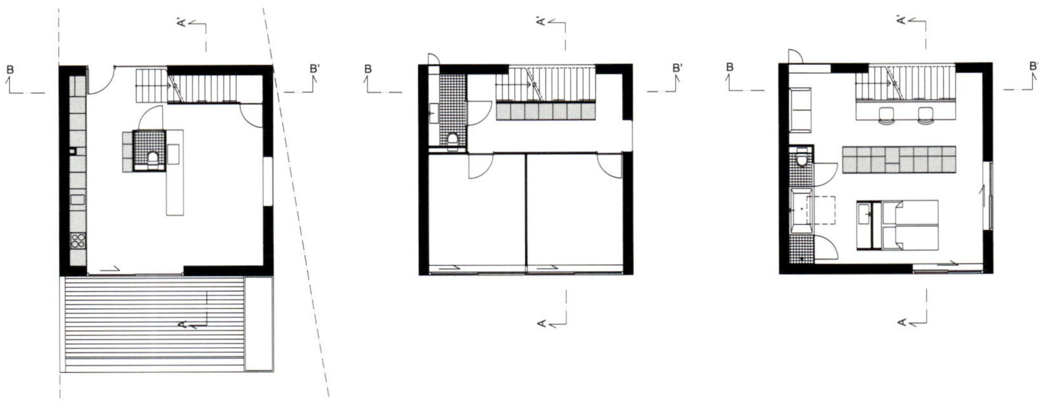

Floor plans

A.GRUPPO

ANDREW NANCE & THAD REEVES

A.GRUPPO is a design + build architecture firm that specializes in sustainable, modern residential and commercial builds throughout the state of Texas. With two Texas offices in the heart of Dallas and San Marcos, A.GRUPPO has proven themselves with an array of unique and timeless buildings and continues to seek innovation, sustainability, and craftsmanship with every new project.
A.GRUPPO architects was founded in 2005 by Andrew Nance and Thad Reeves. The office has been positioned as a vehicle for collaboration between themselves and other designers, architects, manufacturers, and most importantly, clients.
A.GRUPPO engages in a broad range of project types and scales from intimately detailed interior "installations" to large scale master planning and speculative development.

www.agruppo.com
info@agruppo.com

Die A.GRUPPO ist ein Design+Build-Architekturbüro, das sich auf nachhaltige, moderne Wohn- und Gewerbebauten im gesamten Bundesstaat Texas spezialisiert hat. Mit zwei Büros in Texas im Herzen von Dallas und San Marcos hat sich die A.GRUPPO mit einer Reihe einzigartiger und zeitloser Gebäude bewährt und sucht bei jedem neuen Projekt nach Innovation, Nachhaltigkeit und handwerklichem Können.
A.GRUPPO architects wurde 2005 von Andrew Nance und Thad Reeves gegründet. Das Büro wurde als Vehikel für die Zusammenarbeit zwischen ihnen und anderen Designern, Architekten, Herstellern und vor allem Kunden positioniert.
A.GRUPPO beschäftigt sich mit einem breiten Spektrum von Projekttypen und -größen, von intimen, detaillierten „Inneninstallationen" bis hin zu großangelegten Masterplanungen und visionären Entwicklungen.

A.GRUPPO est un cabinet d'architecture spécialisé dans la conception et la construction de bâtiments résidentiels et commerciaux durables et modernes dans tout l'État du Texas. Avec deux bureaux au Texas, au cœur de Dallas et de San Marcos, A.GRUPPO a fait ses preuves avec un éventail de bâtiments uniques et intemporels et continue à rechercher l'innovation, la durabilité et le savoir-faire artisanal avec chaque nouveau projet.
A.GRUPPO architects a été fondé en 2005 par Andrew Nance et Thad Reeves. Le bureau a été positionné comme un véhicule de collaboration entre eux et d'autres concepteurs, architectes, fabricants et, surtout, clients.
A.GRUPPO s'engage dans un large éventail de projets, de types et d'échelles allant des «installations» intérieures intimement détaillées à la planification générale à grande échelle et au développement spéculatif.

A.GRUPPO es una empresa de arquitectura, diseño y construcción que se especializa en proyectos residenciales y comerciales modernos y sostenibles en el estado de Texas. Con dos oficinas en el corazón de Dallas y San Marcos, A.GRUPPO se ha probado a sí mismo con una serie de edificios únicos e intemporales y continúa buscando la innovación, la sostenibilidad y la artesanía con cada nuevo proyecto.
A.GRUPPO fue fundada en 2005 por Andrew Nance y Thad Reeves. La oficina se ha posicionado como un vehículo para la colaboración con otros diseñadores, arquitectos, fabricantes, y lo más importante, clientes.
A.GRUPPO se dedica a una amplia gama de tipos y escalas de proyectos, desde instalaciones de interiores íntimamente detalladas hasta la planificación a gran escala.

TRAMMEL RESIDENCE

The owners purchased two lots to develop two different homes. After going through the design process, they decided to change one of the designs to a custom home for themselves. The only access to the site is from the street, which required the garage to be located on the front of the house. Once accepted as a main design element, the garage was used to help to define the entry courtyard, guiding the adjacent home to the east.
It is a single story house with three bedrooms and two bathrooms and a series of outdoor spaces. The house lays out as a bar running the length of the site, with two wings facing east.

Die Eigentümer kauften zwei Grundstücke, um zwei Spezialimmobilien zu entwickeln. Nachdem sie den Entwurfsprozess durchlaufen hatten, beschlossen sie, einen der Entwürfe in ein individuelles Haus für sich selbst zu ändern. Der einzige Zugang zum Grundstück ist von der Straße aus, weshalb sich die Garage auf der Vorderseite des Hauses befinden musste. Sobald die Garage als herausragendes Designelement akzeptiert war, wurde sie zur Definition des Eingangshofes verwendet, wobei die Realisierung des östlich angrenzenden Hauses den Hof vervollständigen wird.
Es handelt sich um ein einstöckiges Haus mit drei Schlafzimmern und zwei Badezimmern und einer Reihe von Außenräumen. Das Haus ist als Bar über die gesamte Länge des Grundstücks angelegt, wobei sich zwei Flügel nach Osten hin erstrecken.

Les propriétaires ont acheté deux terrains pour y construire deux maisons. Après avoir suivi le processus de conception, ils ont décidé de modifier l'un des modèles pour en faire une maison sur mesure pour eux. Le seul accès au site se fait par la rue, ce qui a nécessité l'installation d'un garage sur la façade de la maison. Une fois accepté comme un élément de conception important, le garage a été utilisé pour aider à définir la cour d'entrée, en réalisant que la maison adjacente à l'Est complétera la cour.
Il s'agit d'une maison d'un seul étage avec trois chambres et deux salles de bain et une série d'espaces extérieurs. La maison se présente comme un bar sur toute la longueur du site, avec deux ailes s'étendant à l'Est.

Los dueños compraron dos terrenos para desarrollar dos casas de lujo. Después de pasar por el proceso de diseño, decidieron cambiar de idea y quedarse con una de las casas. El único acceso a la propiedad es desde la calle, lo que requirió que el garaje se ubicara en la parte delantera de la casa. Una vez aceptado como un elemento de diseño importante, el garaje se utilizó para ayudar a definir el patio de entrada.
Se trata de una casa de una sola planta con tres dormitorios y dos baños y una serie de espacios exteriores, con dos alas que se extienden hacia el este.

LOCATION
Dallas, Texas, USA

PHOTOS
© Dror Baldinger FAIA Architectural Photography

PROJECT ARCHITECT
Jon Beck

6522

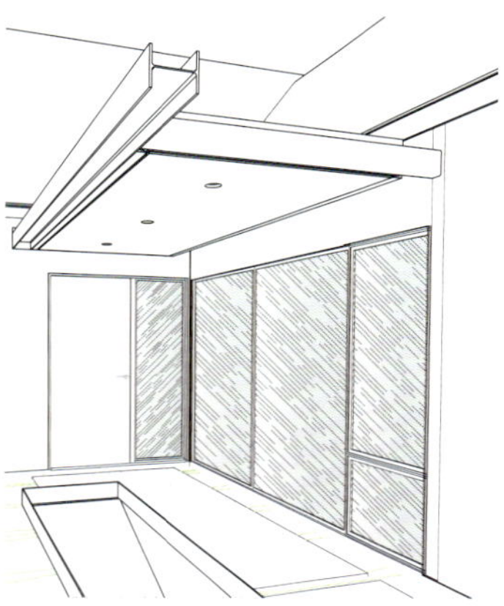

Perspective

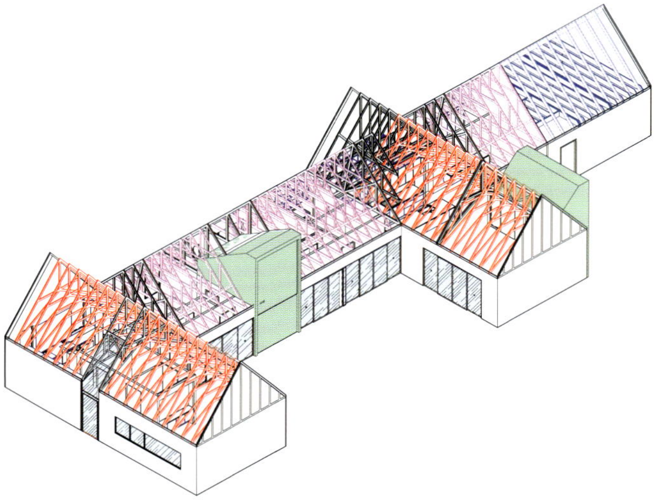

Axonometry roof diagram

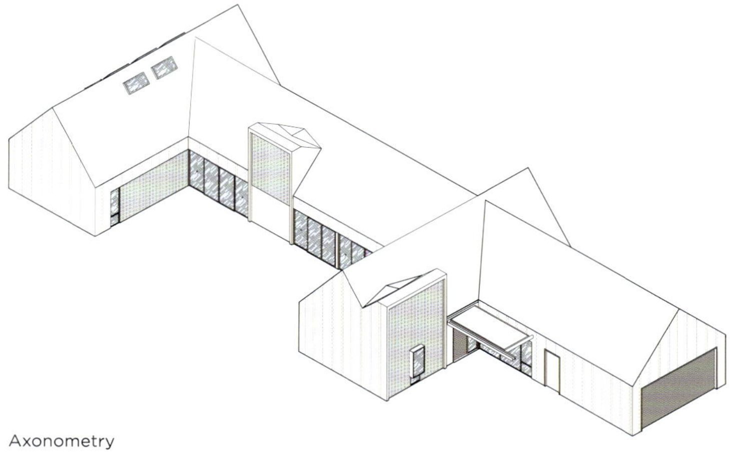

Axonometry

Elevations

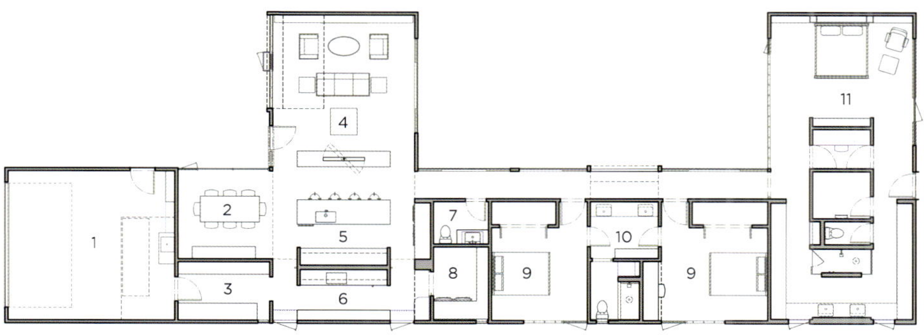

Floor plan

1. Garage
2. Dining room
3. Mudroom
4. Living room
5. Kitchen
6. Butler kitchen
7. Powder room
8. Utility room
9. Bedroom
10. Bathroom
11. Master suite

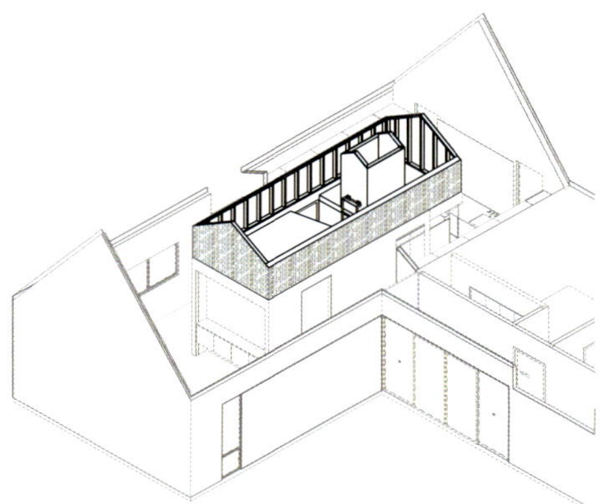

Floor plan

ANONYM
STUDIO

This untitled "ANONYM" is a design studio based in Bangkok, Thailand. Our design phi-osophy is focusing on balancing relationship between spaces, people and contexts as a esult for meaningful design and unique characteristic space that belong to each project. We believe that the great design can be created with diversity, innovation and environ-mentally-friendly condition.
Founded by Phongphat Ueasangkhomset and Parnduangjai Roojnawate, we specialize n architectural and interior design, providing comprehensive design services including architectural design, master planning, landscape design and feasibility study.
We seek for creative solutions for our clients, helping them fulfill their dreams, archive heir goals and find their happiness.

www.anonymstudio.com
anonym@anonymstudio.com

Dieses unbenannte „ANONYM" ist ein Designstudio mit Sitz in Bangkok, Thailand. Un-sere Designphilosophie konzentriert sich darauf, die Beziehung zwischen Räumen, Men-schen und Kontexten auszubalancieren, um ein sinnvolles Design und einen einzigarti-gen charakteristischen Raum zu schaffen, die zu jedem Projekt gehören. Wir glauben, dass großartiges Design mit Vielfalt, Innovation und Umweltfreundlichkeit geschaffen werden kann.
Gegründet von Phongphat Ueasangkhomset und Parnduangjai Roojnawate, sind wir auf Architektur und Innenarchitektur spezialisiert und bieten umfassende Design-Dienst-leistungen an, darunter Architekturdesign, Masterplanung, Landschaftsgestaltung und Machbarkeitsstudien.
Für unsere Kunden suchen wir nach kreativen Lösungen, die ihnen helfen, ihre Träume zu erfüllen, ihre Ziele zu archivieren und ihr Glück zu finden.

« ANONYM » est un studio de design basé à Bangkok, en Thaïlande. Notre philosophie de conception se concentre sur l'équilibre des relations entre les espaces, les personnes et les contextes, ce qui permet d'obtenir un design significatif et un espace caractéris-tique unique qui appartient à chaque projet. Nous croyons que le grand design peut être créé dans la diversité, l'innovation et le respect de l'environnement.
Fondée par Phongphat Ueasangkhomset et Parnduangjai Roojnawate, nous sommes spécialisés dans l'architecture et le design d'intérieur et fournissons des services com-plets de design, y compris la conception architecturale, le plan directeur, le design pay-sager et l'étude de faisabilité.
Nous recherchons des solutions créatives pour nos clients afin de les aider à réaliser leurs rêves, à atteindre leurs objectifs et à trouver leur bonheur.

«ANONYM» es un estudio de diseño con sede en Bangkok, Tailandia. Nuestra filosofía de diseño se centra en el equilibrio de la relación entre los espacios, las personas y los con-textos como resultado de un diseño significativo y un espacio único para cada proyecto. Creemos que el gran diseño puede ser creado a través de la diversidad, la innovación y la condición ecológica.
Fundada por Phongphat Ueasangkhomset y Parnduangjai Roojnawate, nos especiali-zamos en el diseño arquitectónico y de interiores, proporcionando servicios de dise-ño integrales que incluyen la concepción, la planificación, el paisajismo y el estudio de viabilidad.
Buscamos para nuestros clientes soluciones creativas que les ayuden a cumplir sus sue-

BAAN FLOWER CAGE

The owner wanted to renovate this house to provide space that would suit the needs to its full capacity. Architects proposed to adjust the interior space, bring in natural light and add the multipurpose area over the original barn. The new building represents the owner character, strong, energetic, yet gentle and sensitive. The construction was reinforced with aggressive steel structure but it still feels light. The one-hundred and two olive trees enhance the uniqueness of this house.

Der Eigentümer wollte dieses Haus renovieren, um den Bedürfnissen entsprechende Räumlichkeiten in vollem Umfang zur Verfügung zu stellen. Die Architekten schlugen vor, den Innenraum anzupassen, natürliches Licht einzubringen und den Mehrzweckbereich über der ursprünglichen Garage hinzuzufügen. Das neue Gebäude repräsentiert den Charakter des Eigentümers, der stark, energisch, aber gleichzeitig sanft und sensibel ist. Es ist mit einer aggressiven Stahlkonstruktion verstärkt, fühlt sich aber trotzdem leicht an. Erhöhet wird die Zartheit mit den Olivenbaumtöpfen, die speziell von Keramikkünstlern entworfen wurden, dem Symbol der Freiheit, das zwischen den Raum des gesamten Rahmens von 102 Bäumen gesetzt wurde, um die Einzigartigkeit dieses Hauses zu unterstreichen.

Le propriétaire veut rénover cette maison pour offrir un espace adapté aux besoins à sa pleine capacité. Les architectes ont proposé d'ajuster l'espace intérieur, d'apporter de la lumière naturelle et d'ajouter un espace multifonctionnel au-dessus du garage d'origine. Le nouveau bâtiment représente le caractère du propriétaire qui est à la fois fort, énergique, mais aussi doux et sensible. Il est renforcé par une structure en acier agressive, mais il reste léger. La tendresse est accentué avec des pots d'oliviers spécialement conçus par des artistes céramistes, symbole de liberté et placés entre l'espace de l'ensemble du cadre de 102 arbres pour renforcer le caractère unique de cette maison.

El propietario quiso renovar esta casa para conseguir un espacio que se adaptara a sus necesidades de forma completa. Los arquitectos propusieron ajustar el espacio interior, atraer la luz natural y añadir un área multiusos sobre el garaje original. El nuevo edificio representa el carácter fuerte y enérgico del propietario, pero a la vez suave y sensible. La vivienda se ha reforzado con una agresiva estructura de acero, pero aún así sigue destilando sensación de ligereza. Unas vasijas de olivo que han sido específicamente diseñadas por artistas de la cerámica y 102 árboles plantados en el jardín realzan su singularidad.

LOCATION
Bangkok, Thailand

PHOTOS
© Ketsiree Wongwan

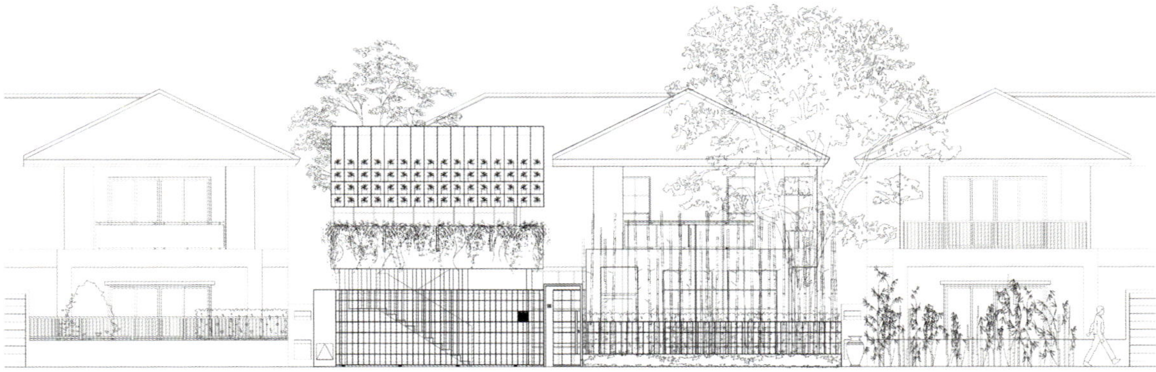

Street elevation

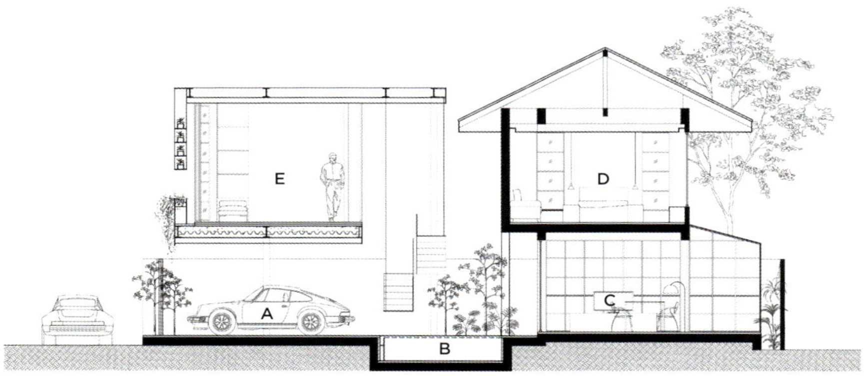

A. Garage
B. Reflecting pool
C. Dining area
D. Master bedroom
E. Multi-purpose area

Building section

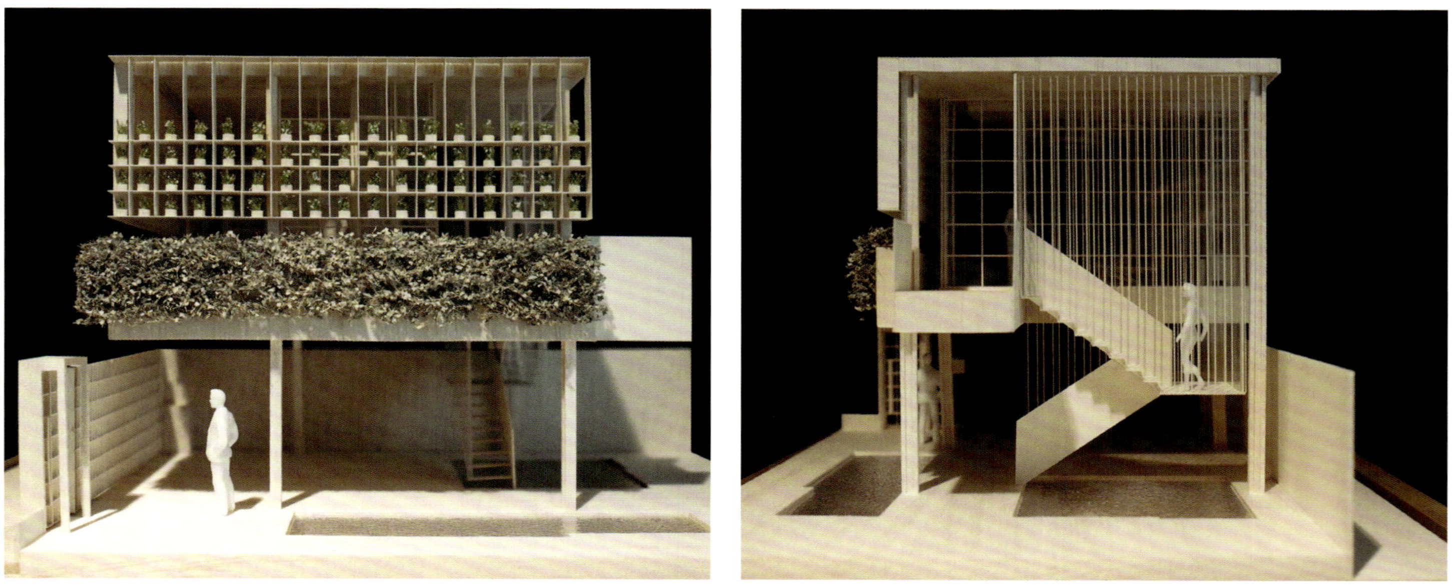

Views of scale model

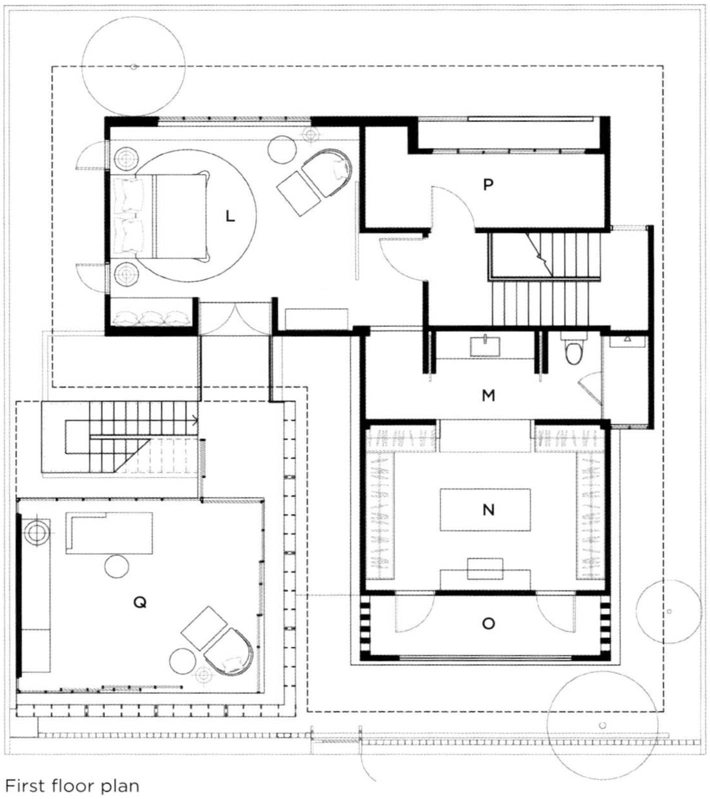

First floor plan

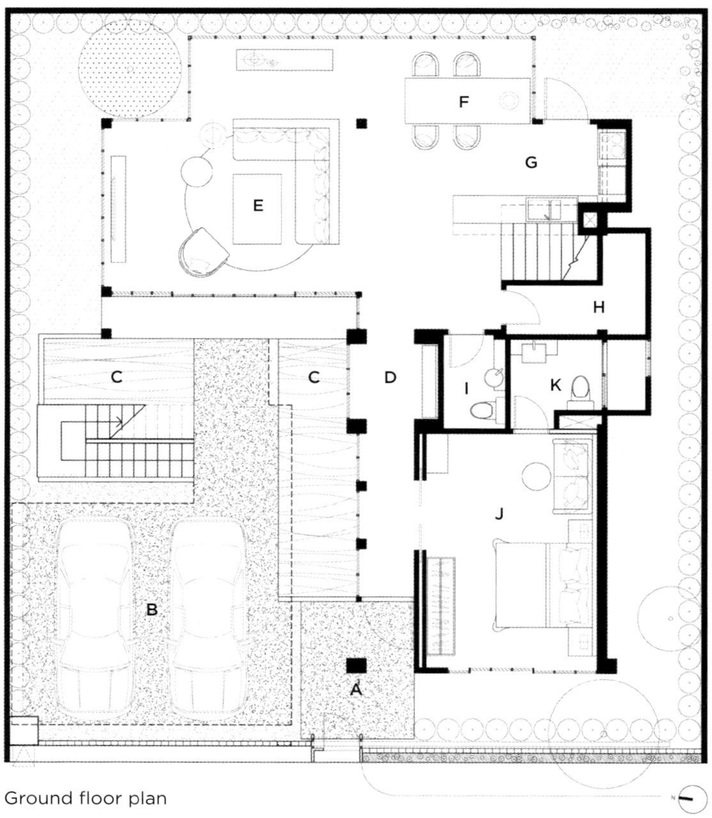

Ground floor plan

A. Entrance
B. Garage
C. Reflecting pool
D. Foyer
E. Living area
F. Dining area
G. Pantry
H. Storage
I. Powder room
J. Bedroom
K. Bathroom
L. Master bedroom
M. Master bathroom
N. Walk-in closet
O. Balcony
P. Laundry room
Q. Multi-purpose area

Wilson's

ANTONELLA MARI

Antonella Mari (Bari, 1966), owner of the AAM44 Architecture Studio, associates teaching and research with professional practice. Graduated with honors from La Sapienza University of Rome, she obtained the Master of Science in Advanced Architectural Design from Columbia University in New York. She received awards for research and design work and in 2001 she won the Fulbright Fellowship in Fine Arts at the American Academy in Rome. She has participated in numerous competitions in Italy, among them, the Diocesan Paths (2014) and the new Madonna del Carmelo parish center in Santa Maria La Carità (finalist). The Casa Petrini-Villani project won the Apulia 2011 Award. The works have been published and exhibited in Italy and abroad.

https://antonellamari.houzz.it
aam44architettura@gmail.com

Antonella Mari (*1966, Bari), Inhaberin des Architekturbüros AAM44, verbindet Lehre und Forschung mit der beruflichen Praxis. Sie schloss ihr Studium an der Universität La Sapienza in Rom mit Auszeichnung ab und erwarb den Master of Science in Advanced Architectural Design an der Columbia University in New York. Sie erhielt Auszeichnungen für Forschungs- und Designarbeiten und gewann 2001 das Fulbright-Stipendium für Bildende Kunst an der American Academy in Rom. Sie hat an zahlreichen Wettbewerben in Italien teilgenommen, unter anderem an den Diözesanwegen (2014) und dem neuen Pfarrzentrum Madonna del Carmelo in Santa Maria La Carità (Finalistin). Das Projekt Casa Petrini-Villani wurde mit dem Preis Apulien 2011 ausgezeichnet. Die Werke wurden in Italien und im Ausland veröffentlicht und ausgestellt.

Antonella Mari (Bari, 1966), propriétaire du studio d'architecture AAM44, associe l'enseignement et la recherche à la pratique professionnelle. Diplômée avec mention de l'université La Sapienza de Rome, elle a obtenu le Master of Science in Advanced Architectural Design de l'université Columbia de New York. Elle a reçu des prix pour ses travaux de recherche et de conception et, en 2001, elle a obtenu la bourse Fulbright en beaux-arts de l'Académie américaine de Rome. Elle a participé à de nombreux concours en Italie, parmi lesquels les Chemins Diocésains (2014) et le nouveau centre paroissial de Madonna del Carmelo à Santa Maria La Carità (finaliste). Le projet de la Casa Petrini-Villani a remporté le prix des Pouilles 2011. Les œuvres ont été publiées et exposées en Italie et à l'étranger.

Antonella Mari (Bari, 1966), propietaria del estudio de arquitectura AAM44, asocia la enseñanza y la investigación con la práctica profesional. Graduada con honores en la Universidad La Sapienza de Roma, obtuvo el Master of Science in Advanced Architectural Design de la Universidad de Columbia en Nueva York. Recibió premios por su trabajo de investigación y diseño y en 2001 ganó la Beca Fulbright en Bellas Artes en la Academia Americana de Roma. Ha participado en numerosos concursos en Italia, entre ellos, los Caminos Diocesanos (2014) y el nuevo centro parroquial de la Virgen del Carmen en Santa Maria La Carità (finalista). El proyecto de Casa Petrini-Villani ganó el Premio Apulia 2011. Las obras han sido publicadas y expuestas en Italia y en el extranjero.

52

CASA PETRINI VILLANI

This project consists of the renovation and extension of an old house. The design focuses on the contrast between the firmness and opacity of the original part and the permeability and lightness of the new floors. While the stone façade remains almost intact, the new upper volume is defined by the use of different materials, opening up a dialogue between the old and the new intervention. The design of the new façade is proposed as a means of optimising the daylight inside. On the roof, a large skylight covers a transparent staircase, allowing natural light to penetrate vertically into the entire building.

Dieses Projekt besteht aus der Renovierung und Erweiterung eines alten Hauses. Das Design konzentriert sich auf den Kontrast zwischen der Festigkeit und Opazität des ursprünglichen Teils und der Durchlässigkeit und Leichtigkeit der neuen Böden. Während die steinerne Fassade nahezu unversehrt geblieben ist, wird das neue obere Volumen durch die Verwendung unterschiedlicher Materialien definiert, wodurch ein Dialog zwischen der alten und der neuen Intervention eröffnet wird. Die Gestaltung der neuen Fassade wird als Mittel zur Optimierung des Tageslichts im Inneren vorgeschlagen. Auf dem Dach überspannt ein großes Oberlicht eine transparente Treppe, die natürliches Licht vertikal in das gesamte Gebäude eindringen lässt.

Ce projet consiste en la rénovation et l'extension d'une vieille maison. La conception se concentre sur le contraste entre la fermeté et l'opacité de la pièce d'origine, ainsi que la perméabilité et la légèreté des nouveaux sols. Si la façade en pierre reste presque intacte, le nouveau volume supérieur est défini par l'utilisation de différents matériaux, ce qui ouvre un dialogue entre l'ancienne structure et la nouvelle intervention. La conception de la nouvelle façade est proposée comme un moyen d'optimiser la lumière du jour à l'intérieur. Sur le toit, une grande lucarne recouvre un escalier transparent, permettant à la lumière naturelle de pénétrer verticalement dans tout le bâtiment.

Este proyecto consiste en la renovación y extensión de una antigua vivienda. El diseño se centra en el contraste entre la firmeza y la opacidad de la parte original y la permeabilidad y la ligereza de los nuevos pisos. Mientras que la fachada de piedra permanece casi intacta, el nuevo volumen superior se define mediante el uso de diferentes materiales, abriendo un diálogo entre la antigua y la nueva intervención. El diseño de la nueva fachada se plantea como medio para optimizar la luz del día en el interior. En la azotea, un gran tragaluz cubre una escalera transparente, permitiendo que la luz natural penetre verticalmente en todo el edificio.

LOCATION
Polignano a Mare, Bari, Italy

PHOTOS
© Michele Cera, Peppino Campanella

Site plan

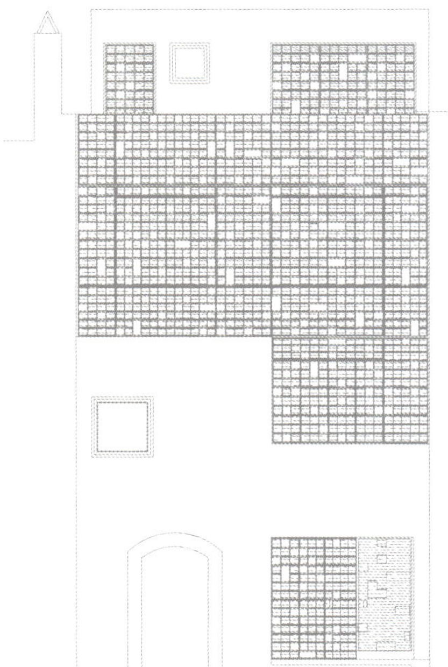

Front elevation

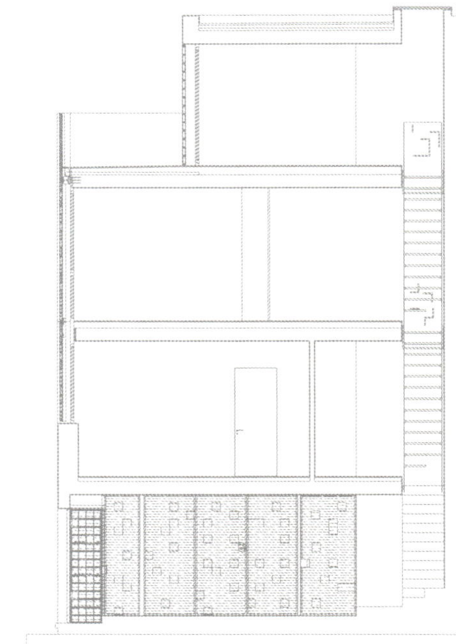

Section

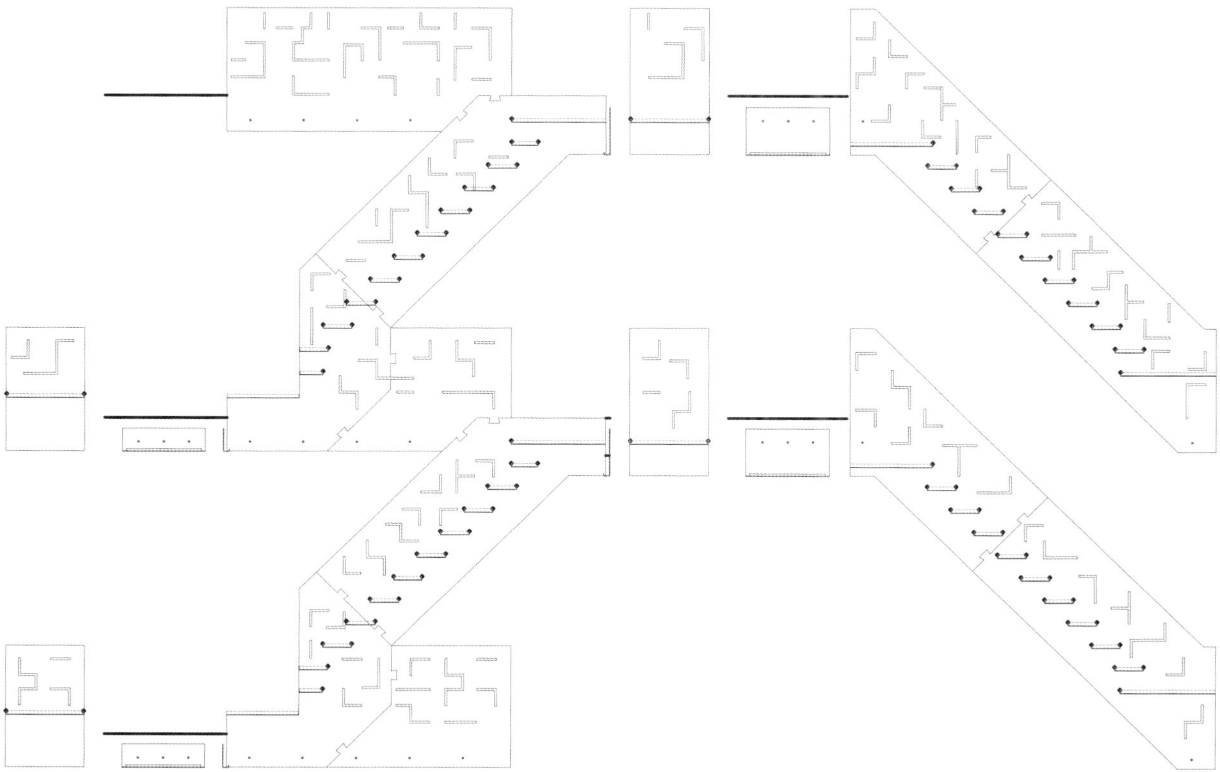

Guardrail elevations

Ground floor plan

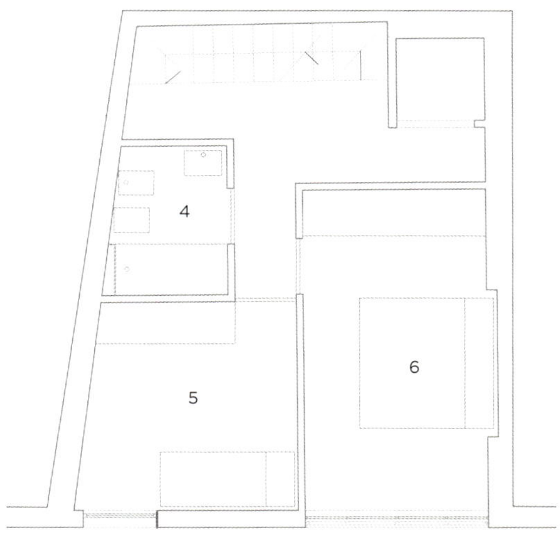

First floor plan

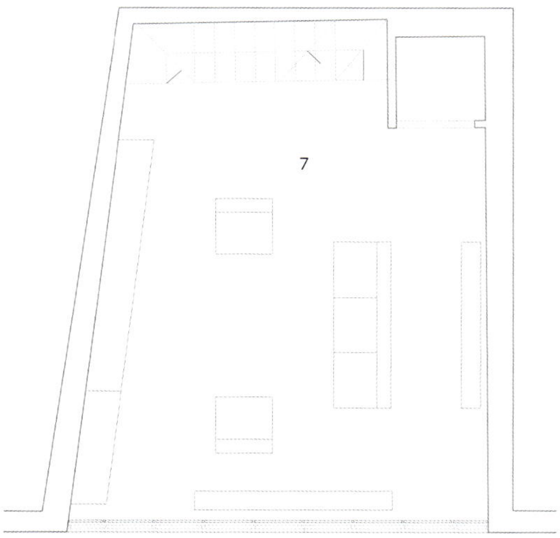

Second floor plan

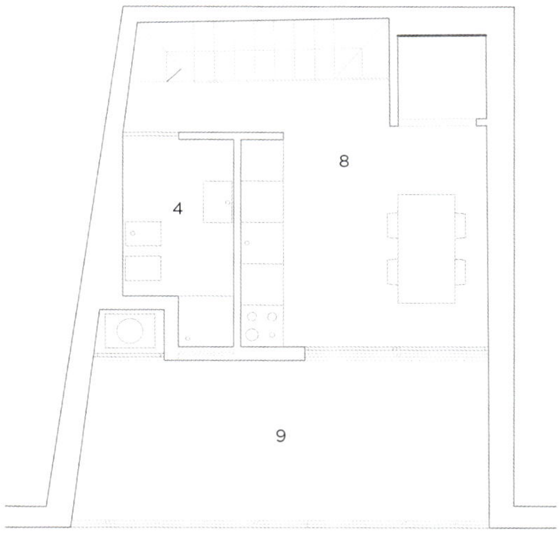

Third floor plan

1. Entry
2. Studio
3. Technical room
4. Bathroom
5. Bedroom
6. Master bedroom
7. Living room
8. Kitchen
9. Terrace

ARCHITE
TM

The Architectural Practice of Tom Maher, B.Arch., Dip. Arch Tech., MRIAI, RIBA is a re-cipient of Ireland's Highest Architectural Awards/ Honours:
The Downes Medal for Excellence in Architectural Design from the Architectural Association of Ireland in 2006 and The Triennial Gold Medal for 2004-2006 from the Royal Institute of Architects of Ireland in 2013.
The work of the practice has also being published both nationally and internationally.

Das Architekturbüro von Tom Maher, B. Arch., Dip. Arch. Tech., MRIAI, RIBA. Ein Empfänger der höchsten irischen Architekturpreise und - ehren:
die Downes-Medaille für herausragendes architektonisches Design von der Architectural Association of Ireland im Jahr 2006 und die dreijährliche Goldmedaille für 2004–2006 vom Royal Institute of Architects of Ireland im Jahr 2013.
Die Arbeit des Büros wurde sowohl national als auch international veröffentlicht.

La pratique architecturale de Tom Maher, B.Arch., Dip. Arch Tech., MRIAI, RIBA. Récipiendaire des plus hautes distinctions architecturales d'Irlande :
la médaille Downes pour l'excellence en conception architecturale de l'Architectural Association of Ireland en 2006 et la médaille d'or triennale pour 2004-2006 du Royal Institute of Architects of Ireland en 2013.
Les travaux du cabinet ont également été publiés au niveau national et international.

El estudio de arquitectura de Tom Maher (B.Arch., Dip. Arch. Tech., MRIAI, RIBA) ha recibido los más altos premios y honores de arquitectura de Irlanda:
la Medalla Downes a la Excelencia en el Diseño Arquitectónico del Colegio de Arquitectos de Irlanda en 2006 y la Medalla de Oro Trienal para 2004-2006 del Real Instituto de Arquitectos de Irlanda en 2013.
La labor del estudio también se ha publicado a nivel nacional e internacional.

www.architectstm.com
office@architectstm.com

K HOUSE

The site location and the city council planning policy conditioned the design of this home. The house takes the form of an inhabited light scoop, to provide spaces for refuge and prospect and extends between two outside rooms, a ramped entrance court with a small water pool and a roof terrace, a place to perch and capture sunsets and the local city skyline. Kitchen and dining mezzanine are on the second level; living and study on first; bedrooms and bathrooms on ground all dressed with untreated copper and lime washed maple.

Der Standort und die Planungspolitik des Stadtrats waren ausschlaggebend für die Gestaltung dieses Hauses. Das Haus hat die Form einer bewohnten Lichtschaufel, die Raum für Zuflucht und Ausblick bietet, und erstreckt sich zwischen zwei Außenräumen, einem rampenförmigen Eingangshof mit einem kleinen Wasserbecken, um die Stadt zu verlangsamen und zu zerstreuen, und einer Dachterrasse, einem Platz, an dem man sich niederlassen und Sonnenuntergänge und die lokale Skyline der Stadt einfangen kann. Bezug nach außen und innen bilden Küche und Esszimmer im zweiten, Wohn- und Arbeitszimmer im ersten Stock, und Schlaf- und Badezimmer auf dem Erdgeschoss, verkleidet mit unbehandeltem Kupfer und mit Kalk gewaschenem Ahorn.

L'emplacement du site et la politique d'aménagement du conseil municipal ont conditionné la conception de cette maison. La maison prend la forme d'un scoop de lumière habité, pour offrir des espaces de refuge et de prospection. Elle s'étend entre deux pièces extérieures et une cour d'entrée en pente avec un petit bassin d'eau pour ralentir et dissiper la ville. On y trouve également une terrasse sur le toit ; un endroit pour se percher et capturer les couchers de soleil et l'horizon de la ville locale. A la fois à l'extérieur et à l'intérieur, formant la cuisine et la mezzanine à manger au second, le salon et le bureau au premier, les chambres et les salles de bain au sol et revêtues de cuivre non traité et d'érable lavé à la chaux.

La ubicación del terreno y la política de planificación del ayuntamiento condicionaron el diseño de esta casa llena de luz que proporciona espacios de refugio y meditación y se extiende entre dos habitaciones exteriores, un patio de entrada con un pequeño estanque que rompe con el ambiente urbano y una azotea, un lugar para contemplar las puestas de sol y el horizonte. En el entresuelo se han situado la cocina y el comedor. En el primer piso se encuentran la sala y el estudio, y en el segundo, los dormitorios y los baños, acabados en cobre sin tratar y madera de arce lavada a la cal.

LOCATION
Ranelagh, Dublin, Ireland

PHOTOS
© Ros Kavanagh

ARCHSTUDIO

Established in 2010 by Han Wenqiang and based in Beijing, ARCHSTUDIO advocates for an harmonious balance among human, nature, history and commerce, pursuing the essence and true way of design and controling the whole process from concept to construction. Currently, the studio mainly focuses on architectural design in natural context, urban architecture renovation & transformation, and upgrade of consumption spaces. During design practices, ARCHSTUDIO insists on the principle of "design of relationships", analyzes reality of uncertainties, and coordinates relations between the large and small, exterior and interior, the new and old, the artificial and natural.

www.archstudio.cn
archstudio@126.com

Das 2010 von Han Wenqiang gegründete und in Peking ansässige ARCHSTUDIO setzt sich für ein harmonisches Gleichgewicht von Mensch, Natur, Geschichte und Handel ein, indem es die Essenz und den wahren Weg des Designs verfolgt und den gesamten Prozess vom Konzept bis zur Konstruktion kontrolliert. Gegenwärtig konzentriert sich das Studio hauptsächlich auf architektonisches Design im natürlichen Kontext, die Renovierung und Umgestaltung städtischer Architektur und die Aufwertung von Konsumräumen. Während der Entwurfspraxis beharrt ARCHSTUDIO auf dem Prinzip der „Gestaltung von Beziehungen", analysiert die Realität der Unsicherheiten und koordiniert die Beziehungen zwischen Groß und Klein, Außen und Innen, Neu und Alt, Künstlich und Natürlich.

Créé en 2010 par Han Wenqiang ARCHSTUDIO est basé à Pékin. Il plaide pour un équilibre harmonieux entre l'homme, la nature, l'histoire et le commerce, en poursuivant l'essence et la véritable manière de concevoir et en contrôlant l'ensemble du processus ; du concept à la construction. Actuellement, le studio se concentre principalement sur la conception architecturale dans un contexte naturel, la rénovation et la transformation de l'architecture urbaine, et l'amélioration des espaces de consommation. Lors des pratiques de conception, ARCHSTUDIO insiste sur le principe de «conception des relations», analyse la réalité des incertitudes et coordonne les relations entre le grand et le petit, l'extérieur et l'intérieur, le nouveau et l'ancien, l'artificiel et le naturel.

Inaugurado en 2010 por Han Wenqiang y con sede en Beijing, ARCHSTUDIO aboga por un equilibrio armonioso entre el ser humano, la naturaleza, la historia y el comercio, persiguiendo la esencia y la verdadera manera de diseñar y controlar todo el proceso, desde el concepto hasta la construcción. Actualmente, el estudio se centra principalmente en el diseño arquitectónico en el contexto natural, la renovación y transformación de la arquitectura urbana y la mejora de los espacios de consumo. Durante el proceso de diseño, ARCHSTUDIO insiste en el principio de «diseño de relaciones», analiza la realidad de las incertidumbres, y coordina las relaciones entre lo grande y lo pequeño, el exterior y el interior, lo nuevo y lo viejo, lo artificial y lo natural.

HAITANG VILLA

The project is a three-story townhouse located in a residential area in the eastern suburbs of Beijing. The first floor and the basement are connected space to be used to receive visitors. The second floor is for daily living. It has separate entrances and exits. The basic concept of the design is to use the changes of material and space to blur the boundary between indoor and outdoor, and the relationship among connections, to create an open environment rich in layers, allowing the interior space to get rid of limited decoration, and return to a natural, simple, quiet and oriental living atmosphere.

Bei diesem Projekt handelt es sich um ein dreistöckiges Stadthaus in einem Wohngebiet in einem östlichen Vorort Pekings. Das erste Stockwerk und das Untergeschoss sind ein zusammenhängender Raum, der für den Empfang von Besuchern genutzt wird. Die zweite Etage dient dem täglichen Leben, sie hat separate Ein- und Ausgänge. Das Grundkonzept des Entwurfs besteht darin, die Veränderungen von Material und Raum zu nutzen, um die Grenze zwischen Innen und Außen und die Beziehung zwischen den Schnittstellen zu verwischen, eine offene, schichtenreiche Umgebung zu schaffen und so den Innenraum von der begrenzenden Dekoration zu befreien und zu einer natürlichen, einfachen, ruhigen und orientalischen Wohnatmosphäre zurückzukehren.

Le projet est une maison de ville de trois étages située dans un quartier résidentiel de la banlieue Est de Pékin. Le premier étage et le sous-sol constituent un espace relié qui sert à recevoir des visiteurs. Le deuxième étage est destiné à la vie quotidienne avec des entrées et des sorties séparées. L'idée de base de la conception est d'utiliser les changements de matériaux et d'espace pour estomper la frontière entre l'intérieur et l'extérieur. Il s'agit également d'utiliser la relation entre les interfaces pour créer un environnement ouvert, riche en couches, pour ainsi faire disparaître la décoration limitée de l'espace intérieur et revenir à une atmosphère de vie naturelle, simple, calme et orientale.

El proyecto es una casa de tres pisos situada en una zona residencial en los suburbios de Beijing. El primer piso y el sótano son un espacio conectado que se utiliza para recibir a los visitantes. El segundo piso está dedicado a la vida diaria y tiene entradas y salidas separadas. El concepto básico del diseño es utilizar los cambios de materiales y espacios para desdibujar la frontera entre el interior y el exterior, creando un ambiente abierto y rico en capas que permita al espacio interior deshacerse de la decoración limitada, volviendo a un ambiente natural, simple, tranquilo y de inspiración oriental.

LOCATION
Chaoyang District, Beijing, China

PHOTOS
© Magic Penny

1. Entry way
2. Living room
3. Main bedroom
4. Guest bedroom
5. Kid's room
6. Kitchen
7. Dining room
8. Main bathroom
9. Guest bedroom
10. Balcony

Second floor plan

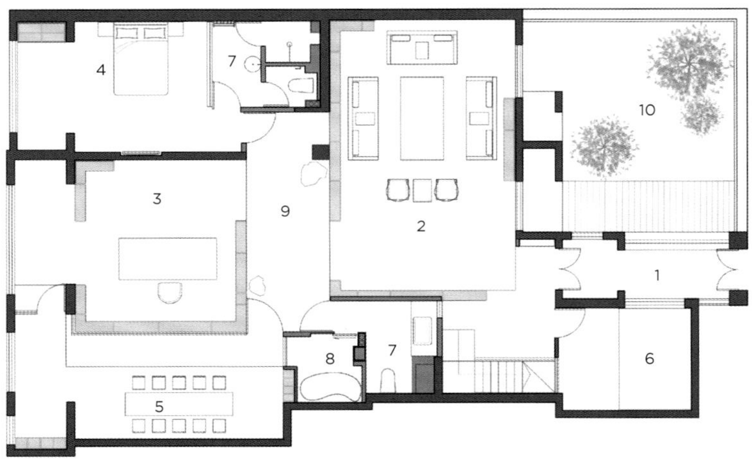

1. Entrance
2. Living room
3. Study
4. Guest room
5. Tea room
6. Bedroom
7. Restroom
8. Bathroom
9. Corridor
10. Sunken courtyard

First floor plan

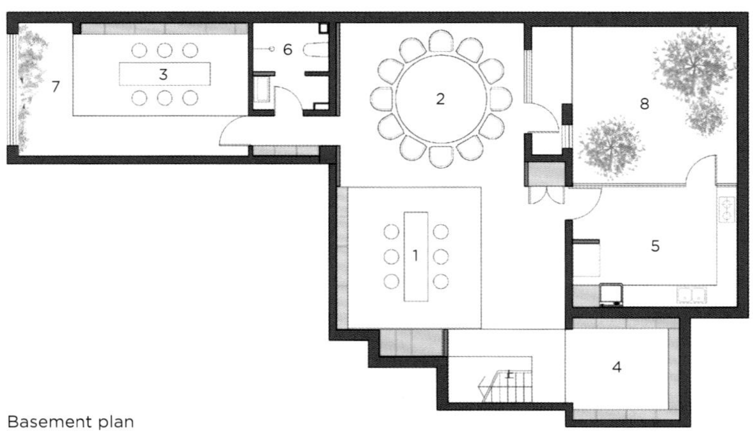

1. Dining room for 6
2. Dining room for 12
3. Tea room
4. Leisure space
5. Kitchen
6. Bathroom
7. Bamboo landscape
8. Exterior courtyard

Basement plan

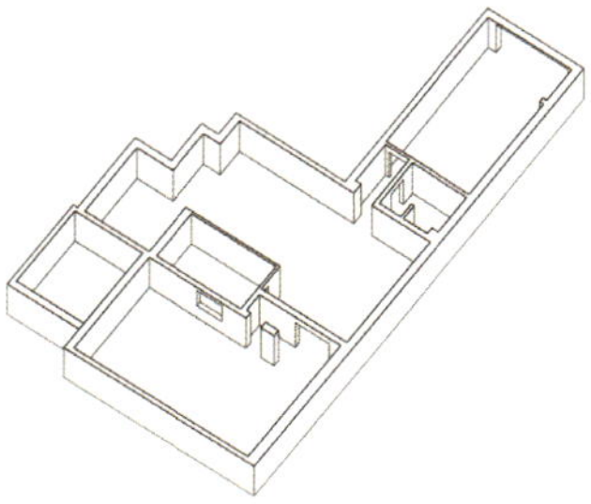

Basement before renovation

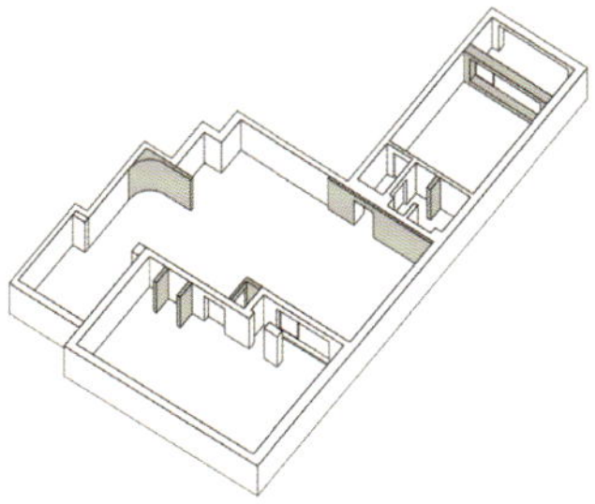

Basement newly built

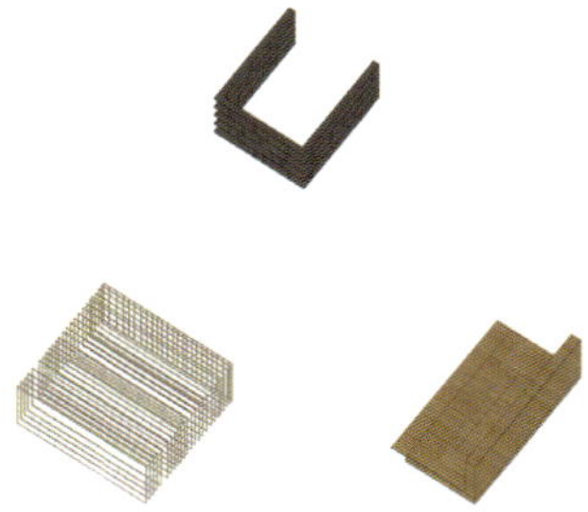

Basement built-in furniture

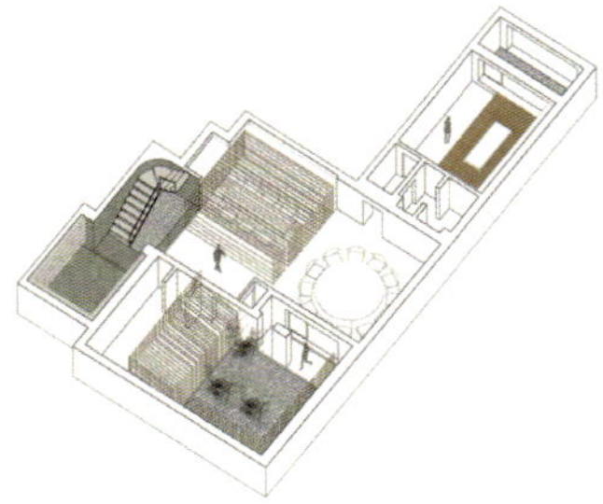

Basement after renovation

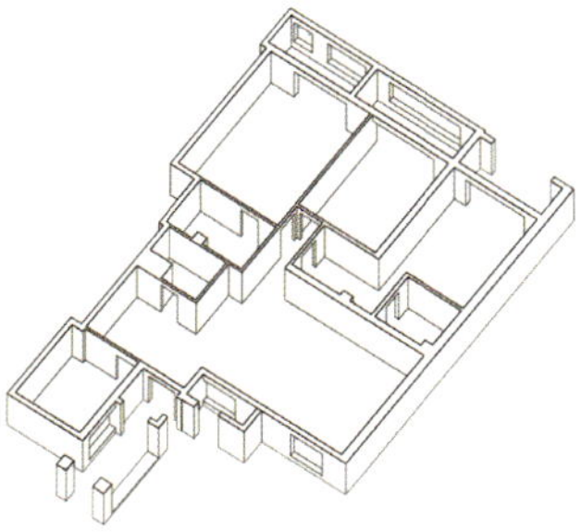

First floor before renovation

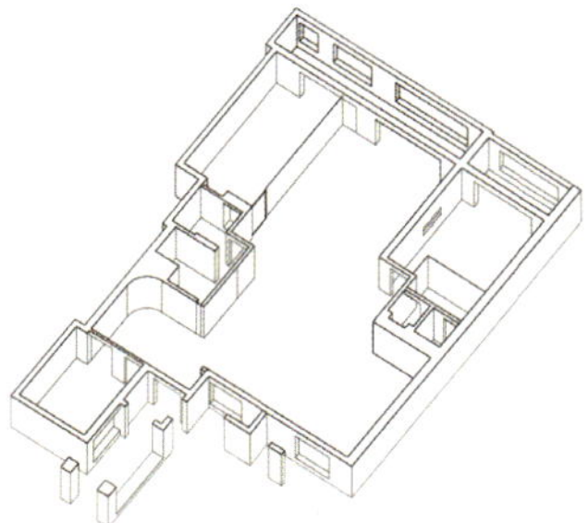

First floor before renovation

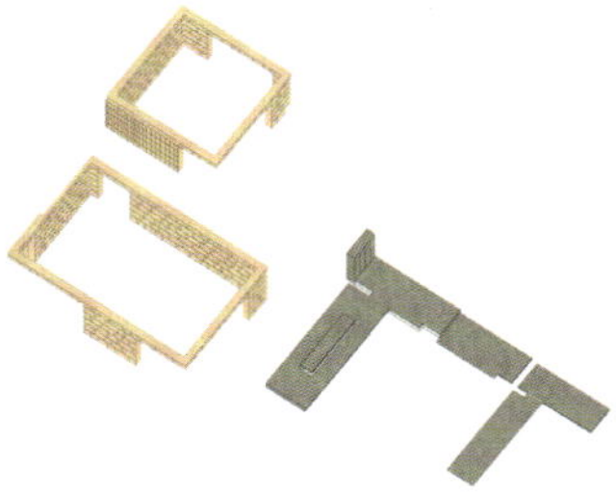

First floor built-in furniture

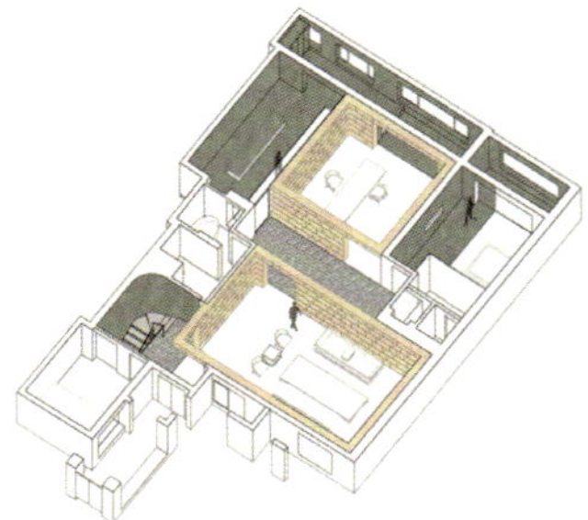

First floor after renovation

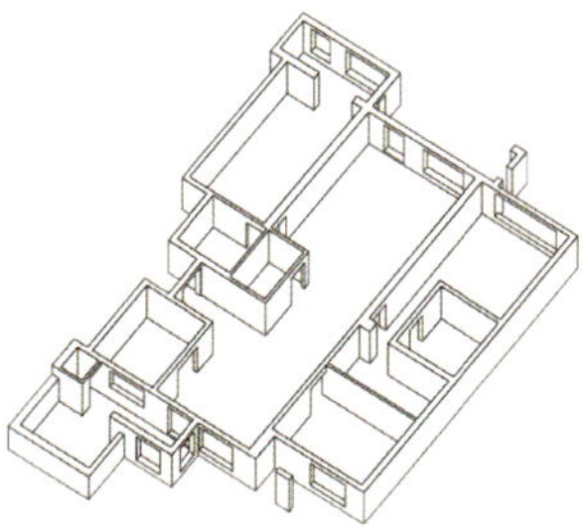

Second floor before renovation

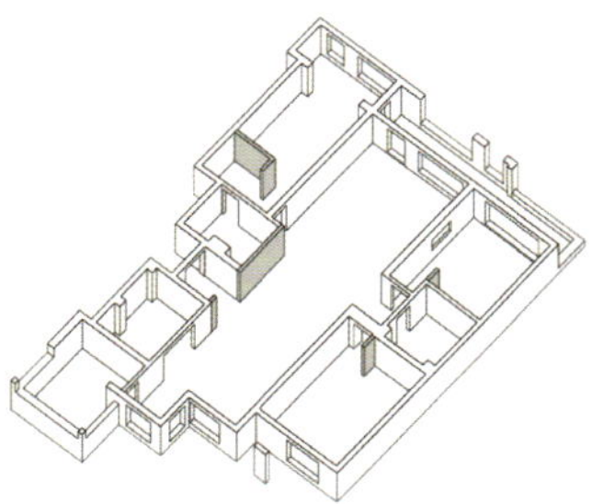

Second floor before renovation

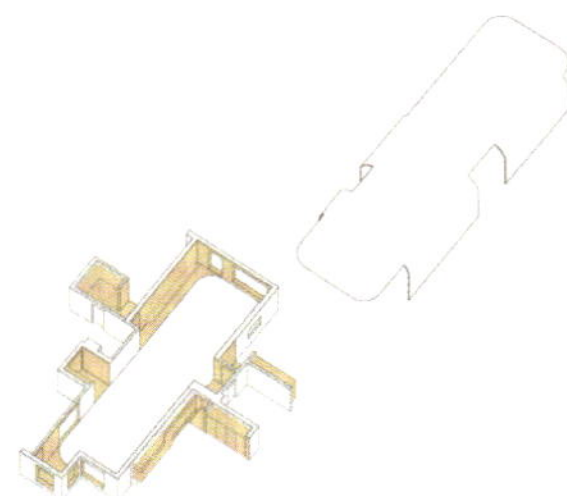

Second floor built-in furniture

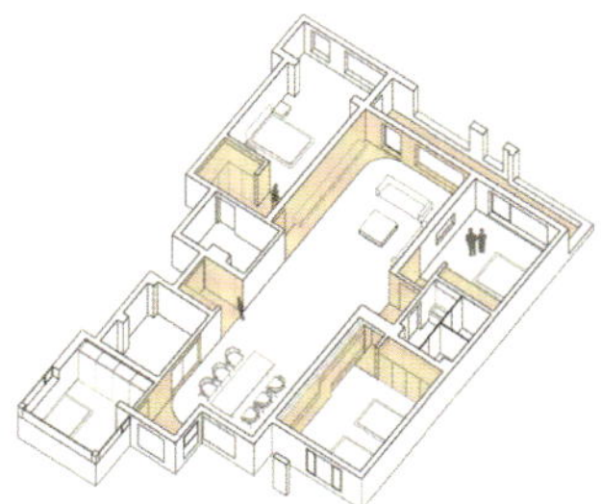

Second floor after renovation

AVENIER CORNEJO ARCHITECTES

Christelle Avenier and Miguel Cornejo (born in Santiago de Chile) studied at the École Supérieure d'Architecture de Paris Malaquais. After their diploma, they worked on projects with various architects —Mathias Klotz in Santiago de Chile, Douglas Deremer in San Francisco and, in France, François Roche, (R&Sie(n)), XTU, Jacques Ferrier, and Galiano & Simon— before founding their own firm in Paris.
Their solo career began with a winning project for the Électra Grant (EDF) in Valparaíso, Chile, followed by projects for private clients, before the firm won a public contract in 2007 for a social housing program. After this, Avenier Cornejo completed a private house in Orsay, a building of ten dwellings for the RIVP in Paris, a kindergarten and a young workers' hostel and kindergarten at Paris's Porte des Lilas. Today, Avenier Cornejo is in the preliminary design phase of a number of schemes of diverse tipology.

www.avenier-cornejo.com
agence@avenier-cornejo.com

Christelle Avenier und Miguel Cornejo (geboren in Santiago de Chile) haben an der École Supérieure d'Architecture de Paris Malaquais studiert. Nach ihrem Diplom arbeiteten sie an Projekten mit verschiedenen Architekten – Mathias Klotz in Santiago de Chile, Douglas Deremer in San Francisco und, in Frankreich, François Roche, (R&Sie(n)), XTU, Jacques Ferrier und Galiano & Simon – bevor sie ihr eigenes Büro in Paris gründeten.
Ihre Solokarriere begann mit einem Siegerprojekt für den Électra Grant (EDF) in Valparaíso, Chile, gefolgt von Projekten für Privatkunden, bevor die Firma 2007 einen öffentlichen Auftrag für ein Sozialwohnungsprogramm erhielt. Danach stellte Avenier Cornejo ein Privathaus in Orsay, ein Gebäude mit zehn Wohnungen für das RIVP in Paris, einen Kindergarten sowie ein Wohnheim und einen Kindergarten für junge Arbeiter an der Pariser Porte des Lilas fertig. Heute befindet sich Avenier Cornejo in der Vorentwurfsphase einer Reihe von Entwürfen unterschiedlicher Typologie.

Christelle Avenier et Miguel Cornejo (né à Santiago du Chili) ont étudié à l'École supérieure d'architecture de Paris Malaquais. Après leur diplôme, ils ont travaillé sur des projets avec différents architectes - Mathias Klotz à Santiago du Chili, Douglas Deremer à San Francisco et, en France, François Roche, (R&Sie(n)), XTU, Jacques Ferrier et Galiano & Simon. Ils ont ensuite fondé leur propre cabinet à Paris.
Leur carrière solo a commencé par un projet gagnant pour la bourse Électra (EDF) à Valparaíso, au Chili, suivi de projets pour des clients privés, avant que le cabinet ne remporte un contrat public en 2007 pour un programme de logement social. Par la suite, Avenier Cornejo a réalisé une maison privée à Orsay, un bâtiment de dix logements pour le RIVP à Paris, une école maternelle et un foyer de jeunes travailleurs et une école maternelle à la Porte des Lilas à Paris. Aujourd'hui, l'Avenier Cornejo est en phase de conception préliminaire d'un certain nombre de projets de topologie diverse.

Christelle Avenier y Miguel Cornejo (nacido en Santiago de Chile) estudiaron en la École Supérieure d'Architecture de Paris Malaquais. Después de su diploma y antes de fundar su propia firma en París, colaboraron en proyectos con varios arquitectos: Mathias Klotz en Santiago de Chile, Douglas Deremer en San Francisco y, en Francia, con François Roche, (R&Sie(n)), XTU, Jacques Ferrier y Galiano & Simon.
Su carrera en solitario comenzó con un proyecto ganador de la Beca Électra (EDF) en Valparaíso, Chile, seguido de proyectos para clientes privados, antes de que la empresa ganara un contrato público en 2007 para un programa de vivienda social. A continuación, Avenier Cornejo completó una casa privada en Orsay, un edificio de diez viviendas en París, un jardín de infancia y un albergue para jóvenes en la Porte des Lilas (París). Hoy en día, Avenier Cornejo se encuentra en la fase de anteproyecto de varios proyectos de diversa tipología.

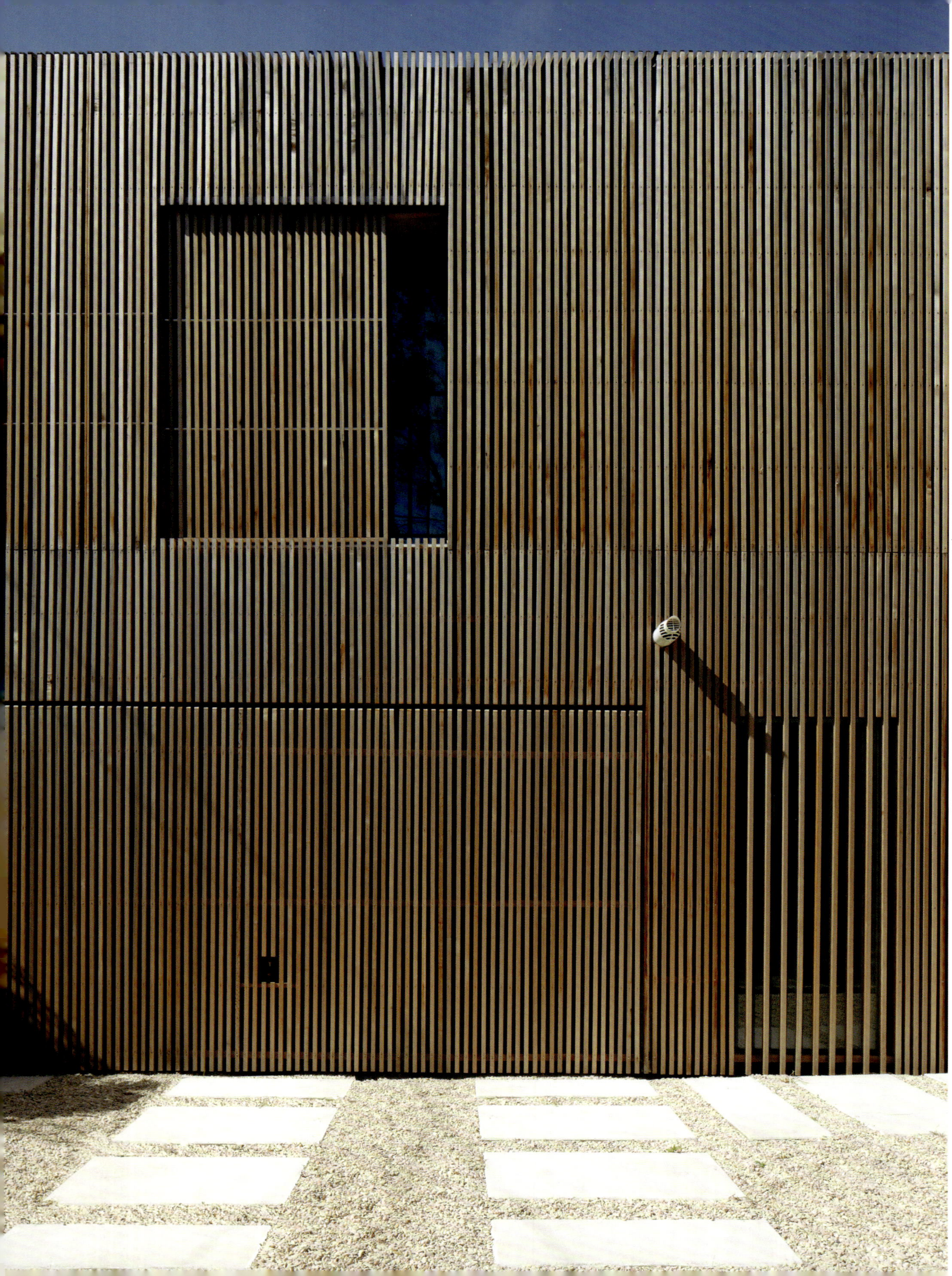

HOUSE 2G

LOCATION
Orsay, France

PHOTOS
© Christobal Palma, Stéphane Chalmeau

The challenge was to set a contemporary ecological house in a traditional suburban environment, making the most of the view on the park. The sober exterior offsets and enhances the sculpted interior, where one large volume links the two levels of the building. An indoor patio provides additional light for the bedrooms and bathroom. A staircase structures the ground floor. The original layout offers optimal views of the landscaped garden. Over time, the untreated wood cladding will gradually take on a silver-grey patina that will age gracefully, blending gently into its surroundings.

Die Herausforderung des Projekts bestand darin, ein modernes ökologisches Haus in einem traditionellen Vorort zu errichten. Das nüchterne Äußere versetzt und verstärkt das skulpturale Innere, in dem ein großes Volumen die beiden Ebenen des Hauses vereint. Ein Innenhof sorgt für zusätzliches Licht für die Schlafzimmer und das Bad, die Treppe strukturiert das Erdgeschoss, und der ursprüngliche Grundriss bietet eine optimale Aussicht auf den Landschaftsgarten. Mit der Zeit wird die unbehandelte Holzverkleidung nach und nach eine silbergraue Patina annehmen, die sich anmutig und sanft in die Umgebung einfügt.

Le défi du projet était d'installer une maison écologique contemporaine dans une banlieue traditionnelle. L'extérieur sobre compense et met en valeur l'intérieur sculpté, où un grand volume réunit les deux niveaux de la maison. Un patio intérieur apporte un éclairage supplémentaire pour les chambres et la salle de bain, l'escalier structure le rez-de-chaussée et la disposition originale offre des vues optimales sur le jardin paysager. Avec le temps, le revêtement en bois non traité prendra progressivement une patine gris argenté qui vieillira avec grâce et se fondra doucement dans son environnement.

El desafío del proyecto consistía en establecer una casa ecológica contemporánea en un suburbio tradicional. El sobrio exterior compensa y realza el interior, donde un gran volumen une los dos niveles de la casa. Un patio interior proporciona luz adicional para los dormitorios y el baño. La escalera estructura la planta baja, logrando óptimas vistas del jardín. Con el tiempo, el revestimiento de madera sin tratar irá adquiriendo gradualmente una pátina gris plateada que envejecerá con estilo y se mezclará suavemente con su entorno.

Site plan

Elevations

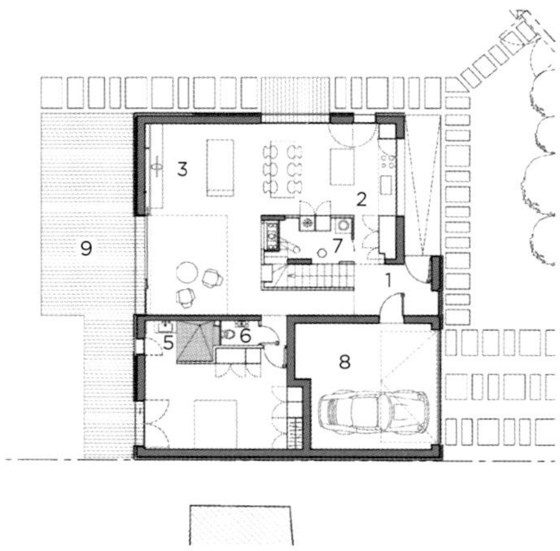

Ground floor plan

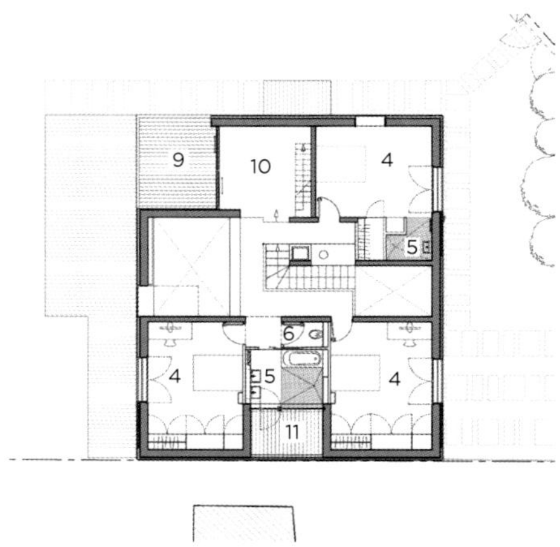

First floor plan

1. Entry
2. Kitchen
3. Living/dining room
4. Bedroom
5. Bathroom
6. Toilet
7. Laundry/cellar
8. Garage
9. Terrace
10. Gameroom
11. Courtyard
12. Open space above the entry
13. Open space above the living room
14. Mezzanine

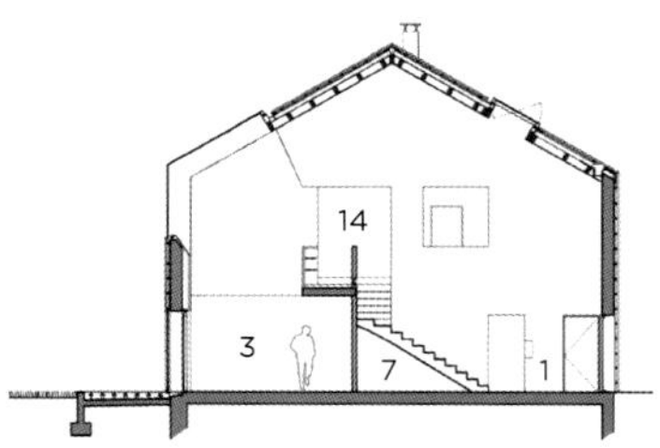

Section

dmvA ARCHITECTEN

DAVID DRIESEN AND TOM VERSCHUEREN

David Driesen and Tom Verschueren mutual passion for architecture led to dmvA, 'door middel van Architectuur' ('by means of Architecture'). A noble goal to provide a critical answer using architecture to respond to social, economic and collective matters. The work of dmvA can be described as expressive and meticulous, achieving maximalism through minimalism. By claiming to have no defined style, the entire range of styles is in fact appropriated.
dmvA focuses on the design process and is always looking for the architectural added value while designing. dmvA likes to act as scriptwriters: they transform a plan into a scenario, spaces into sequences and buildings into storytellers.

www.dmva-architecten.be
info@dmva-architecten.be

Die gemeinsame Leidenschaft von David Driesen und Tom Verschueren für Architektur führte zur dmvA, „door middel van Architectuur" („mittels der Architektur"), mit dem hehren Ziel, eine kritische Antwort zu geben, indem die Architektur als Antwort auf soziale, wirtschaftliche und kollektive Angelegenheiten verwendet wird. Die Arbeit der dmvA kann als expressiv und akribisch beschrieben werden, wobei durch Minimalismus das Maximum erreicht wird. Durch die Behauptung, keinen definierten Stil zu haben, wird in der Tat die gesamte Bandbreite der Stile verfügbar.
Die dmvA konzentriert sich auf den Entwurfsprozess und sucht beim Entwerfen immer nach dem architektonischen Mehrwert. Die dmvA tritt gerne als Drehbuchautorin: Sie verwandelt einen Plan in ein Szenario, Räume in Sequenzen und Gebäude in Geschichtenerzähler.

La passion commune de David Driesen et Tom Verschueren pour l'architecture a donné naissance à la dmvA, «door middel van Architectuur» (« par le biais de l'architecture »). Un noble objectif : apporter une réponse critique en utilisant l'architecture pour répondre à des questions sociales, économiques et collectives. Le travail de la dmvA peut être décrit comme expressif et méticuleux, atteignant le maximalisme par le minimalisme. En prétendant n'avoir aucun style défini, toute la gamme des styles est en fait appropriée.
dmvA se concentre sur le processus de conception et recherche toujours la valeur ajoutée architecturale lors de la conception. dmvA aime jouer le rôle de scénariste : elle transforme un plan en scénario, des espaces en séquences et des bâtiments en conteurs.

La pasión mutua de David Driesen y Tom Verschueren por la arquitectura les llevó a formar dmvA, «door middel van Architectuur» («por medio de la arquitectura»), un objetivo noble de dar respuesta crítica usando la arquitectura para reaccionar a los asuntos sociales, económicos y colectivos. El trabajo del dmvA puede describirse como expresivo y meticuloso, logrando el maximalismo a través del minimalismo.
dmvA se centra en el proceso de diseño, buscando siempre el valor arquitectónico añadido. A dmvA les gusta actuar como guionistas; transforman un plano en un escenario, los espacios en secuencias y los edificios en narradores de historias.

ZONE
UITGEZONDERD

HOUSE OF LORRAINE

LOCATION
Mechelen, Belgium

PHOTOS
© Sergio Pirrone

This project consists of rehabilitating an emblematic corner in the Grote Markkt. The main objectives were the high quality of life and urban integration, respecting the history of the building. The form and rhythm of the original facades were maintained; thus the houses are small and vertical and all are white although with different materials. The facades are open, but ensure enough privacy. Because of its arrangement, the house on the corner received little light; as a solution, an interior street was created between the houses, allowing light to reach it. The interior street also functions as a meeting place for the residents.

Dieses Projekt besteht in der Sanierung einer emblematischen Ecke im Grote Markt. Die Hauptziele waren hohe Lebensqualität und die städtische Integration unter Berücksichtigung der Geschichte des Gebäudes. Die Form und der Rhythmus der ursprünglichen Fassaden wurden beibehalten; so sind die Häuser klein und vertikal und alle weiß, wenn auch mit unterschiedlichen Materialien. Die Fassaden sind offen, gewährleisten aber eine ausreichende Privatsphäre. Aufgrund seiner Lage erhielt das Haus an der Ecke wenig Licht; als Lösung wurde eine innere Straße zwischen den Häusern geschaffen, die das Licht erreichen konnte. Die innere Straße dient auch als Treffpunkt für die Bewohner.

Ce projet consiste à réhabiliter un coin emblématique de la Grand-Place. Les principaux objectifs étaient la haute qualité de vie et l'intégration urbaine, dans le respect de l'histoire du bâtiment. La forme et le rythme des façades d'origine ont été maintenus. Ainsi, les maisons sont petites, verticales et toutes sont blanches, malgré l'utilisation de matériaux différents. Les façades sont ouvertes, mais assurent une intimité suffisante. En raison de sa position, la maison du coin recevait peu de lumière. La solution a été de créer une rue intérieure entre les maisons, permettant à la lumière de l'atteindre. La rue intérieure fonctionne également comme un lieu de rencontre pour les habitants.

Este proyecto consiste en rehabilitar una emblemática esquina en el Grote Markkt. Los principales objetivos eran la alta calidad de vida y la integración urbana, respetando la historia del edificio. Se mantuvieron la forma y el ritmo de las fachadas originales; así las viviendas son pequeñas y verticales y todas son blancas aunque con materiales diferentes. Las fachadas son abiertas, pero aseguran suficiente privacidad. Por su posición, la casa de la esquina recibía poca luz; como solución, se creó una calle interior entre las viviendas, permitiendo que la luz llegara a esta. La calle interior también funciona como un lugar de encuentro para los residentes.

Site plan

Facades

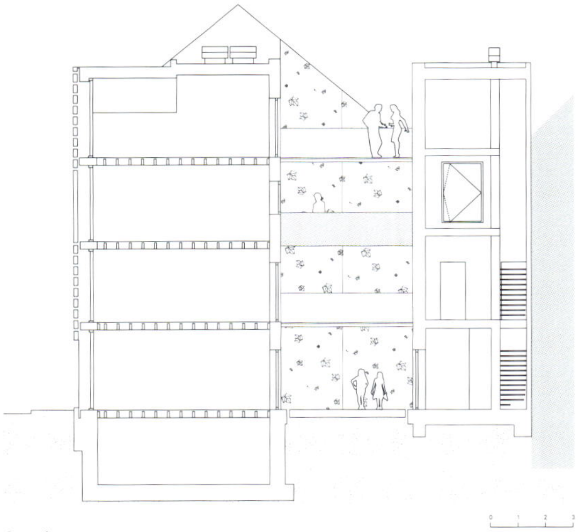

Section

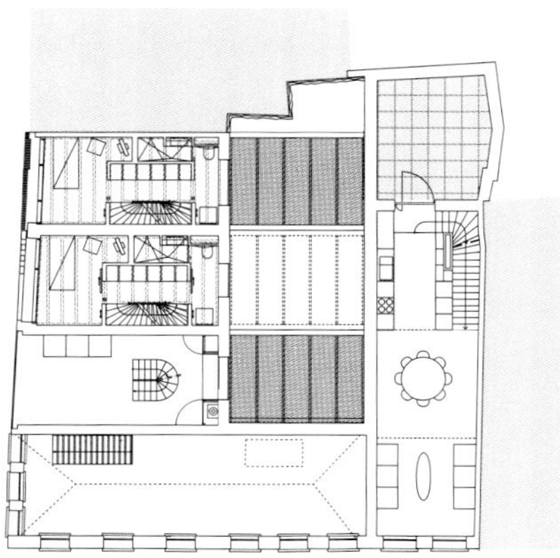

Second floor plan

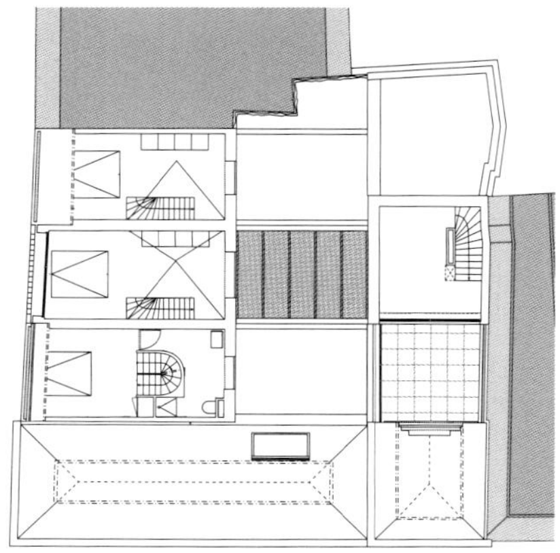

Third floor plan

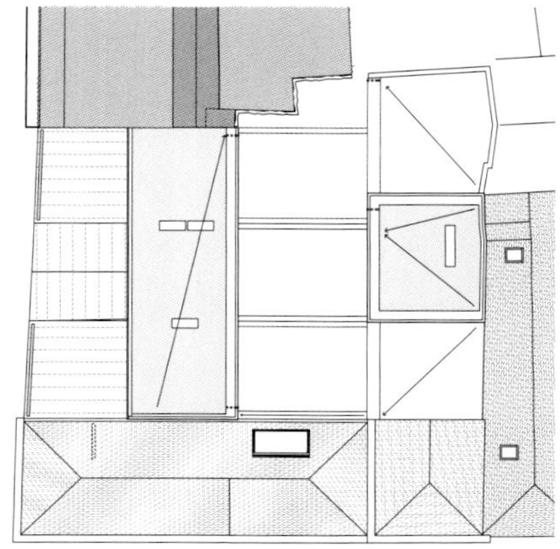

Roof plan

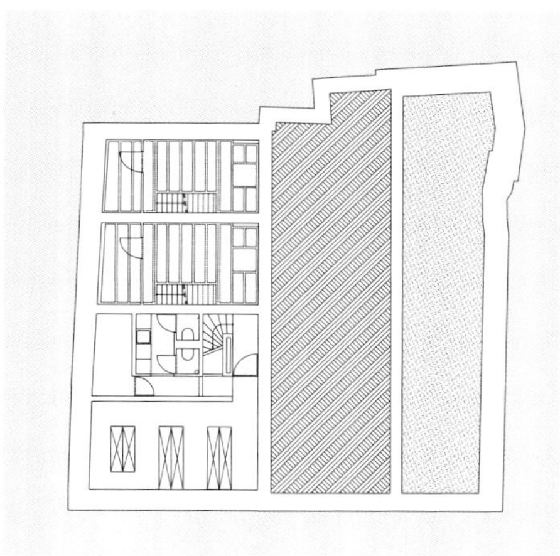

Basement plan

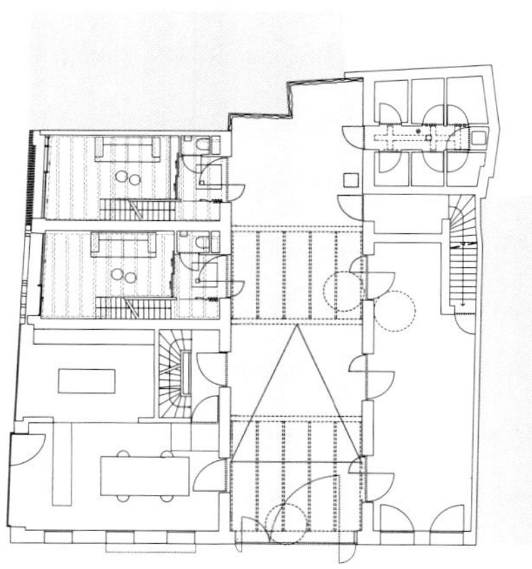

Ground floor plan

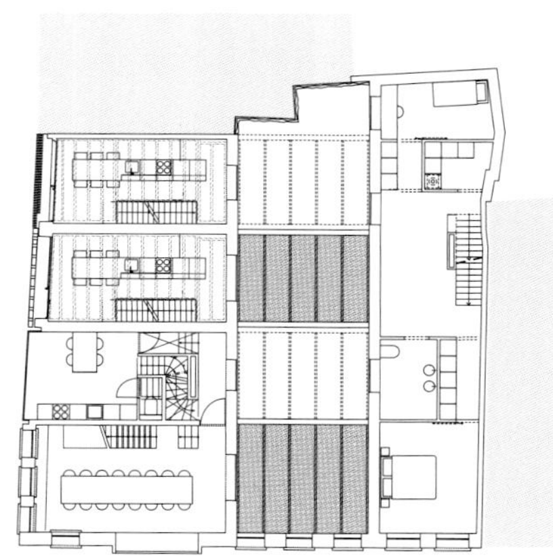

First floor plan

ELUA ARCHITECTURE

Founded in September 2006 by Clément Miglierina, the elua® studio works on a wide variety of projects, public and private, from scenography to collective housing, from educational programs to cultural programs including the design of objects.
By tilting a universal shape by a few degrees, the studio elua® distorts the traditional geometry of the small suburban house to turn it into a new volume, abstract and immaculate. A rebirth that galvanises the inside space and disrupts the conventions of urban space.

Das elua® Studio wurde im September 2006 von Clément Miglierina gegründet und arbeitet an einer Vielzahl von öffentlichen und privaten Projekten, von Szenografie bis zu kollektivem Wohnen, von Bildungsprogrammen bis zu Kulturprogrammen, einschließlich der Gestaltung von Objekten.
Indem das Studio elua® eine universelle Form um einige Grad kippt, verzerrt es die traditionelle Geometrie des kleinen Vorstadthauses, um es in ein neues, abstraktes und makelloses Volumen zu verwandeln. Eine Wiedergeburt, die den Innenraum belebt und die Konventionen des Stadtraums aufbricht.

Fondé en septembre 2006 par Clément Miglierina, le studio elua® travaille sur des projets très variés, publics et privés, de la scénographie à l'habitat collectif, des programmes éducatifs aux programmes culturels en passant par le design d'objets.
En inclinant une forme universelle de quelques degrés, le studio elua® déforme la géométrie traditionnelle de la petite maison de banlieue pour la transformer en un nouveau volume, abstrait et immaculé. Une renaissance qui galvanise l'espace intérieur et bouleverse les conventions de l'espace urbain.

Fundado en septiembre de 2006 por Clément Miglierina, el estudio elua® trabaja en una amplia variedad de proyectos públicos y privados, desde la escenografía hasta la vivienda colectiva, desde programas educativos hasta programas culturales, incluido el diseño de objetos.
Al inclinar unos grados una forma universal, el estudio elua® distorsiona la geometría tradicional de la pequeña casa suburbana para convertirla en un nuevo volumen, abstracto e inmaculado. Un renacimiento que galvaniza el espacio interior y rompe las convenciones del espacio urbano tradicional.

www.elua.eu
studio@elua.eu

GONE WITH THE WIND

This house makes the most of the land to offer practical interior space and as much garden space as possible. The construction, with a gable roof and sloping to the west, is inspired by the old farm sheds worn out by time and climate. Under the roof structure, a house painted in Klein blue, which seems to float in space, contains two bedrooms, a bathroom, a toilet and a small open attic. The staircase draws a graphic thread linking the two floors; but it is also a small interior balcony, a platform to live and look through the large triangular window on the gable wall.

Dieses Haus nutzt das Land optimal aus, um praktischen Innenraum und möglichst viel Gartenfläche zu bieten. Die Konstruktion mit einem Satteldach und einer Neigung nach Westen ist inspiriert von den alten, durch Zeit und Wetter abgenutzten Schuppen. Unter der Dachkonstruktion befindet sich ein in Klein-Blau gestrichenes Haus, das im Raum zu schweben scheint, mit zwei Schlafzimmern, einem Badezimmer, einer Toilette und einem kleinen offenen Dachboden. Die Treppe zieht einen grafischen Faden, der die beiden Stockwerke verbindet; sie ist aber auch ein kleiner Innenbalkon, eine Plattform zum Leben und zum Blick durch das große dreieckige Fenster an der Giebelwand.

Cette maison tire le meilleur parti du terrain sur laquelle elle est implantée pour offrir un espace intérieur pratique et une surface maximale jardin. La structure, avec un toit à pignon et en pente vers l'ouest, est inspirée des anciennes remises des fermes, usées par le temps et le climat. Sous la structure du toit, la maison peinte en bleu Klein, qui semble flotter dans l'espace, contient deux chambres à coucher, une salle de bains, des toilettes et un petit grenier ouvert. L'escalier dessine un fil graphique reliant les deux étages ; mais il s'agit là aussi d'un petit balcon intérieur, d'une plate-forme où vivre et regarder à travers la grande fenêtre triangulaire située sur le mur pignon.

Esta casa saca el máximo provecho del terreno para ofrecer un espacio interior práctico y el mayor espacio posible de jardín. La construcción, con tejado a dos aguas e inclinada hacia el oeste se inspira en los viejos cobertizo de las granjas ajados por el tiempo y el clima. Bajo la estructura del tejado, una casa pintada en azul Klein, que parece flotar en el espacio, contiene dos dormitorios, un baño, un aseo y un pequeño ático abierto. La escalera dibuja un hilo gráfico que une los dos pisos; pero también es un pequeño balcón interior, una plataforma para vivir y mirar a través de la gran ventana triangular de la pared del frontón.

LOCATION
Mérignac, Bordeaux, France

PHOTOS
© elua

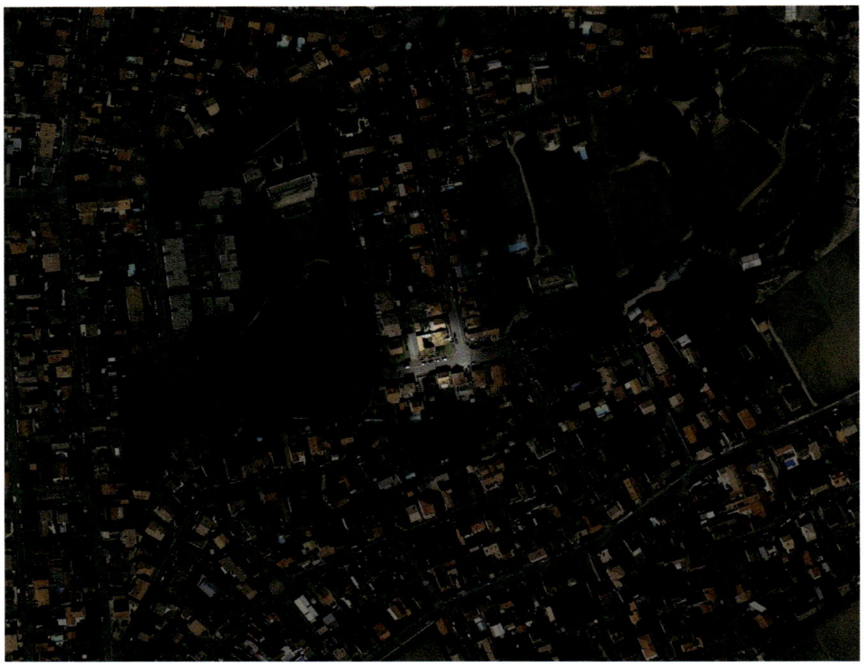

Site plan

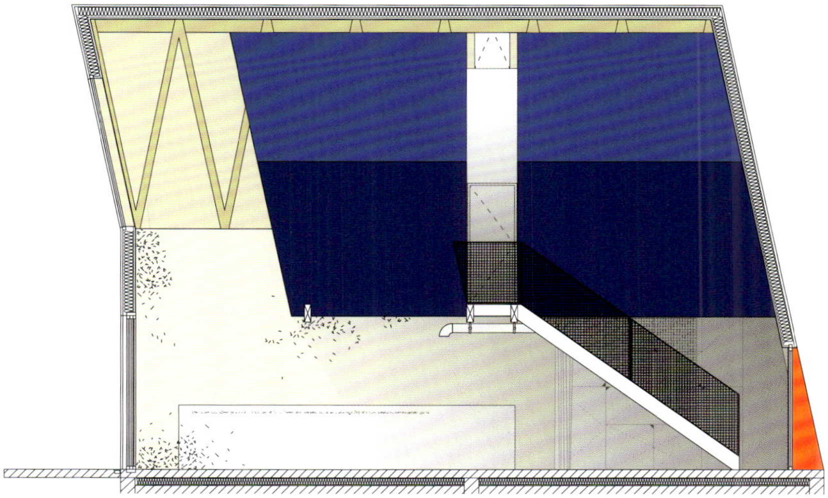
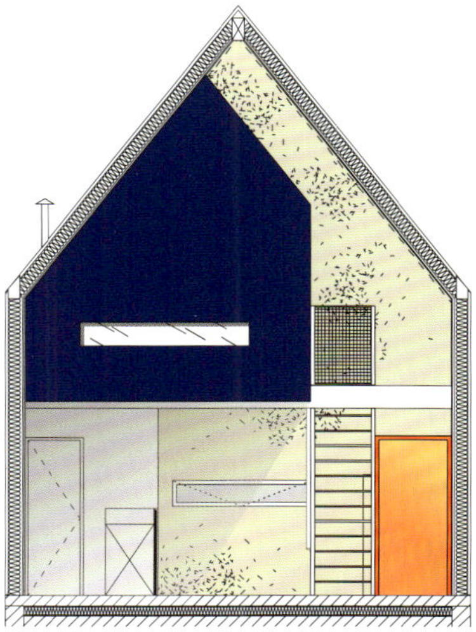

Sections

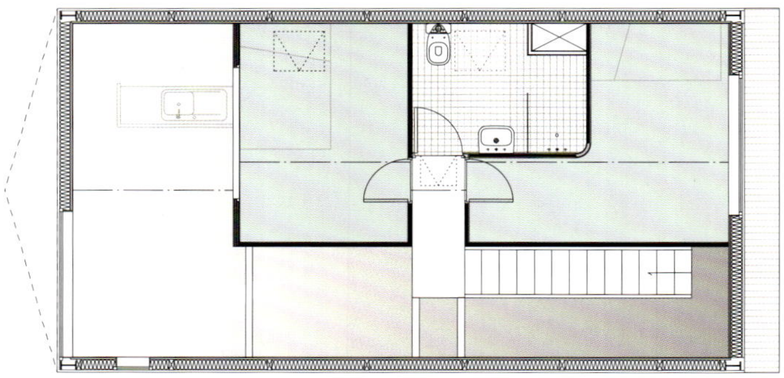

First floor plan

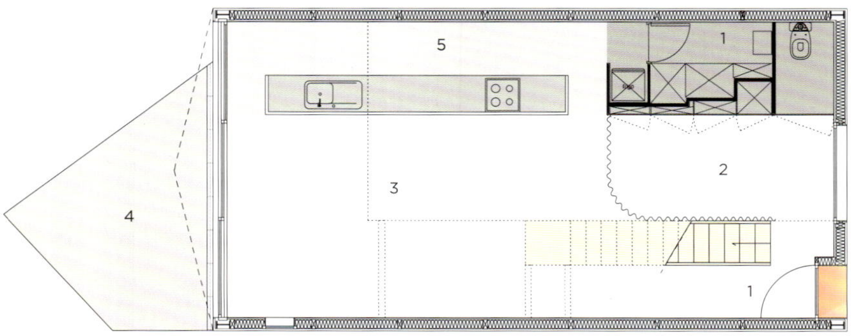

1. Entry
2. Modular space
3. Living room
4. Terrace
5. Kitchen
6. Cellar

Ground floor plan

FUMIASO

ARCHITECT & ASSOCIATES

When one architecture is born, it is born with a lot of thoughts and expectations.
I dream of becoming an architect that will be loved by many people.
When one architecture is born, history already exists there.
Taking into account the history of the place, the memories of the builder, the experience of the designer, and their context, a new history (architecture) is born.
To be loved for a long time and continue to live.
The builder's thought is the architecture itself.
By all means, I would like to be involved as a designer in an architecture that brings out the "thoughts" and "expectations" of such a person.
We aim to listen to the owner, listen to the site, and create a beloved architecture that can only be found here.

www.fumiaso-aa.com
fumiaso@fumiaso-aa.com

Wenn eine Architektur geboren wird, geschieht das mit vielen Gedanken und Erwartungen.
Ich träume davon, eine Architektur zu schaffen, die von vielen Menschen geliebt wird.
Wenn eine Architektur geboren wird, existiert dort bereits Geschichte.
Wenn man die Geschichte des Ortes, die Erinnerungen des Erbauers, die Erfahrung des Entwerfenden und ihren Kontext berücksichtigt, wird eine neue Geschichte (Architektur) geboren.
Für lange Zeit geliebt zu werden und weiterzuleben.
Der Gedanke des Erbauers ist die Architektur selbst.
Auf jeden Fall möchte ich als Entwerfender an einer Architektur beteiligt sein, die die „Gedanken" und „Erwartungen" einer solchen Person zum Ausdruck bringt.
Unser Ziel ist es, dem Bauherrn zuzuhören, der Website zuzuhören und eine geliebte Architektur zu schaffen, die nur hier zu finden ist.

Quand une architecture naît, elle naît avec beaucoup de pensées et d'attentes.
Je rêve de devenir une architecture qui sera aimée par beaucoup de personnes.
Lorsqu'une architecture naît, l'histoire y est déjà présente.
En tenant compte de l'histoire du lieu, des souvenirs du constructeur, de l'expérience du concepteur et de leur contexte, une nouvelle histoire (l'architecture) naît.
Pour être aimé longtemps et continuer à vivre.
La pensée du constructeur est l'architecture elle-même.
Par tous les moyens, je voudrais être impliqué en tant que designer dans une architecture qui fait ressortir les «pensées» et les «attentes» d'une telle personne.
Notre objectif est d'écouter le propriétaire, d'écouter le site et de créer une architecture bien-aimée qui ne peut être trouvée qu'ici.

Cuando nace una arquitectura, lo hace llena de pensamientos y expectativas.
Sueño con conseguir una arquitectura que sea amada por mucha gente.
Cuando nace una arquitectura, la historia está ya presente.
Teniendo en cuenta la historia del lugar, los recuerdos del constructor, la experiencia del diseñador y su contexto, nace una nueva historia (arquitectura).
Para ser amado durante mucho tiempo y continuar viviendo.
El pensamiento del constructor es la propia arquitectura.
Por supuesto, me gustaría involucrarme como diseñador en una arquitectura que sacara a relucir los pensamientos» y «expectativas» de la gente.
Nuestro objetivo es escuchar al propietario, entender el contexto, y crear una arquitec-

MOON HOUSE

An unnamed space was created in this house by inserting one wall in a square volume giving richness to a living space that becomes a gentle area that makes everyday life stand out. A quiet and soft space and an active room are now back-to-back, making it a place for families to come and go.

Eine Wand, die in ein quadratisches Volumen eingefügt wurde, breitet sich aus und hat eine Lücke, so dass in diesem Haus ein unbenannter Raum geschaffen wurde, der dem Wohnraum Reichtum und Ausflug verleiht. Dies ist ein leerer Raum zwischen der Stadt und diesem Haus. Dieser Raum ist zu einem sanften Raum geworden, der das alltägliche Leben zur Geltung bringt. So liegen ein ruhiger und weicher Raum und ein aktiver und alltäglicher Raum Rücken an Rücken und erzeugen einen Ort, an dem Familien kommen und gehen können.

Un mur inséré dans un volume carré s'étale et présente un vide, de sorte qu'un espace sans nom a été créé dans cette maison. Cela procure richesse et excursion à l'espace de vie. Il s'agit d'un espace vide entre la ville et cette maison. Cet espace est devenu un espace doux qui fait ressortir la vie quotidienne. Un espace calme et doux et un espace actif et quotidien se trouvent dos à dos, ce qui en fait un lieu d'allées et venues pour les familles.

El cuerpo original consistía en una pared insertada en una adición en forma de volumen cuadrado, por lo que se creó un espacio que diera riqueza al espacio, un espacio que se ha convertido en refugio para la vida cotidiana; un espacio tranquilo pero activo, un lugar que invita a salir y entrar.

LOCATION
Sakai, Osaka Prefecture, Japan

PHOTOS
© Kenta Hasegawa

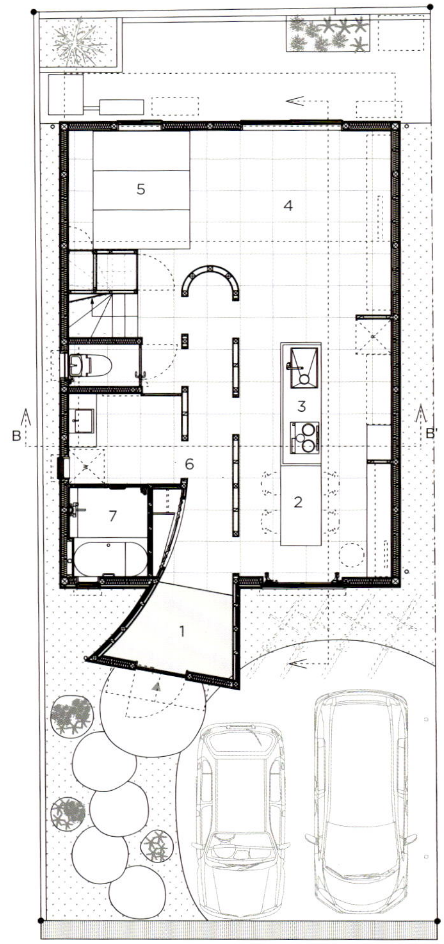

Ground floor plan

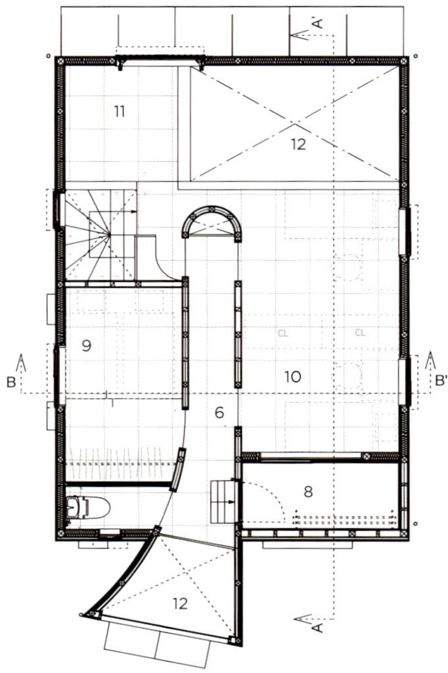

Second floor plan

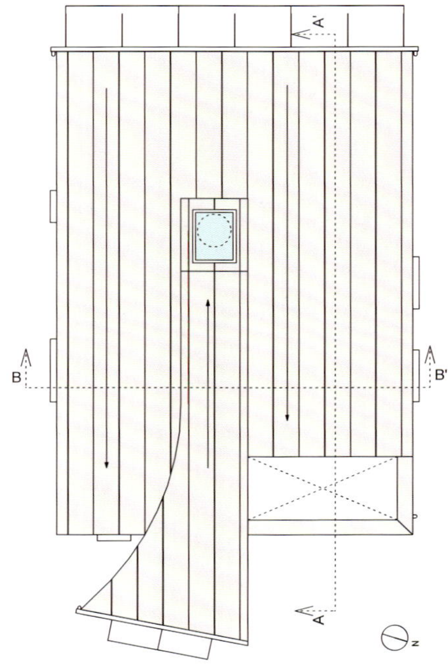

Third floor plan

1. Entrance
2. Dining room
3. Kitchen
4. Living room
5. Tatami
6. Margin space
7. Bathroom
8. Terrace
9. Space 1
10. Space 2
11. Cloak
12. Void

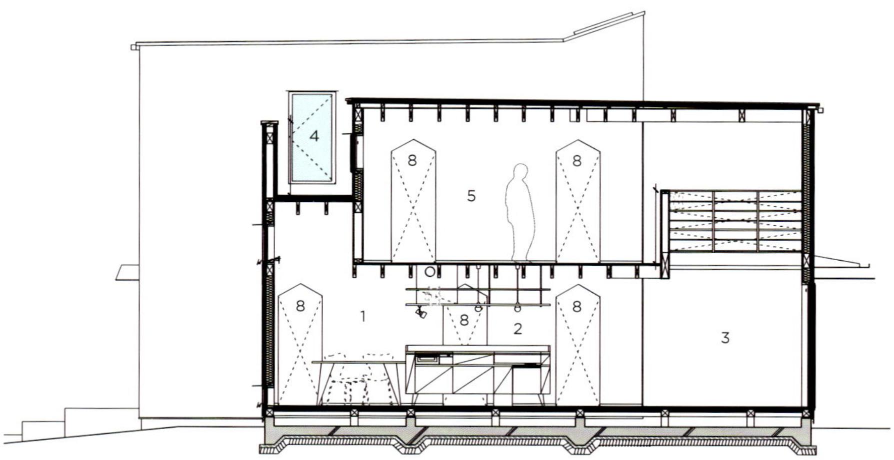

A-A′ section

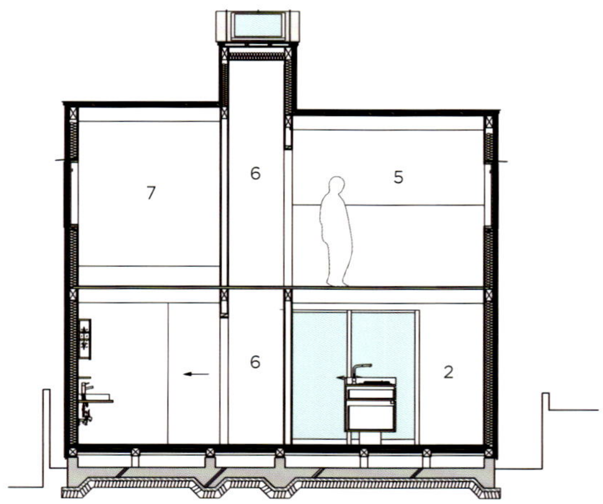

B-B′ section

1. Dining room
2. Kitchen
3. Living room
4. Terrace
5. Space 2
6. Margin space
7. Space 1
8. Open

HAT HOUSE

When new architecture is born, there is still a history behind.The history of the place, the memories of the residents and the own designer's experience help to create a new history (architecture). When a new architecture project is born, many thoughts and expectations are set out; I hope that this architecture will be loved by many people from now on.

Wenn eine neue Architektur geboren wird, gibt es bereits Geschichte. Die Geschichte des Ortes, die Erinnerungen der Bewohner und die Erfahrung des Planers durch ihren Kontext schaffen eine neue Geschichte (Architektur). So kann diese Architektur für lange Zeit geliebt und am Leben erhalten werden. Wenn eine Architektur geboren wird, sind darin viele Gedanken und Erwartungen verankert. Ich hoffe, dass sie von nun an zu dieser Architektur wird, die von vielen Menschen geliebt wird.

Quand une nouvelle architecture naît, il y a déjà de l'histoire. L'histoire du lieu, les souvenirs des habitants et l'expérience du concepteur, du fait de leur contexte, créent une nouvelle histoire (l'architecture). L'idée est que cette architecture soit aimée pendant longtemps et qu'elle reste vivante. Lorsqu'une architecture naît, de nombreuses pensées et attentes y sont inscrites. J'espère qu'elle deviendra cette architecture aimée par beaucoup de gens à partir de maintenant.

Cuando nace una nueva arquitectura ya hay detrás una historia que contar. La historia del lugar, los recuerdos de los residentes, la experiencia del diseñador, la tradición del contexto en el que se construye... esto es la arquitectura y una forma de mantenerla viva y amada. Espero seguir generando de ahora en adelante una arquitectura que sea amada y recordada por la gente.

LOCATION
Kobe, Hyogo Prefecture, Japan

PHOTOS
© Shigeo Ogawa

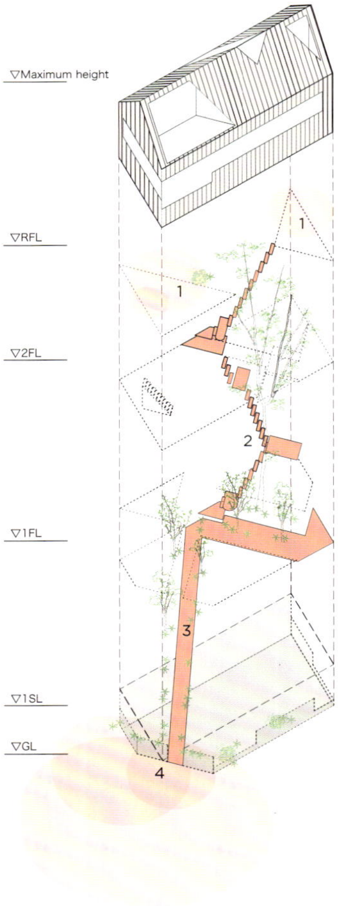

Three-dimensional alley

Alley connects town and architecture, and guides people into this house.

People come and go as the architecture breathes.

1. Terrace
2. Courtyard
3. Alley
4. Approach

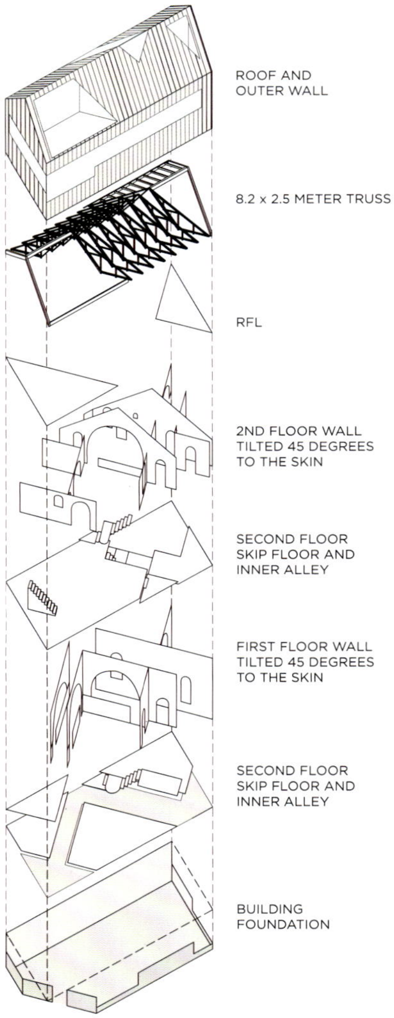

Architecture composition

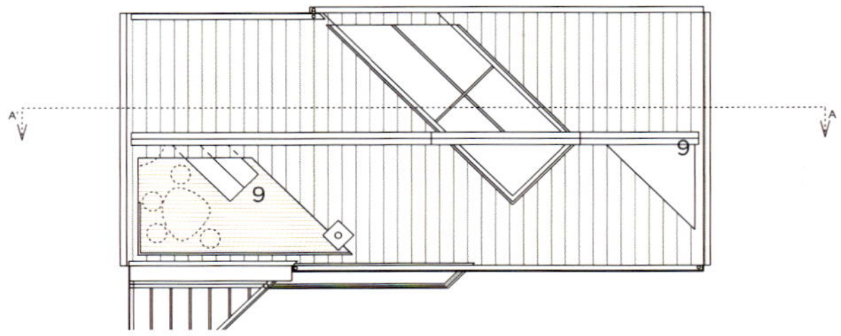

Roof plan

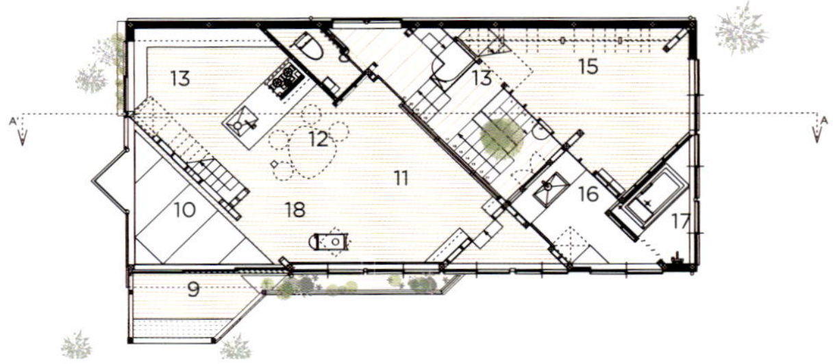

First floor plan

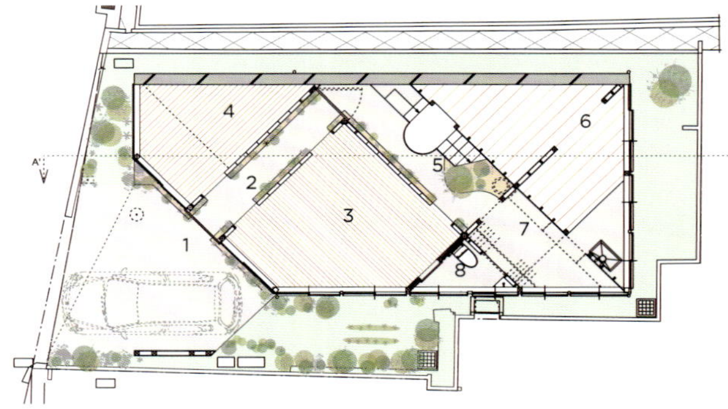

Ground floor plan

1. Approach
2. Alley
3. Atelier 1
4. Atelier 2
5. Courtyard
6. Space A
7. Garage
8. WC
9. Terrace
10. Japanese room
11. Living
12. Dining
13. Kitchen
14. Courtyard
15. Space B
16. Washroom
17. Bathroom
18. Loft

A-A section

1. Space A
2. Space B
3. Courtyard
4. Atelier 1
5. Atelier 2
6. Alley
7. Living
8. Dining
9. Kitchen
10. Public road

G20 ARCHITECTS

G20 was founded in 2011 by Michele Grazzini and Stephan Obermaier. We have learned that only an open and constant discussion about the approaches to the various tasks leads to success. The goal of G20 is to realize individual and sustainable architectures that have an emotional and aesthetically perceptible component. To achieve this, we work in intensive exchange with all project participants, the city, the builders, specialist planners, experts from other areas and the end users.
Our experiences so far range from furniture designs to the conception of large urban structures. Timelessness and cost-effectiveness influence our daily responsibility, "think global, act local" plays an important role in this.

www.g2o-arch.eu
info@g2o-arch.eu

Die G20 wurde 2011 von Michele Grazzini und Stephan Obermaier gegründet. Wir haben gelernt, dass nur eine offene und ständige Diskussion über die Herangehensweise an die verschiedenen Aufgaben zum Erfolg führt. Das Ziel von G20 ist es, individuelle und nachhaltige Architekturen zu realisieren, die eine emotionale und ästhetisch wahrnehmbare Komponente haben. Um dies zu erreichen, arbeiten wir im intensiven Austausch mit allen Projektbeteiligten, der Stadt, den Bauherren, Fachplanern, Experten aus anderen Bereichen und den Endnutzern.
Unsere bisherigen Erfahrungen reichen vom Möbeldesign bis hin zur Konzeption großer Stadtstrukturen. Zeitlosigkeit und Kosteneffizienz beeinflussen unsere tägliche Verantwortung. „Think global, act local" spielt dabei eine wichtige Rolle.

Le G20 a été fondé en 2011 par Michele Grazzini et Stephan Obermaier. Nous avons appris que seule une discussion ouverte et constante sur les approches des différentes tâches mène au succès. L'objectif de G20 est de réaliser des architectures individuelles et durables qui ont une composante émotionnelle et esthétiquement perceptible. Pour y parvenir, nous travaillons dans le cadre d'un échange intensif avec tous les participants au projet : la ville, les constructeurs, les planificateurs spécialisés, les experts d'autres domaines et les utilisateurs finaux.
Nos expériences jusqu'à présent vont de la conception de meubles à la conception de grandes structures urbaines. L'intemporalité et la rentabilité influencent notre responsabilité quotidienne, « penser globalement, agir localement » joue un rôle important à cet égard.

El estudio G20 fue fundado en 2011 por Michele Grazzini y Stephan Obermaier. Hemos aprendido que sólo una discusión abierta y constante sobre los enfoques de las diversas tareas conduce al éxito. El objetivo del G20 es una arquitectura individual y sostenible que tenga un componente emocional y estéticamente perceptible. Para lograrlo, trabajamos en un intenso intercambio con todos los participantes del proyecto, la ciudad, los constructores, los planificadores especializados, los expertos de otras áreas y los usuarios finales.
Nuestras experiencias hasta el momento van desde el diseño de muebles hasta la concepción de grandes estructuras urbanas. La intemporalidad y la rentabilidad influyen en nuestra responsabilidad diaria, «pensar globalmente, actuar localmente».

ES PO 356H
120

OS66.1 HOUSE

This house for working and living preserved the spirit of a traditional Stuttgart Rückgebäude. Four apartments and an office floor were created, with the associated parking spaces and a new amber tree. The result was equipped with an external lift -staircase combination.
Monolithic and monochrome on the outside, individually on the inside, each unit is designed to the needs of residents and users. Old brick walls visibly contrast with the light grey design of the house. Built-in furniture becomes part of the architecture. Energetically, the building meets the "Passive House" standard.

Der Geist eines traditionellen Stuttgarter Rückgebäudes, eines Hauses zum Arbeiten und Wohnen, wurde bewahrt. So entstanden vier Wohnungen und eine Büroetage mit den dazugehörigen Parkplätzen und einem neuen Bernsteinbaum. Das Ergebnis wurde mit einer außenliegenden Aufzug-/Treppenhaus-Kombination ausgestattet.
Außen monolithisch und monochrom, innen individuell: Jede Einheit ist auf die Bedürfnisse der Bewohner und Nutzer ausgerichtet. Alte Ziegelsteinmauern kontrastieren sichtbar mit dem hellgrauen Design des Hauses. Einbaumöbel werden Teil der Architektur. Energetisch entspricht das Gebäude dem Passivhausstandard.

L'esprit d'un Rückgebäude traditionnel de Stuttgart a été préservé : une maison pour travailler et vivre. Ainsi, quatre appartements et un étage de bureaux ont été créés, avec les places de parking associées et un nouvel arbre d'ambre. Le résultat a été équipé d'une combinaison ascenseur/escalier extérieur.
Monolithique et monochrome à l'extérieur, individuel à l'intérieur : chaque unité est conçue en fonction des besoins des résidents et des utilisateurs. Les vieux murs en briques contrastent visiblement avec le design gris clair de la maison. Les meubles intégrés font partie de l'architecture. Sur le plan énergétique, le bâtiment répond à la norme des maisons passives.

El proyecto consiste en una casa para trabajar y vivir que sigue en su concepción el espíritu de un *Rückgebäude*, un trastero tradicional típico de Stuttgart. Se crearon cuatro apartamentos y un piso de oficinas, con los correspondientes espacios de aparcamiento. El resultado se equipó con una combinación de ascensor/escalera exterior.
Monolítico y monocromo en el exterior, en el interior cada unidad está diseñada para las necesidades de los residentes y usuarios. Las viejas paredes de ladrillo contrastan visiblemente con el diseño gris claro de la casa. Los muebles empotrados se convierten en parte de la arquitectura. Energéticamente, el edificio cumple con el estándar de Casa Pasiva.

LOCATION
Stuttgart, Germany

PHOTOS
© Brigida González

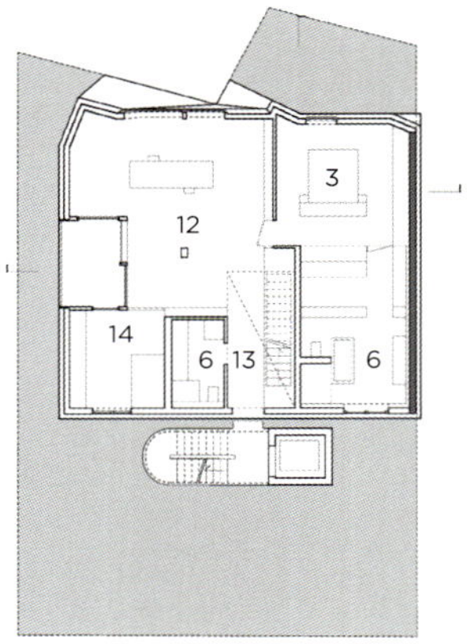

Third floor plan

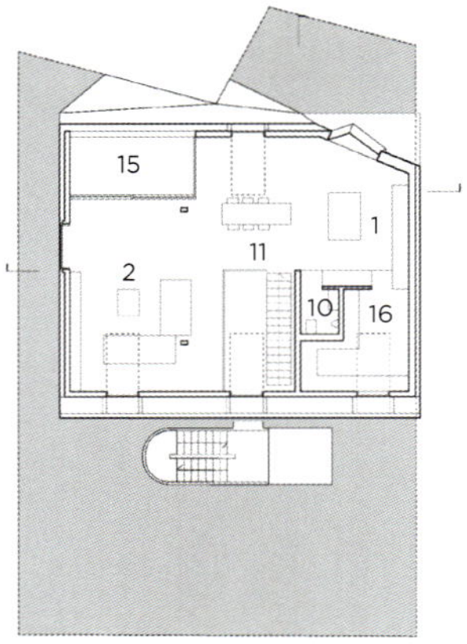

Fourth floor plan

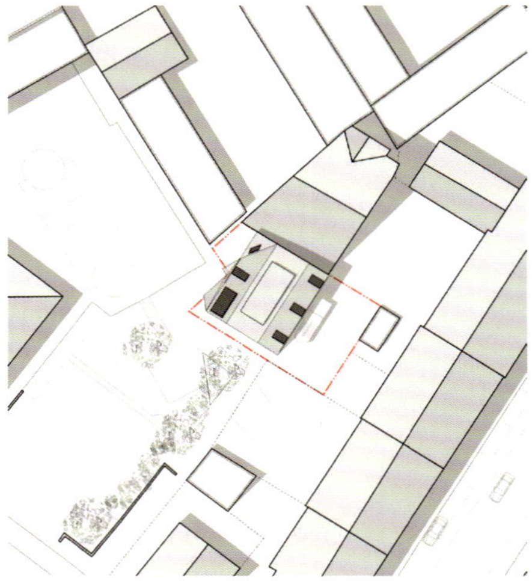

Site plan

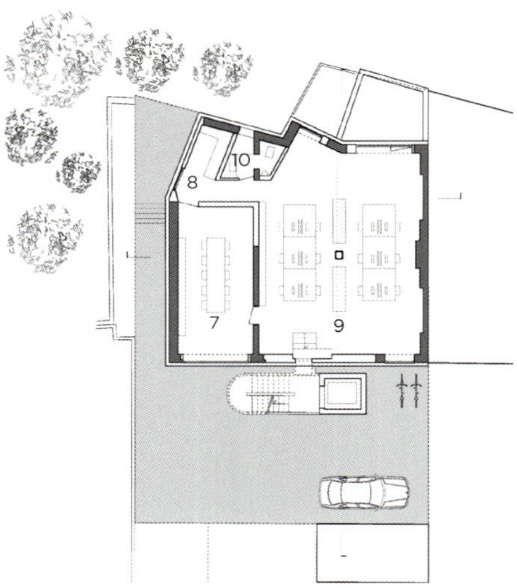

First floor plan

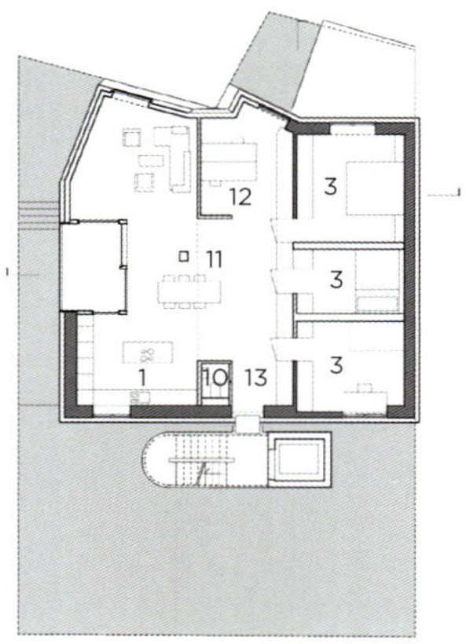

Second floor plan

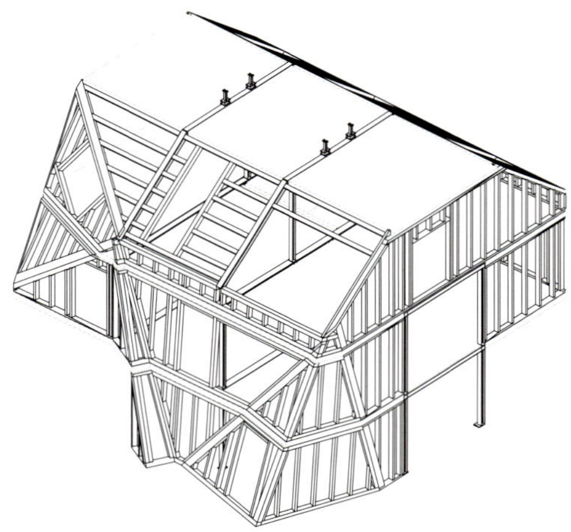

Axonometry

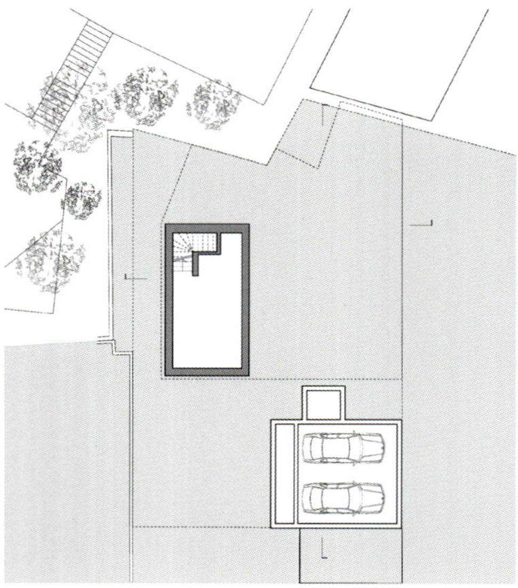

Basement plan

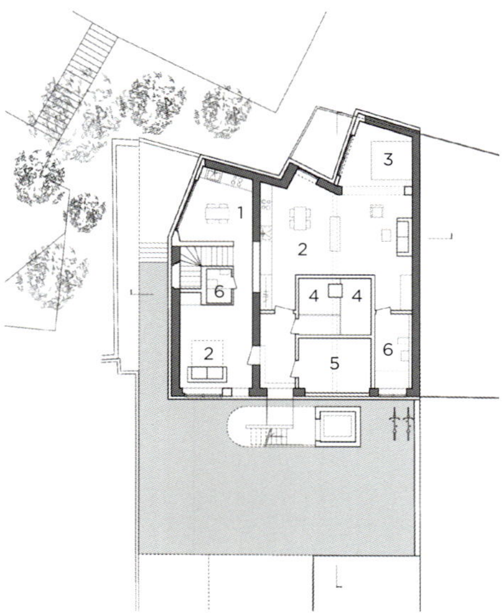

Ground floor plan

1. Kitchen
2. Living room
3. Bedroom
4. Cellar
5. Technical room
6. Bathroom
7. Meeting room
8. Kitchenette
9. Working space
10. Toilet
11. Dining room
12. Office
13. Hall
14. Guest room
15. Winter garden
16. Store

GRAUX & BAEYENS

ARCHITECTEN

GRAUX & BAEYENS architecten was established in 2005 in Ghent, Belgium, by Koen Baeyens and Basile Graux. The practice operates in the field of contemporary architecture, interior and product design and has developed a distinct architectural vision during the last 15 years. The office is realizing a variety of projects in Belgium, ranging from single family dwellings, offices and design furniture.
GBA strives to create ideas that result in one clear concept that emerge through continuous questioning and production. From the start, they resolutely opted for a total approach: from urban scale to the interior and its details. They try to distil the right questions in every assignment and answer with a clear vision and proposal. Their design logic starts from a synergy. The context of building in a saturated Flanders inspires GBA to create its own architectural language, giving answers to the contemporary urban complexity with an apparent simplicity.

www.graux-baeyens.be
info@graux-baeyens.be

GRAUX & BAEYENS Architecten wurde 2005 in Gent, Belgien, von Koen Baeyens und Basile Graux gegründet. Das Büro ist auf dem Gebiet der zeitgenössischen Architektur, des Innen- und Produktdesigns tätig und hat in den letzten 15 Jahren eine eigene architektonische Vision entwickelt. Das Büro realisiert eine Vielzahl von Projekten in Belgien, von Einfamilienhäusern über Büros bis hin zu Designmöbeln.
GBA ist bestrebt, Ideen zu entwickeln, die zu einem klaren Konzept führen, das durch kontinuierliche Befragung und Produktion entsteht. Von Anfang an entschieden sie sich entschieden für einen Gesamtansatz: vom städtischen Maßstab bis zum Innenraum und seinen Details. Sie versuchen, in jeder Aufgabe die richtigen Fragen zu destillieren und mit einer klaren Vision und einem klaren Vorschlag zu beantworten. Ihre Designlogik geht von einer Synergie aus. Der Kontext des Bauens in einem gesättigten Flandern inspiriert GBA dazu, eine eigene Architektursprache zu schaffen, die mit scheinbarer Einfachheit Antworten auf die zeitgenössische städtische Komplexität gibt.

GRAUX & BAEYENS architectes a été fondée en 2005 à Gand, en Belgique, par Koen Baeyens et Basile Graux. La pratique opère dans le domaine de l'architecture contemporaine, de la décoration intérieure et de la conception de produits et a développé une vision architecturale distincte au cours des 15 dernières années. Le bureau réalise une variété de projets en Belgique, allant des maisons unifamiliales aux bureaux et au mobilier design.
GBA s'efforce de créer des idées qui aboutissent à un concept clair qui émerge à travers un questionnement et une production continus. Dès le départ, ils ont résolument opté pour une approche globale: de l'échelle urbaine à l'intérieur et aux détails. Ils essaient de distiller les bonnes questions dans chaque mission et répondent avec une vision et une proposition claires. Leur logique de conception part d'une synergie. Le contexte de la construction dans une Flandre saturée inspire GBA à créer son propre langage architectural, donnant des réponses à la complexité urbaine contemporaine avec une simplicité apparente.

GRAUX & BAEYENS architecten se fundó en 2005 en Gante, Bélgica, por Koen Baeyens y Basile Graux. La práctica opera en el campo de la arquitectura contemporánea, el diseño de interiores y productos y ha desarrollado una visión arquitectónica distinta durante los últimos 15 años. Realizan una variedad de proyectos en Bélgica, que van desde viviendas unifamiliares a oficinas y muebles de diseño.
GBA se esfuerza por crear ideas que den como resultado un concepto claro que surja a través de preguntas y producción continuas. Desde el principio, decidieron decididamente un enfoque total: desde la escala urbana hasta el interior y sus detalles. Intentan destilar las preguntas correctas en cada tarea y responder con una visión y propuesta claras. Su lógica de diseño parte de una sinergia. El contexto de la construcción en un Flandes saturado inspira a GBA a crear su propio lenguaje arquitectónico, dando respuestas a la complejidad urbana contemporánea con una aparente simplicidad.

HOUSE L-C

LOCATION
Anzegem, Belgium

PHOTOS
© Jeroen Verrecht Photographs

The project was conceived on an empty trapezium shape plot that forced the architects to a creative solution. A semi-open house was designed, which begins very narrowly on the street side opening up to the back of the plot. The design of the house manifests itself as a composition of three cubes and varying roof heights. The rectangular spaces with functions as office, kitchen and living room are connected with their corners, by opening them. This creates an interesting relationship, accentuated by the concrete beams that support the upper level and roof.

Das Projekt wurde auf einem leeren trapezförmigen Grundstück realisiert, das die Architekten zu einer kreativen Lösung zwang. Es entstand ein halboffenes Haus, das sehr schmal an der Straßenseite beginnt und sich zur Rückseite des Grundstücks hin öffnet. Der Entwurf des Hauses manifestiert sich als eine Komposition aus drei Kuben und unterschiedlichen Dachhöhen. Die rechteckigen Räume mit den Funktionen Büro, Küche und Wohnzimmer sind mit ihren Ecken verbunden, indem sie sich öffnen. Dadurch entsteht eine interessante gegenseitige Beziehung, die durch die Betonbalken, die die obere Ebene und das Dach tragen, noch verstärkt wird.

Le projet a été réalisé sur une parcelle vide en forme de trapèze qui a obligé les architectes à trouver une solution créative. Une maison semi-ouverte a été créée, qui commence très étroitement du côté de la rue et s'ouvre sur l'arrière de la parcelle. La conception de la maison se manifeste par une composition de trois cubes et des hauteurs de toit variables. Les espaces rectangulaires aux fonctions de bureau, de cuisine et de salon sont reliés par leurs angles tout en les ouvrant. Cela crée une relation mutuelle intéressante, accentuée par les poutres en béton qui soutiennent le niveau supérieur et le toit.

El proyecto se realizó en una parcela vacía en forma de trapecio que obligó a los arquitectos a una solución creativa. Se creó una casa semi abierta, que empieza muy estrecha en el lado de la calle y se abre al fondo del terreno. El diseño se basa en una composición de tres cubos y diferentes alturas de techo. Los espacios rectangulares con funciones de oficina, cocina y sala de estar se conectan en sus esquinas, lo que crea una interesante relación mutua, acentuada por las vigas de hormigón que soportan el nivel superior y el techo.

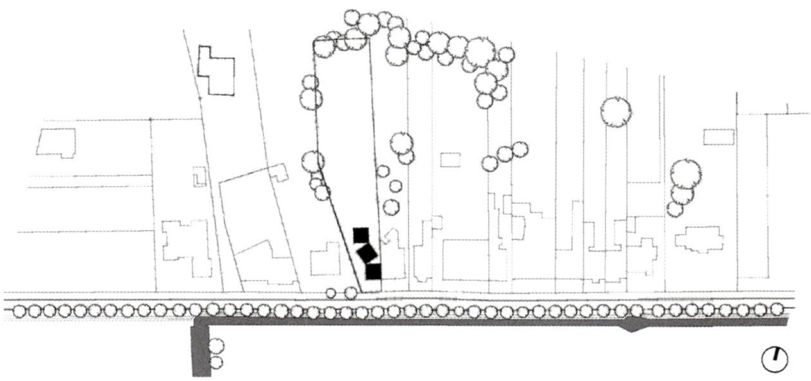

Site plan

Concept diagram

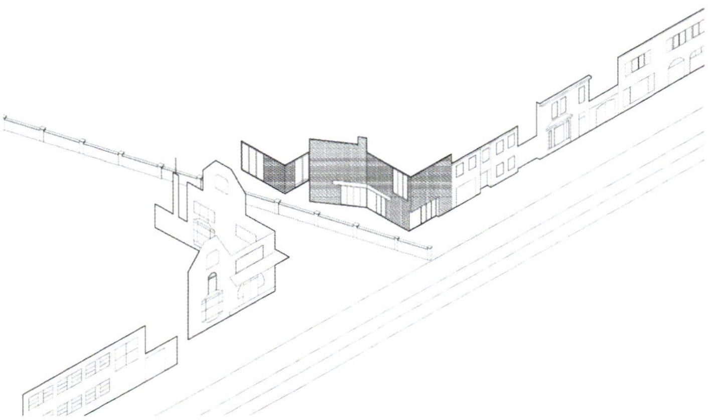

Site plan

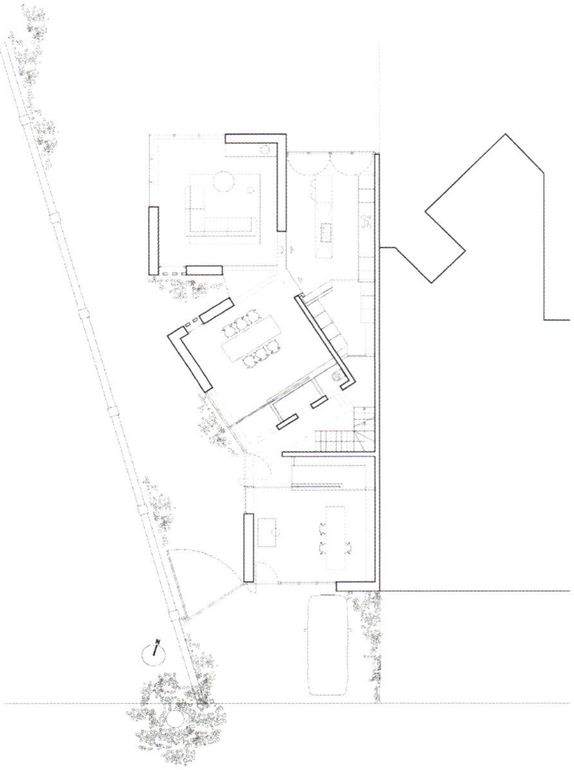

Ground floor plan

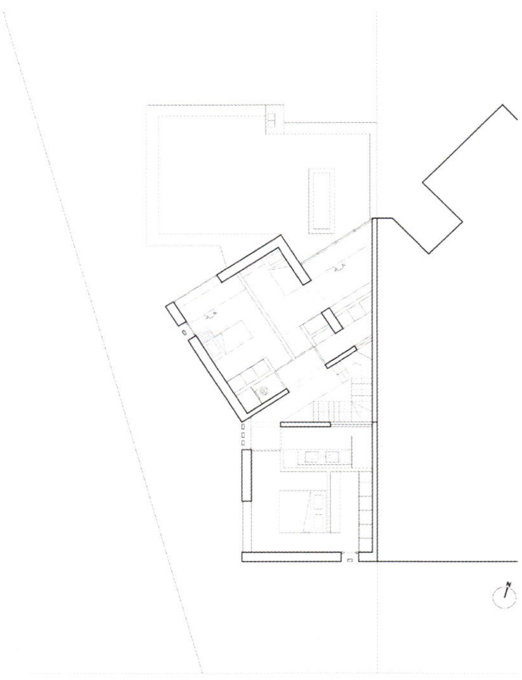

First floor plan

HOUSE VP-VA

This new city dwelling in a suburb of the middle-sized city Ghent has an enriching relationship with its surroundings. The generous front and rear façades enter into a dialogue with the street through the various outdoor areas. This forms a fascinating game of positive and negative spaces. Designed as a so-called 'through-lit house', the different living spaces are also vertically connected by skylights. The vertical, stacked living is therefore experienced as space release.

Diese neue Stadtwohnung in einem Vorort der mittelgroßen Stadt Gent hat eine bereichernde Beziehung zu ihrer Umgebung. Die großzügigen Vorder- und Rückfassaden treten durch die verschiedenen Außenbereiche in einen Dialog mit der Straße, der durch das teilweise Zurückziehen der Fassade entsteht. Dadurch entsteht ein faszinierendes Spiel von positiven und negativen Räumen. Als sogenanntes „durchleuchtetes Haus" konzipiert, sind die verschiedenen Wohnräume auch vertikal durch Hohlräume und Oberlichter miteinander verbunden. Das vertikale/gestapelte Wohnen wird daher als räumlich befreiend erlebt.

Ce nouveau logement urbain, situé dans une banlieue de la ville moyenne de Gand, entretient une relation enrichissante avec son environnement. Les généreuses façades de l'avant et de l'arrière entrent en dialogue avec la rue par le biais des différents espaces extérieurs créés par la rétraction partielle de la façade. Cela crée un jeu fascinant d'espaces positifs et négatifs. Conçues comme une « maison éclairée par la lumière du jour », les différentes zones d'habitation sont également reliées verticalement par des vides et des lucarnes. La vie verticale / superposée de la structure est donc vécue comme une libération spatiale.

Esta nueva ciudad que habita en un suburbio de la ciudad de Gante tiene una relación enriquecedora con su entorno. Las generosas fachadas delantera y trasera entran en diálogo con la calle a través de las diversas zonas exteriores, creadas por la retracción parcial de la fachada. Esto crea un fascinante juego de espacios positivos y negativos. Diseñada como una «casa iluminada», los diferentes espacios habitables están también conectados verticalmente por vacíos y tragaluces. La vida en «vertical» se experimenta por lo tanto como una liberación espacial.

LOCATION
Ghent, Belgium

PHOTOS
© Dennis De Smet

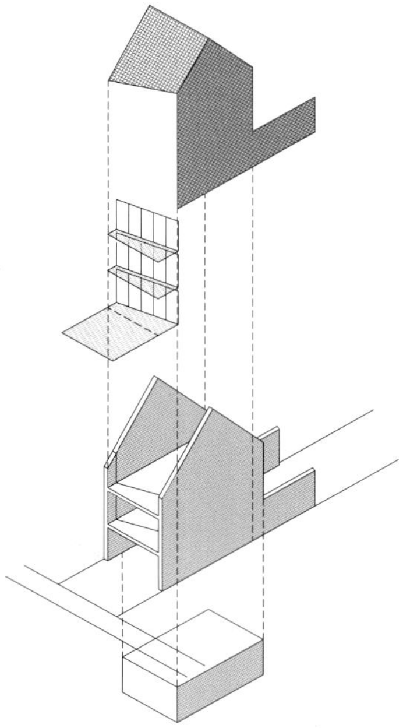

Axonometry exploded

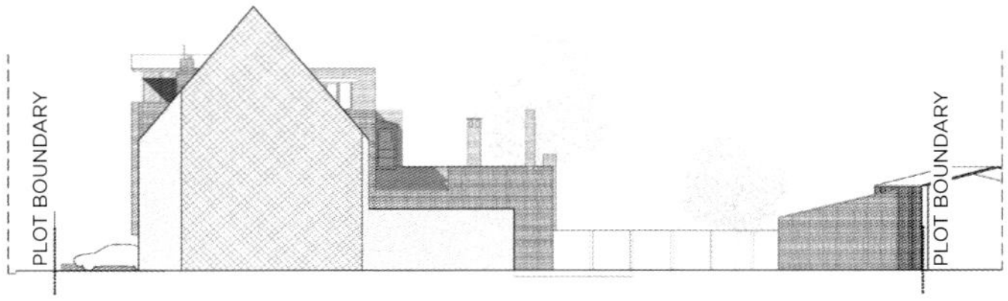

South elevation

West elevation

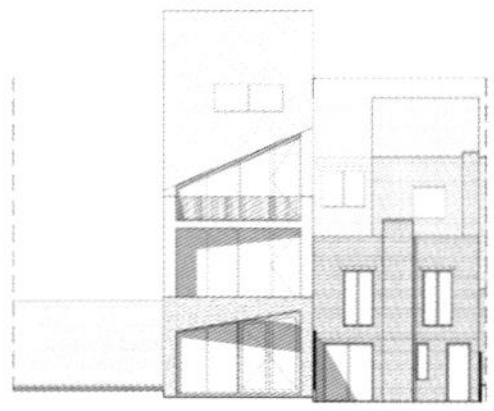

East elevation

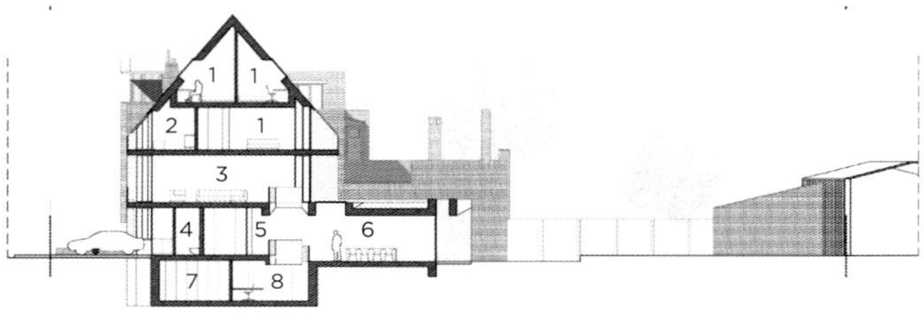

Section

1. Bedroom
2. Bathroom
3. Living room
4. Toilet
5. Kitchen
6. Dining room
7. Storage room
8. Office

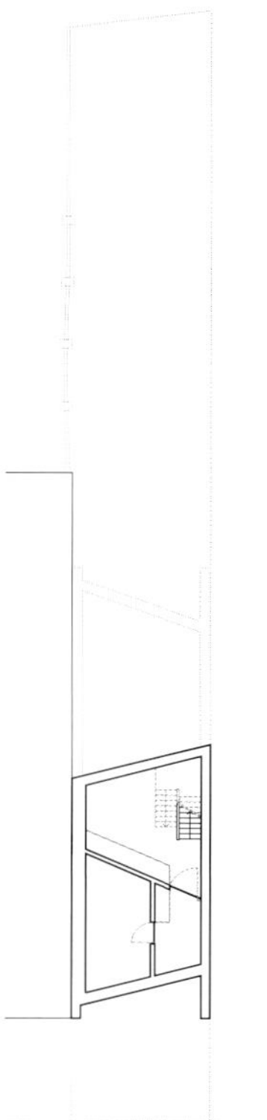

Level -1

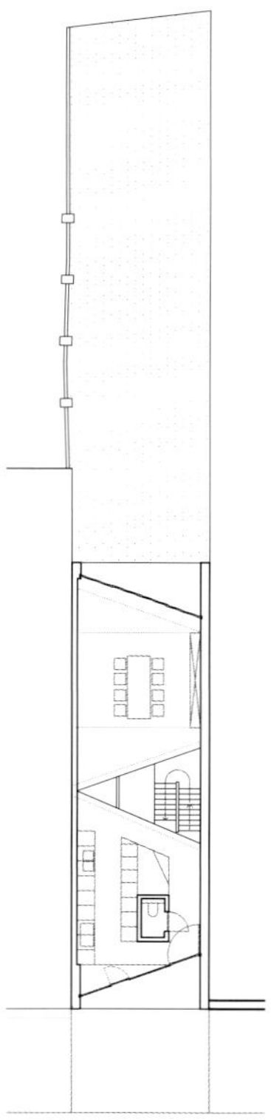

Level +0

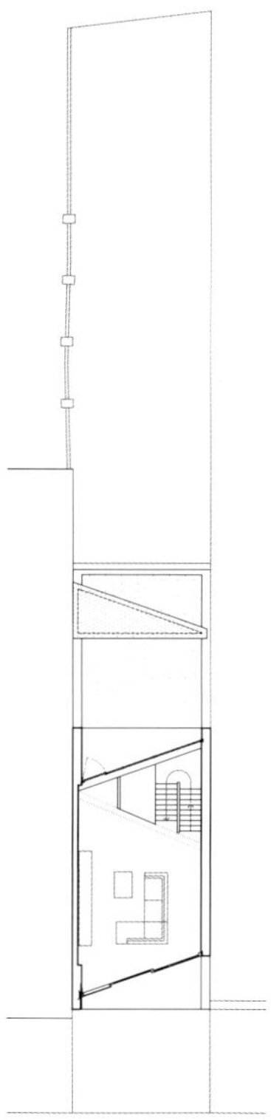

Level +1

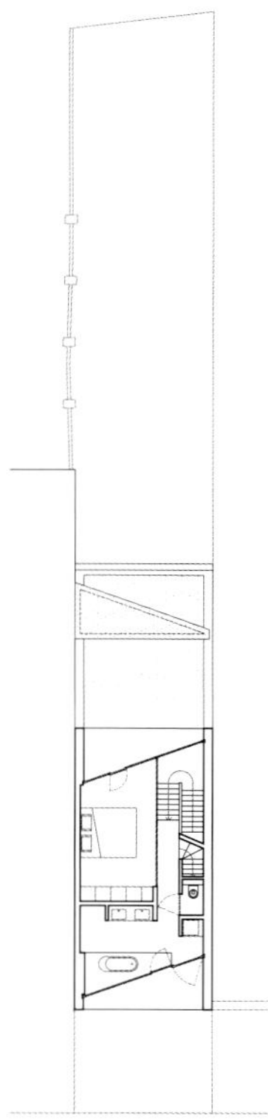

Level +2

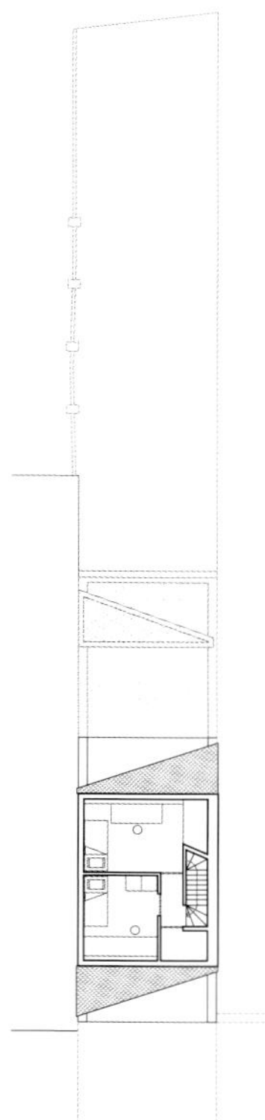

Level +3

HENNING STUMMEL ARCHITECTS

We are a small, award-winning architectural practice, founded by Henning Stummel in 2000. We are passionate about architecture, design and place-making, working closely with our clients to develop the brief and deliver projects which engage and delight. We are a dedicated team who enjoy attention to detail.
Prior to setting up the practice, Henning worked with Sir David Chipperfield (1993 to 2000) and with Lord Foster (1992-93).
He has a general interest in all aspects of design, ranging from consumer products to the pressing issues raised by rapidly expanding conurbations. Fascinated by simple, functional design, there is a great appreciation of the things that transcend time, order, serenity and tranquillity.

www.henningstummelarchitects.com
mail@henningstumelarchitects.com

Wir sind ein kleines, preisgekröntes Architekturbüro, das im Jahr 2000 von Henning Stummel gegründet wurde. Unsere Leidenschaft gilt der Architektur, dem Design und der Gestaltung von Orten. Wir arbeiten eng mit unseren Kunden zusammen, um den Auftrag zu entwickeln und Projekte zu realisieren, die begeistern. Wir sind ein engagiertes Team, das die Liebe zum Detail genießt.
Vor der Gründung des Büros arbeitete Henning Stummel mit Sir David Chipperfield (1993–2000) und mit Lord Foster (1992–93) zusammen.
Er hat ein allgemeines Interesse an allen Aspekten des Designs, von Konsumgütern bis hin zu den drängenden Fragen, die in schnell wachsenden Ballungsräumen aufgeworfen werden. Er ist fasziniert von einfachem, funktionellem Design und hat eine große Wertschätzung für die Dinge, die über Zeit, Ordnung, Ruhe und Gelassenheit hinausgehen.

Nous sommes un petit cabinet d'architectes primé, fondé par Henning Stummel en 2000. Nous sommes passionnés par l'architecture, le design et la création de lieux et nous travaillons en étroite collaboration avec nos clients pour élaborer des projets qui engagent et ravissent. Nous sommes une équipe dévouée qui aime l'attention au détail.
Avant de créer le cabinet, Henning a travaillé avec Sir David Chipperfield (1993 à 2000) et avec Lord Foster (1992-93).
Il s'intéresse à tous les aspects de la conception, des produits de consommation aux questions urgentes soulevées par l'expansion rapide des agglomérations. Fasciné par un design simple et fonctionnel, il apprécie beaucoup les choses qui transcendent le temps, l'ordre, la sérénité et la tranquillité.

Somos un pequeño y premiado estudio de arquitectura fundado por Henning Stummel en el año 2000. Nos apasiona la arquitectura, el diseño y la creación de lugares, trabajando estrechamente con nuestros clientes para desarrollar el concepto y entregar proyectos que se comprometan y deleiten. Somos un equipo que disfruta de la atención al detalle.
Antes de establecer el estudio, Henning trabajó con Sir David Chipperfield (1993-2000) y con Lord Foster (1992-1993).
El estudio tiene un interés general en todos los aspectos del diseño, desde los productos de consumo hasta las cuestiones urgentes que plantean las aglomeraciones urbanas en rápida expansión. Fascinado por el diseño simple y funcional, aprecia las cosas que trascienden el tiempo, el orden, la serenidad y la tranquilidad.

TIN HOUSE

Set in a Victorian neighbourhood, this back country site is overlooked on all sides. Our response was to develop a low, inward looking courtyard house, offering both visual and acoustic privacy.
The design is a composition of pavilions and each one accommodates a room. These spaces have pyramidal roofs with a generous top light over the centre. The roof shape maximizes spatial volume. The top light above brings the spaces to life. The roof-lights can be opened and on warm days the stack effect ensures that fresh cool air is drawn in from above the pool. Secondary spaces such as washrooms are concealed within the double walls in between the pavilions.

LOCATION
London, UK
PHOTOS
© Tim Soar, Zac Nicholson, Gavriil Papadiotis

Diese in einer viktorianischen Nachbarschaft gelegene Stätte im Hinterland wird von allen Seiten eingesehen. Unsere Antwort war die Entwicklung eines niedrigen, nach innen gerichteten Hofhauses, das sowohl visuelle als auch akustische Privatsphäre bietet.
Der Entwurf besteht aus einer Komposition von Pavillons, die jeweils einen Raum beherbergen. Diese Räume haben Pyramidendächer mit einem großzügigen Oberlicht über der Mitte. Die Dachform maximiert das räumliche Volumen. Das Oberlicht darüber erweckt die Räume zum Leben. Die Oberlichter können geöffnet werden, und an warmen Tagen sorgt der Stapeleffekt dafür, dass frische, kühle Luft von über dem Pool angesaugt wird. Nebenräume wie z. B. Waschräume sind in den Doppelwänden zwischen den Pavillons verborgen.

Situé dans un quartier victorien, ce site d'arrière-pays est surplombé de tous côtés. Notre réponse a été de développer une maison basse avec cour intérieure, offrant une intimité visuelle et acoustique.
La conception est une composition de pavillons, chacun d'eux abritant une pièce. Ces espaces ont des toits pyramidaux avec une lumière généreuse en haut au centre. La forme du toit maximise le volume de l'espace. La lumière du haut au-dessus donne vie aux espaces. Les lanterneaux peuvent être ouverts et, les jours chauds, l'effet de cheminée permet d'aspirer l'air frais du dessus de la piscine. Les espaces secondaires, comme les toilettes, sont dissimulés dans les doubles parois entre les pavillons.

El proyecto consistió en construir una casa baja con patio interior en un barrio de estilo Victoriano; una vivienda que ofreciera privacidad visual y acústica.
El diseño se basó en una composición de pabellones en la que cada uno de ellos alberga una habitación. Son espacios con techos piramidales con una generosa luz natural reflejada en la parte central. La forma del techo maximiza el volumen espacial, mientras que la luz cenital da vida a los espacios. Las claraboyas permiten que, en días cálidos, el aire fresco se cuele desde el jardín. Los baños quedan ocultos dentro de las dobles paredes entre pabellones.

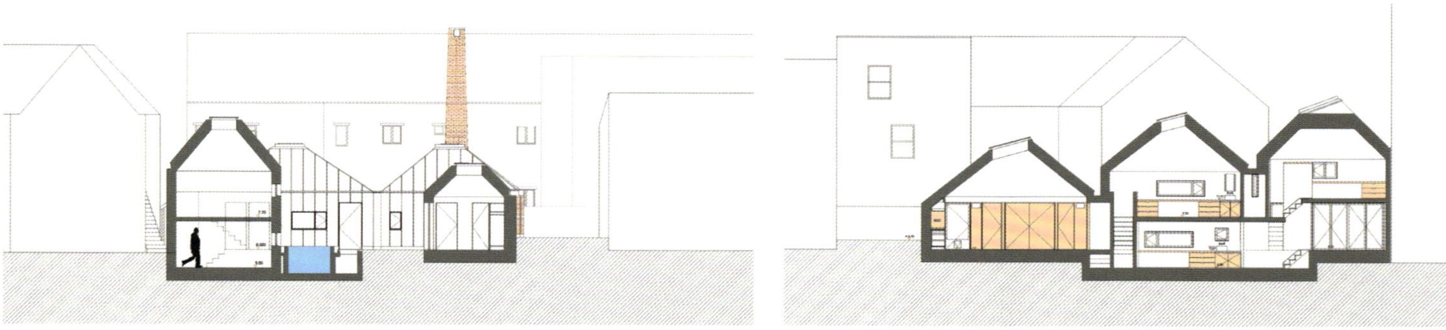

Sections

Sections

Rendering

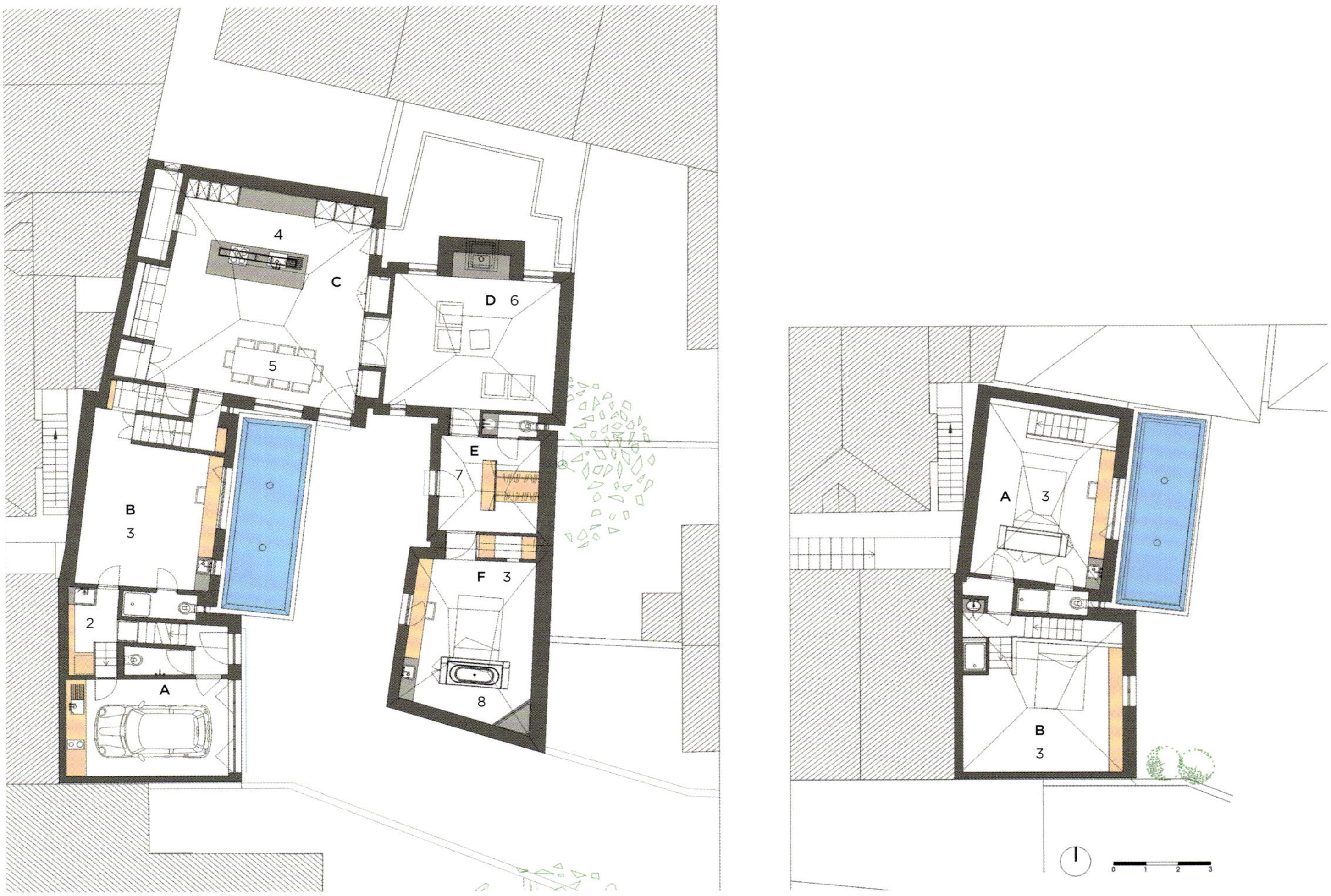

Ground floor and first floor plan

A. Building 1
B. Building 2
C. Building 3
D. Building 4
E. Building 5
F. Building 6

1. Garage / living space
2. Utility room
3. Bedroom
4. Dining area
5. Kitchen
6. Living room
7. Entrance hall
8. Bathroom

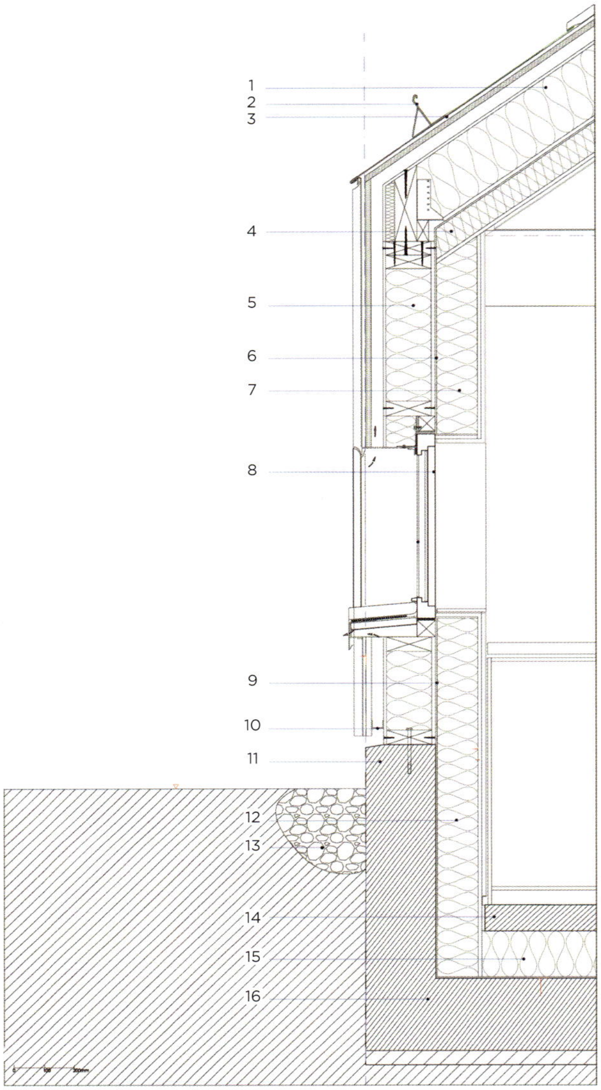

Detailed section of building 3. Backyard

1. Roof Fibrelam or Parallam Timber stand LSL 200 mm Bitvent (or similar) deck
2. Newell Gutter sheet
3. Newell roofing
4. Rigid insulation
5. Wall Fibrelam or Parallam Timber stand LSL 150 mm Bitvent (or similar) deck
6. Air barrier
7. Rigid insulation Thickness 136.5 mm
8. Fixed wooden window
9. Air barrier
10. Insect mesh
11. Concrete upstand Thickness 231.5 mm
12. Joists and insulations 150.5 mm
13. Back filled with gravel
14. Powerfloated polished concrete floor Thickness 90 mm
15. Rigid insulation Thickness 160 mm
16. Concrete slab Thickness 250 mm

IODICE ARCHITETTI

FRANCESCO IODICE, GIUSEPPE IODICE

The iodicearchitetti studio has been working on national and international projects and competitions for a long time.
The design scopes are from an urban architecture scale down to the detail of interior design. Our aim is to answer to complex design programs demands at any scale. In opposition to the latest tendencies, iodicearchitetti group pays attention to the relation between shapes and programs, container and content; a good architecture cannot be separated by a conscious fusion of these two aspects.
We think that architecture, such as literature, music and painting, is a basic component of culture, of any culture and at any time.

Das Atelier iodicearchitetti arbeitet seit Langem an nationalen und internationalen Projekten und Wettbewerben.
Die Gestaltungsmöglichkeiten reichen vom Maßstab der Stadtarchitektur bis hin zum Detail der Innenarchitektur. Unser Ziel ist es, den Anforderungen komplexer Entwurfsprogramme in jeder Größenordnung gerecht zu werden. Im Gegensatz zu den jüngsten Tendenzen achtet die Gruppe iodicearchitetti auf die Beziehung zwischen Formen und Programmen, Behältern und Inhalten; eine gute Architektur lässt sich nicht durch eine bewusste Verschmelzung dieser beiden Aspekte trennen.
Wir sind der Meinung, dass Architektur, wie Literatur, Musik und Malerei, ein grundlegender Bestandteil der Kultur ist, jeder Kultur und zu jeder Zeit.

Le studio iodicearchitetti travaille depuis longtemps sur des projets et des concours nationaux et internationaux.
Les domaines de conception vont de l'échelle de l'architecture urbaine aux détails de la décoration intérieure. Notre objectif est de répondre aux demandes de programmes de design complexes à toute échelle. Contrairement aux dernières tendances, le groupe iodicearchitetti est attentif à la relation entre les formes et les programmes, le contenant et le contenu. Une bonne architecture ne peut être séparée par une fusion consciente de ces deux aspects.
Nous pensons que l'architecture, comme la littérature, la musique et la peinture, est une composante fondamentale de la culture ; de toute culture et à tout moment.

El estudio iodicearchitetti ha estado trabajando en proyectos y concursos nacionales e internacionales durante mucho tiempo.
Los ámbitos de diseño van desde la arquitectura urbana de gran escala hasta el detalle del diseño interior aunque nuestro objetivo es responder a las demandas de programas de diseño complejos a cualquier escala. En oposición a las últimas tendencias, el grupo iodicearchitetti presta especial atención a la relación entre formas y programas, contenedor y contenido; una buena arquitectura no puede separarse por una fusión consciente de estos dos aspectos.
Pensamos que la arquitectura, como la literatura, la música y la pintura, es un componente básico de la cultura, de cualquier cultura y en cualquier momento.

www.iodicearchitetti.com
studio@iodicearchitetti.it

CASA DOPPIA DOUBLE HOUSE

In this house the different parts of the building are organized around several courtyards, each one with its own identity and specific character. The glass surfaces of the ground floor situate the living area in a continuous relationship with the exterior space of the different gardens; unlike the first floor where the volumes are much more compact and where the bedrooms and a small library are located. The two floors are spatially connected by a generous double height characterized by the presence of a skylight formed by large exposed concrete beams.

In diesem Haus sind die verschiedenen Teile des Gebäudes um mehrere Höfe herum organisiert, von denen jeder eine eigene Identität und einen spezifischen Charakter hat. Die Glasflächen des Erdgeschosses stellen den Wohnbereich in eine kontinuierliche Beziehung zum Außenraum der verschiedenen Gärten – im Gegensatz zum ersten Stock, wo die Volumen viel kompakter sind und wo sich die Schlafzimmer und eine kleine Bibliothek befinden. Die beiden Stockwerke sind räumlich durch eine großzügige doppelte Höhe verbunden, die sich durch ein Oberlicht aus großen Sichtbetonbalken auszeichnet.

Dans cette maison, les différentes parties du bâtiment sont organisées autour de plusieurs cours, chacune ayant sa propre identité et son caractère spécifique. Les surfaces vitrées du rez-de-chaussée situent l'espace de vie dans une relation continue avec l'espace extérieur des différents jardins ;contrairement au premier étage où les volumes sont beaucoup plus compacts et où se trouvent les chambres et une petite bibliothèque. Les deux étages sont reliés dans l'espace par une double hauteur généreuse caractérisée par la présence d'un puits de lumière formé par de grandes poutres apparentes en béton.

Las diferentes partes de esta vivienda se organizan en torno a varios patios, cada uno con su propia identidad y un carácter específico. Las superficies acristaladas de la planta baja sitúan la zona de estar en continua relación con el espacio exterior de los distintos jardines; a diferencia de la primera planta donde los volúmenes son mucho más compactos y donde se encuentran los dormitorios y una pequeña biblioteca. Los dos pisos están conectados espacialmente por de una generosa doble altura caracterizada por la presencia de un tragaluz formado por grandes vigas de hormigón expuestas.

LOCATION
San Marcellino, Caserta, Italy

PHOTOS
© Archivio Iodicearchitetti

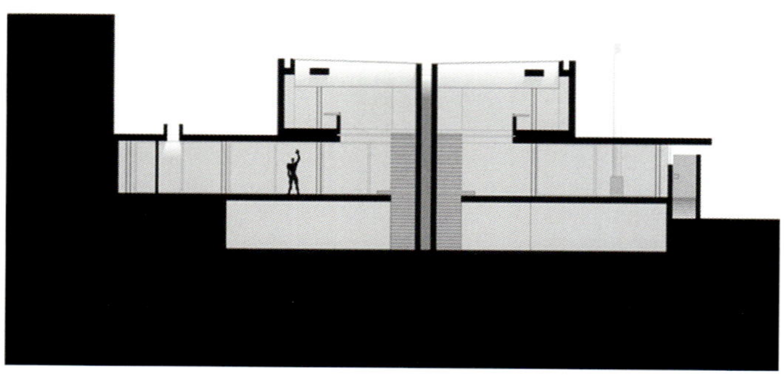

Cross section

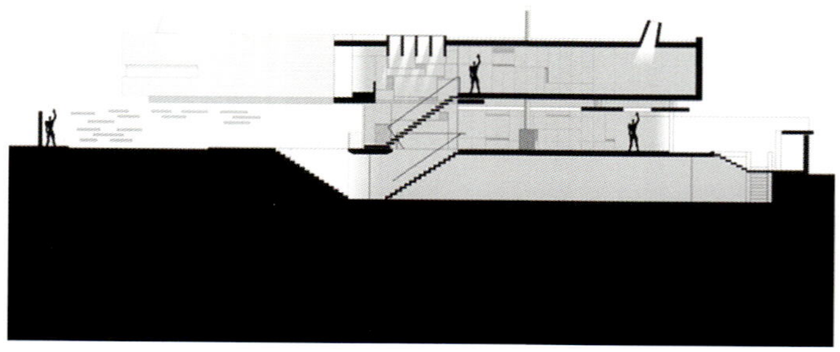

Longitudinal section

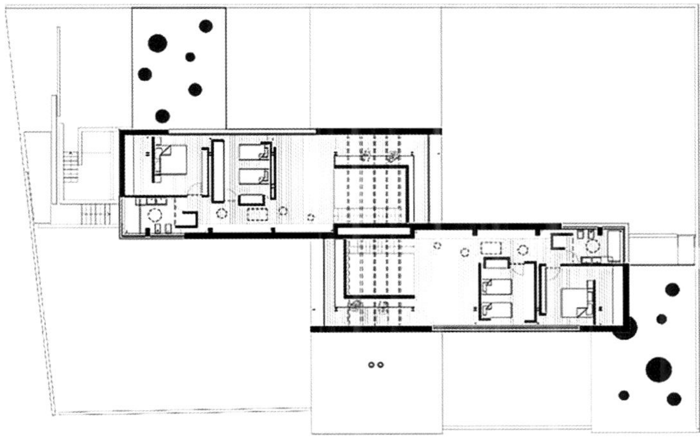

First floor plan

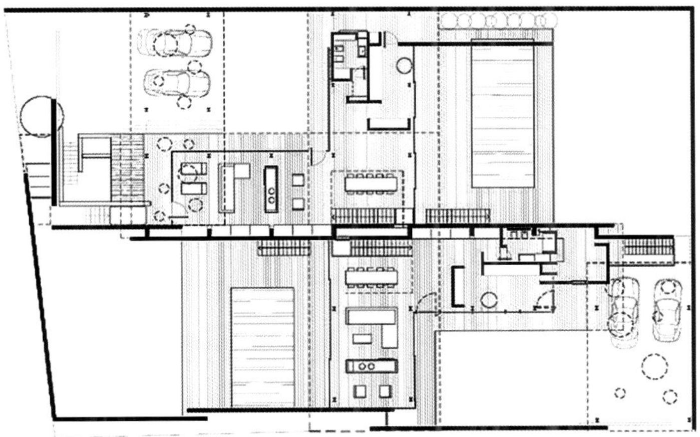

Ground floor plan

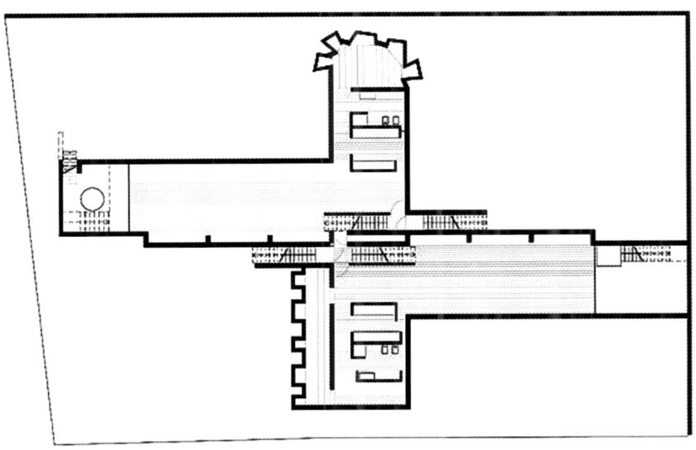

Basement plan

ITN
ARCHITECTS

Nigel Grigg is board member of ITN Architects whose practice specializes in single and smaller multi-residential projects, as well as commercial projects including bars, restaurants and cinemas.

Nigel Grigg ist Vorstandsmitglied von ITN Architects, dessen Büro sich auf Einzel- und kleinere Mehrfamilienhausprojekte sowie auf kommerzielle Projekte wie Bars, Restaurants und Kinos spezialisiert hat.

Nigel Grigg est membre du conseil d'administration d'ITN Architects. Le cabinet est spécialisé dans les projets de maisons individuelles et de petits immeubles résidentiels, ainsi que dans les projets commerciaux tels que les bars, les restaurants et les cinémas.

www.itnarchitects.com
nigel@itnarchitects.com

Nigel Grigg es miembro de la junta directiva de ITN Architects, cuya práctica se especializa en proyectos residenciales individuales y pequeños proyectos multi residenciales, así como en proyectos comerciales que incluyen bares, restaurantes y cines.

CATHERINE HOUSE

This project is a renovation and extension to an Edwardian house, built around 1900. The new building at the rear of the house is in part one and two stories and forms a large open plan kitchen, living and dining area with glass doors across the rear of the extension. Upstairs is a master bedroom wing of the house with views over the rooftops to other buildings of interest nearby. A slatted timber storage cage stair links the two floors, with remnant brick fireplaces retained throughout the renovated house. The old front part of the house has also been renovated and upgraded throughout including new bathrooms and side windows.

Bei diesem Projekt handelt es sich um die Renovierung und Erweiterung eines um 1900 erbauten Hauses aus Edwardian. Das neue Gebäude auf der Rückseite des Hauses ist teilweise ein- und zweistöckig und bildet einen großen offenen Küchen-, Wohn- und Essbereich mit Glastüren auf der Rückseite des Anbaus. Im Obergeschoss befindet sich ein Hauptschlafzimmerflügel des Hauses mit Blick über die Dächer auf andere interessante Gebäude in der Nähe. Eine Holzlamellen-Lagerkäfigtreppe verbindet die beiden Stockwerke, wobei im gesamten renovierten Haus noch Reste von gemauerten Kaminen erhalten sind. Der alte vordere Teil des Hauses wurde ebenfalls renoviert und durchgehend aufgewertet, einschließlich neuer Badezimmer und Seitenfenster.

Ce projet est une rénovation et une extension d'une maison édouardienne construite vers 1900. Le nouveau bâtiment à l'arrière de la maison est en partie de un et deux étages et forme une grande cuisine ouverte, un salon et une salle à manger avec des portes en verre à l'arrière de l'extension. À l'étage, une aile de la maison avec une chambre principale offre une vue sur les toits et sur d'autres bâtiments intéressants situés à proximité. Un escalier en bois à caillebotis relie les deux étages. Les cheminées en briques sont conservées dans toute la maison rénovée. L'ancienne partie avant de la maison a également été rénovée et modernisée, avec de nouvelles salles de bain et des fenêtres latérales.

Este proyecto consiste en una renovación y ampliación de una casa de estilo Eduardiano, construida alrededor del año 1900. El nuevo edificio añadido en la parte trasera de la casa tiene dos niveles y contiene una gran cocina de planta abierta, sala de estar y comedor con puertas de cristal. La parte superior aloja el dormitorio principal en una de las alas con vistas sobre los tejados de otros edificios cercanos. Una escalera de madera con listones une los dos pisos, en los que se han conservado las chimeneas de ladrillo. La parte delantera de la vivienda también ha sido renovada y mejorada, incluyendo nuevos baños y ventanas laterales.

LOCATION
Melbourne, Victoria, Australia

PHOTOS
© Katya Menshikova

Elevations

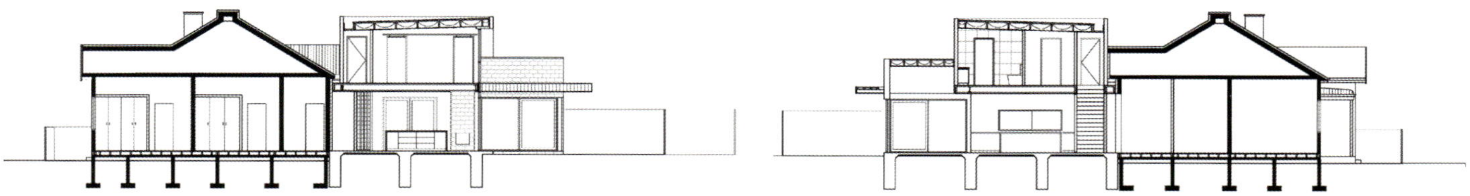

Sections

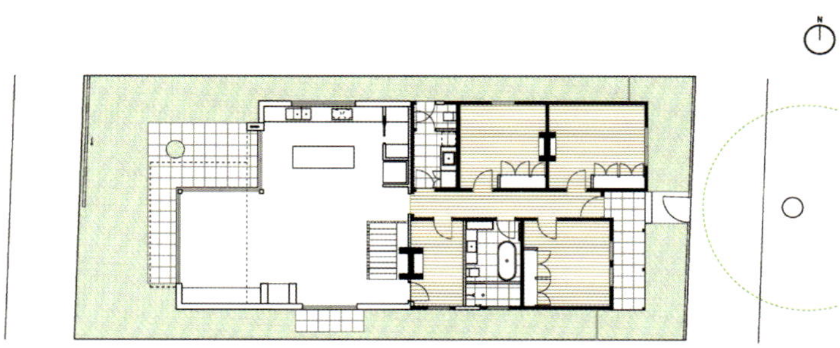

Ground floor plan

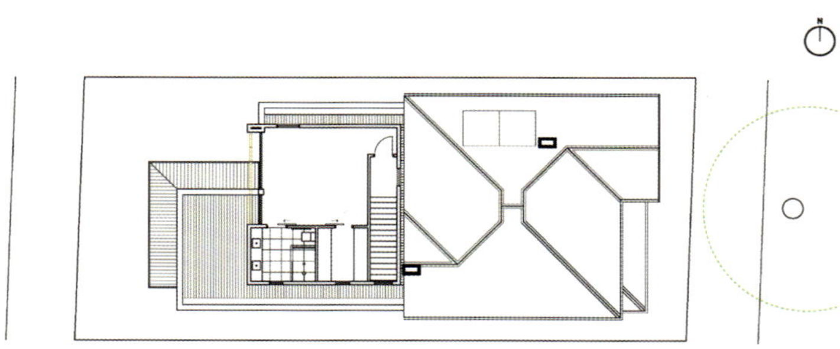

First floor plan

MABIRE
REICH

MABIRE REICH is an agency created in Nantes in 2006 by Antoine Mabire and Marie-Hélène Reich, trained at INSA Strasbourg (ENSAIS).
At the start, there were Antoine Mabire and Marie-Hélène Reich who met at the Strasbourg School of Architecture. Since then, settled in Paris, each of the architects worked separately to finally found their joint agency in Nantes. A choice of discipline but also of life that architects are not ready to forget.
Considering that the act of planning aims to change an existing situation to adapt it to new uses and thereby improve it, MABIRE REICH places its action in an optimistic vision. Each project is an opportunity to create a new urban situation, to consider Architecture in terms of the landscape captured and created.

https://mabire-reich.com
agence@mabire-reich.com

MABIRE REICH ist eine Agentur, die 2006 in Nantes von Antoine Mabire und Marie-Hélène Reich, ausgebildet an der INSA Straßburg (ENSAIS), gegründet wurde.
Antoine Mabire und Marie-Hélène Reich lernten sich an der Straßburger Architekturschule kennen. Danach arbeiteten die beiden Architekten, die sich in Paris niedergelassen hatten, getrennt voneinander, um schließlich ihre gemeinsame Agentur in Nantes zu gründen. Eine Wahl der Disziplin, aber auch des Lebens, das die Architekten nicht zu vergessen bereit sind.
In Anbetracht der Tatsache, dass der Akt der Planung darauf abzielt, eine bestehende Situation zu verändern, um sie an neue Nutzungen anzupassen und sie dadurch zu verbessern, stellen MABIRE REICH ihr Handeln in eine optimistische Vision. Jedes Projekt ist eine Gelegenheit, eine neue städtebauliche Situation zu schaffen und die Architektur im Hinblick auf die erfasste und geschaffene Landschaft zu betrachten.

MABIRE REICH est une agence créée à Nantes en 2006 par Antoine Mabire et Marie-Hélène Reich, formés à l'INSA de Strasbourg (ENSAIS).
Au départ, il y avait Antoine Mabire et Marie-Hélène Reich qui se sont rencontrés à l'école d'architecture de Strasbourg. Depuis, installés à Paris, chacun des architectes a travaillé séparément pour finalement fonder leur agence commune à Nantes. Un choix de discipline mais aussi de vie que les architectes ne sont pas près d'oublier.
Considérant que l'acte de planification vise à changer une situation existante pour l'adapter à de nouveaux usages et ainsi l'améliorer, MABIRE REICH place son action dans une vision optimiste. Chaque projet est une opportunité de créer une nouvelle situation urbaine, de considérer l'Architecture en termes de paysage capté et créé.

MABIRE REICH es una agencia creada en Nantes en 2006 por Antoine Mabire y Marie-Hélène Reich, ambos formados en el INSA de Estrasburgo (ENSAIS).
Desde entonces e instalados en París, cada uno de los arquitectos trabajó por separado para finalmente fundar su agencia conjunta en Nantes, en una elección de disciplina pero también de vida que los arquitectos no están dispuestos a olvidar.
Considerando que el acto de proyectar pretende cambiar una situación existente para adaptarla a nuevos usos, mejorándola, MABIRE REICH sitúa su acción en una visión optimista: cada proyecto es una oportunidad para crear una nueva situación urbana, para considerar la arquitectura en términos del paisaje capturado y creado.

PUZZLE HOUSE

LOCATION
Nantes, France

PHOTOS
© Guillaume Satre

To extend a house is to add an extra layer in an existing building, which sometimes allows to see the previous ones, and this house is a clear example of it. Originally as a single floor interior, this house was first extended aside and eventually partly raised up. Instead of erasing its history, we completed the puzzle by raising up the initial building in order to form a new volume reasonable with the first extension. We painted the façade according to this patchwork. Then we add a wood mesh, giving a new character to the whole building while offering diverse relationships between the inside and the outside.

Ein Haus zu erweitern bedeutet zu einem bestehenden Gebäude eine zusätzliche Schicht hinzuzufügen, die manchmal den Blick auf die vorherigen erlaubt, und dieses Haus ist ein deutliches Beispiel dafür. Zuvor einstöckig, wurde dieses Haus zunächst seitlich erweitert und schließlich teilweise hochgezogen. Anstatt diese Geschichte auszulöschen, haben wir das Puzzle vervollständigt, indem wir das ursprüngliche Gebäude hochgezogen haben, um ein neues Volumen zu bilden, das mit der ersten Erweiterung kohärent ist. Wir haben die Fassade mit dem Ziel bemalt, dieses Patchwork zu harmonisieren. Dann fügten wir ein Holzgeflecht hinzu, das dem ganzen Gebäude einen neuen Charakter verleiht und gleichzeitig verschiedene Beziehungen zwischen dem Inneren und dem Äußeren bietet.

Agrandir une maison, c'est ajouter une couche supplémentaire dans un bâtiment existant, ce qui permet parfois de voir les précédentes. Cette maison en est un exemple évident. Ayant initialement un seul étage, cette maison a d'abord été agrandie à l'écart, puis partiellement surélevée. Au lieu d'effacer cette histoire, nous avons complété le puzzle en surélevant le bâtiment initial afin de former un nouveau volume cohérent avec la première extension. Nous avons peint la façade dans le but d'harmoniser ce patchwork. Nous avons ensuite ajouté un treillis de bois, donnant un nouveau caractère à l'ensemble du bâtiment tout en offrant des relations diverses entre l'intérieur et l'extérieur.

Ampliar una casa es añadir una capa extra a un edificio existente. Esto permite, en ocasiones, ver las capas anteriores. Este proyecto es un claro ejemplo. Originariamente vivienda de una sola planta, fue primero ampliada en uno de sus lados. Más tarde se levantó parcialmente pero en lugar de borrar la historia, se completó el rompecabezas levantando el edificio inicial para formar un nuevo volumen coherente con la primera construcción. Se pintó la fachada con el objetivo de armonizar el mosaico y se añadió una malla de madera, dando un nuevo carácter a todo el edificio y ofreciendo diversas relaciones entre el interior y el exterior.

Site plan

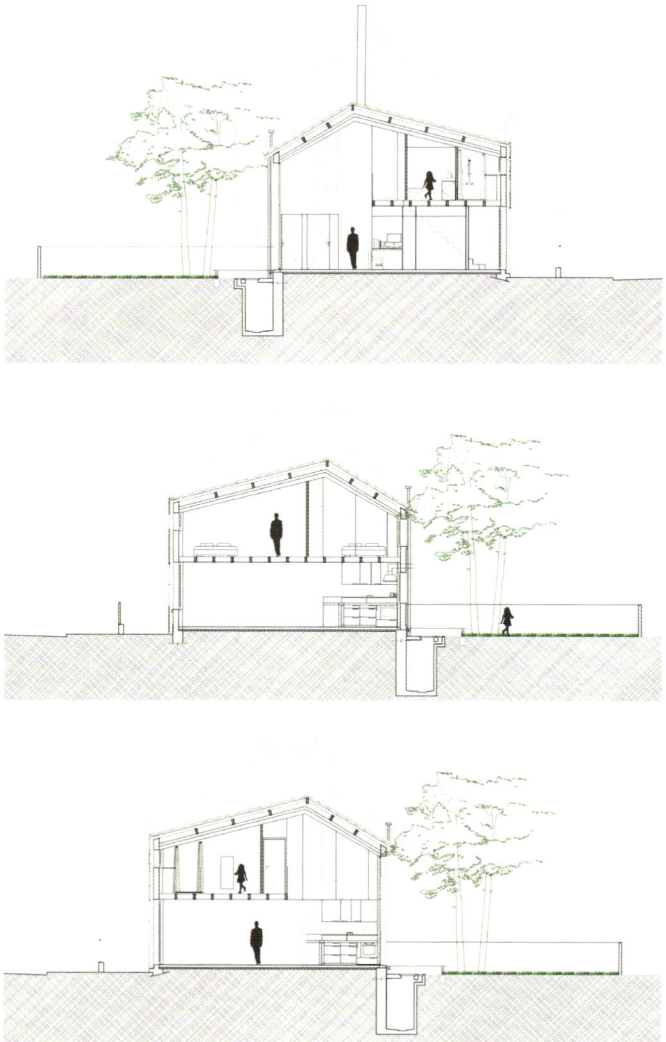

Sections

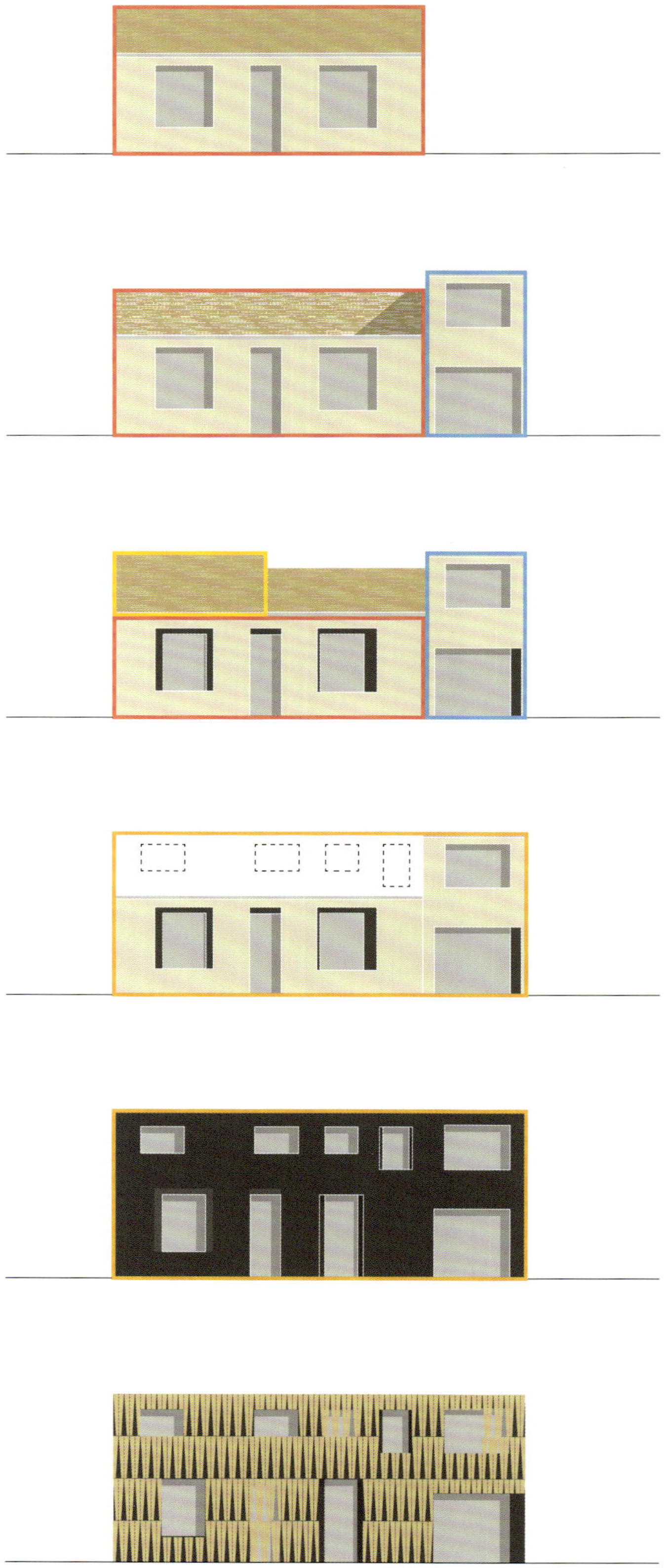

Elevations

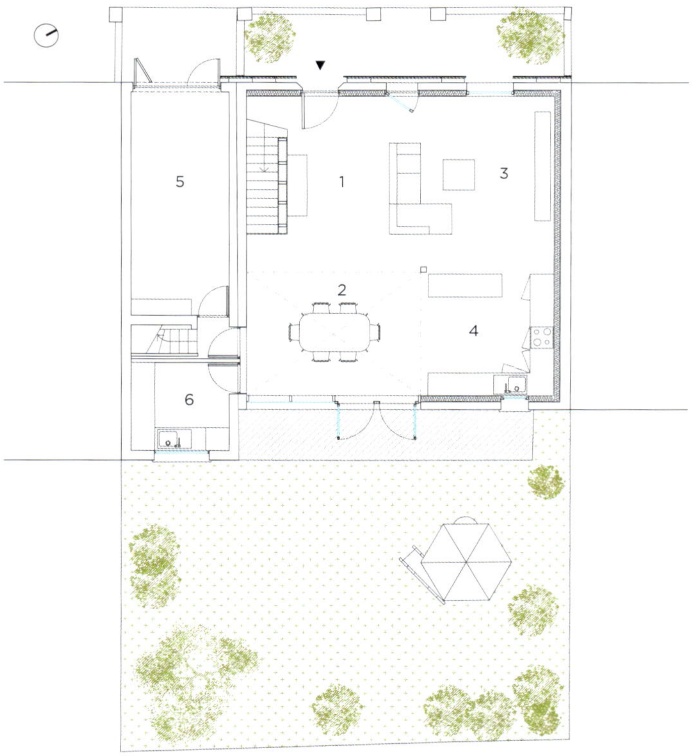

Ground floor plan

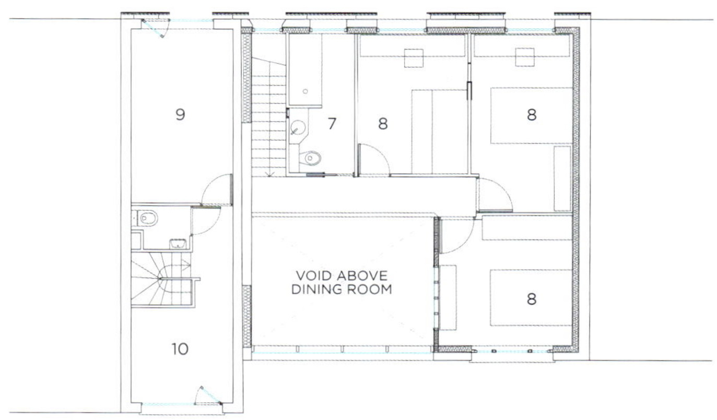

First floor plan

1. Hall
2. Dining room
3. Living room
4. Kitchen
5. Reception / garage
6. Laundry
7. Bathroom
8. Bedroom
9. Consulting room
10. Waiting room

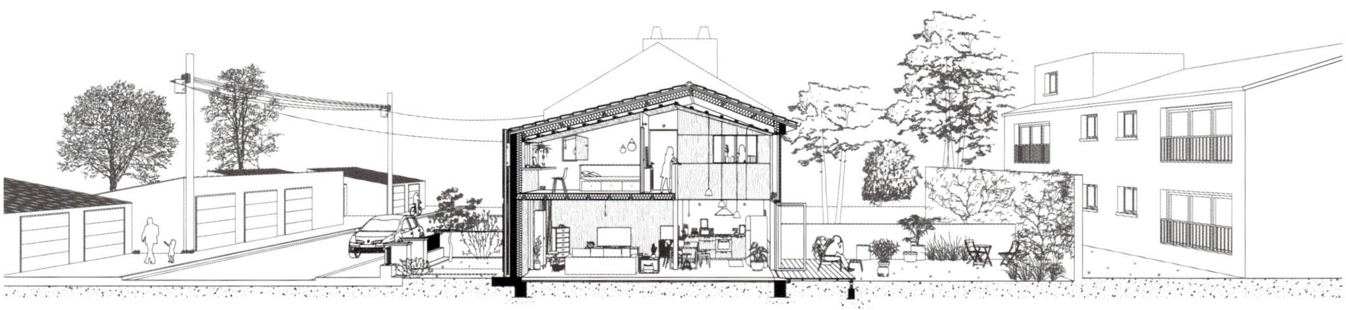

Section

NAT OFFICE

CHRISTIAN GASPARINI ARCHITETTO

Established in 2001 in Reggio Emilia by Christian Gasparini, NAT OFFICE turns its attention to the relationship between architecture, city and landscape and investigates modular structures, intertwining scales, typologies, spaces for a new identity between place and people: Architecture becomes a medium between Nature and Technology, able to give a sense to the antropic presence in the nature.
Christian Gasparini graduates in architecture at the Politecnico of Milan, where he teaches and works as researcher of urban and architectural planning. Expert in bioclimatic planning, he worked in 2000 in Chile, being selected for the international workshop 'Valparaíso de Chile: ideas y proyectos para el casco histórico'. Many are the participations in international meetings and conferences. He has also experience as an Architecture editor and Publisher.

info@natoffice.it
www.natoffice.it

NAT OFFICE wurde 2001 in Reggio Emilia von Christian Gasparini gegründet und konzentriert sich auf die Beziehung zwischen Architektur, Stadt und Landschaft. Es untersucht modulare Strukturen, die Skalen, Typologien und Räume für eine neue Identität zwischen Ort und Mensch miteinander verflechten: Architektur wird zum Medium zwischen Natur und Technologie, die in der Lage ist, der antropischen Präsenz in der Natur einen Sinn zu geben.
Christian Gasparini hat einen Abschluss in Architektur am Politecnico in Mailand, wo er lehrt und als Forscher für Stadt- und Architekturplanung arbeitet. Als Experte für bioklimatische Planung arbeitete er im Jahr 2000 in Chile und wurde für den internationalen Workshop „Valparaíso de Chile: Ideen und Projekte für die Geschichte des Lebens" ausgewählt. Viele nehmen an internationalen Tagungen und Konferenzen teil. Er hat auch Erfahrung als Architekturredakteur und Verleger.

Créée en 2001 à Reggio Emilia par Christian Gasparini, NAT OFFICE s'intéresse aux relations entre architecture, ville et paysage et explore les structures modulaires, les échelles entrelacées, les typologies, les espaces pour une nouvelle identité entre le lieu et les personnes: l'architecture devient un médium entre la nature et la technologie, capable de donner un sens à la présence antropique dans la nature.
Christian Gasparini est diplômé en architecture du Politecnico de Milan, où il enseigne et travaille comme chercheur en urbanisme et architecture. Expert en planification bioclimatique, il a travaillé en 2000 au Chili, étant sélectionné pour l'atelier international « Valparaíso de Chile: ideas y proyectos para el casco histórico ». Nombreuses sont les participations aux réunions et conférences internationales. Il a également de l'expérience en tant qu'éditeur et éditeur d'architecture.

Fundada en 2001 en Reggio Emilia por Christian Gasparini, NAT OFFICE centra su atención en la relación entre arquitectura, ciudad y paisaje e investiga estructuras modulares, escalas entrelazadas, tipologías, espacios para una nueva identidad entre el lugar y las personas: la arquitectura se convierte en un medio entre la naturaleza y Tecnología, capaz de dar sentido a la presencia antrópica en la naturaleza.
Christian Gasparini se graduó en arquitectura en el Politecnico de Milán, donde enseña y trabaja como investigador de planificación urbana y arquitectónica. Experto en planificación bioclimática, trabajó en 2000 en Chile, siendo seleccionado para el taller internacional «Valparaíso de Chile: ideas y proyectos para el casco histórico». Muchas son las participaciones en reuniones y conferencias internacionales. También tiene experiencia como editor y editor de arquitectura.

PIANELLA

HLBH HOUSELEVEL HOMEOFFICE

An ancient and listed building, heritage of the past, becomes a new home/office, intertwining a dialog between indoor and outdoor, place and space, voids and levels, walls and glasses. The building, originally established as a stable and barn, is redefined by an innovative use of inner office/house spaces that emphasize volumes and original spatiality in a continuous dialogue between innovation and tradition. The originality of the project lies on the flexibility and multiplicity use of the spaces, which are configured for an offices' headquarter, that may become a house without any modifications of the walls or interior rooms.

Ein altes und denkmalgeschütztes Gebäude wird zu einem neuen Heim/Büro, das einen Dialog zwischen Innen und Außen, Ort und Raum, Hohlräumen und Ebenen, Wänden und Gläsern in sich birgt. Das Gebäude, das ursprünglich als Stall und Scheune errichtet wurde, wird durch eine innovative Nutzung der inneren Büro-/Hausräume neu definiert, die Volumen und originelle Räumlichkeit in einem kontinuierlichen Dialog zwischen Innovation und Tradition betonen. Die Originalität des Projekts liegt in der Flexibilität und Vielfältigkeit der Nutzung der Räume, die für den Sitz eines Büros konfiguriert sind, das ohne Änderungen der Wände oder Innenräume zu einem Haus werden kann.

Un bâtiment ancien et classé devient une nouvelle maison/bureau, entremêlant un dialogue entre intérieur et extérieur, lieu et espace, vides et niveaux, murs et vitres. Le bâtiment, initialement établi comme une écurie et une grange, est redéfini par une utilisation innovante des espaces intérieurs de bureaux/maisons qui mettent en valeur les volumes et la spatialité originale dans un dialogue continu entre innovation et tradition. L'originalité du projet réside dans la flexibilité et la multiplicité d'utilisation des espaces, qui sont configurés pour un siège de bureaux, qui peut devenir une maison sans aucune modification des murs ou des pièces intérieures.

Un edificio antiguo y protegido, herencia del pasado, se convierte en un nuevo hogar/oficina, entrelazando un diálogo entre interior y exterior, lugar y espacio, vacíos y niveles, paredes y cristales. El edificio, originalmente establo y granero, se redefine mediante un uso innovador de los espacios interiores de oficina/casa que enfatizan los volúmenes y la espacialidad original en un diálogo continuo entre la innovación y la tradición. La originalidad del proyecto radica en la flexibilidad y la multiplicidad de uso de los espacios, que se configuran como oficinas, que pueden convertirse en una casa sin modificar las paredes o las habitaciones interiores.

LOCATION
Cavriago, Reggio Emilia, Italy

PHOTOS
© HLBH - Filippo Poli
Portrait Photo CGA - Davide Galli

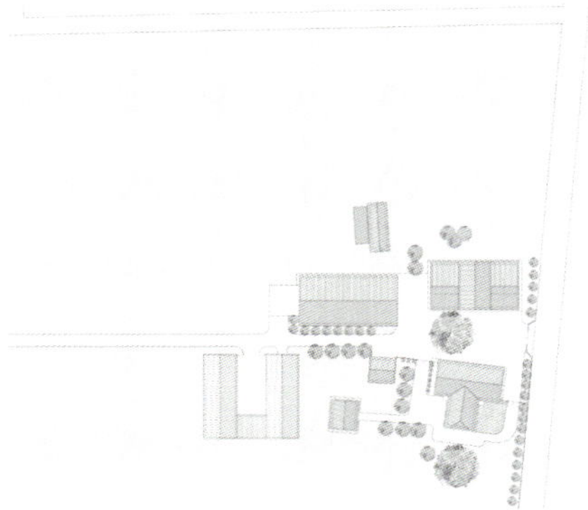

Site plan

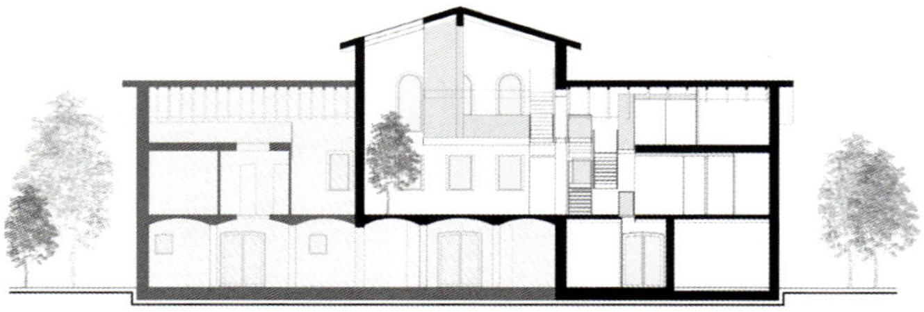

A-A' section

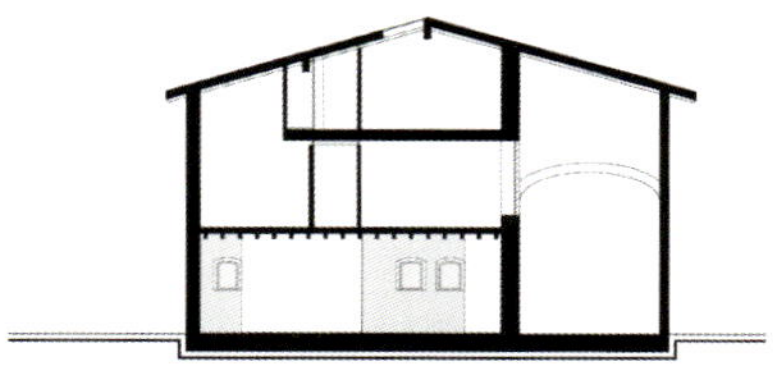

B-B' section

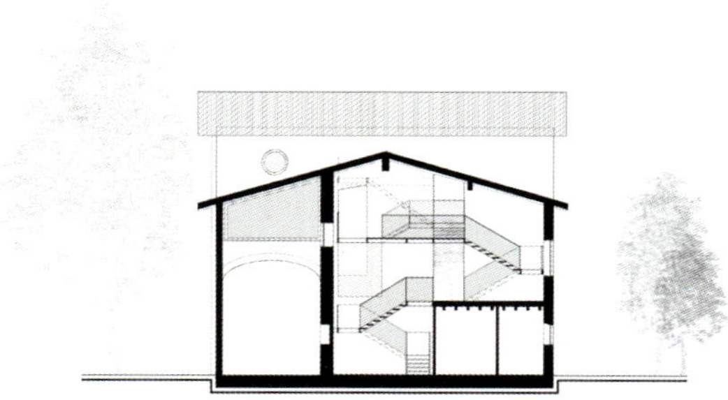

C-C' section

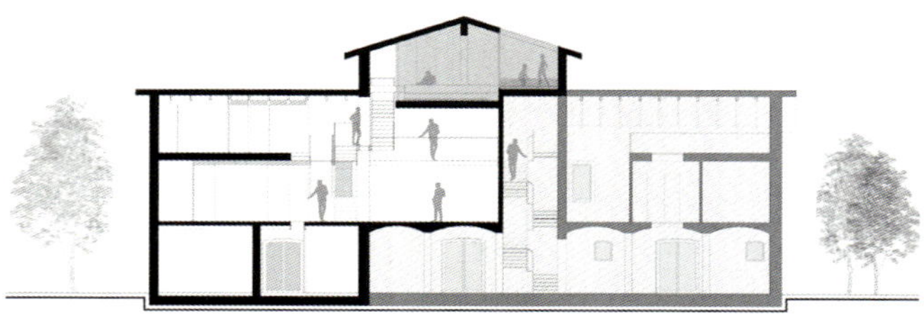

D-D' section

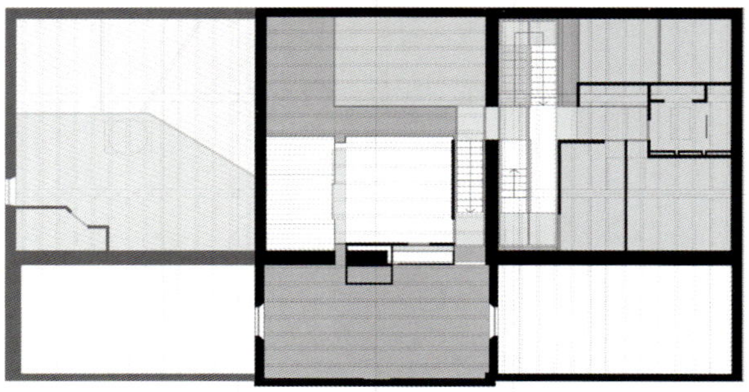

Roof plan

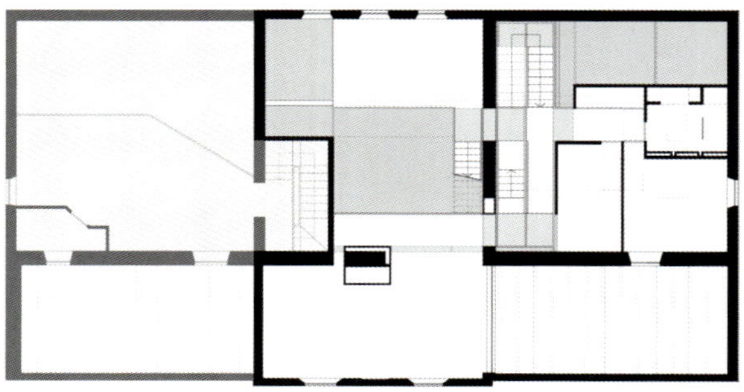

Second floor plan

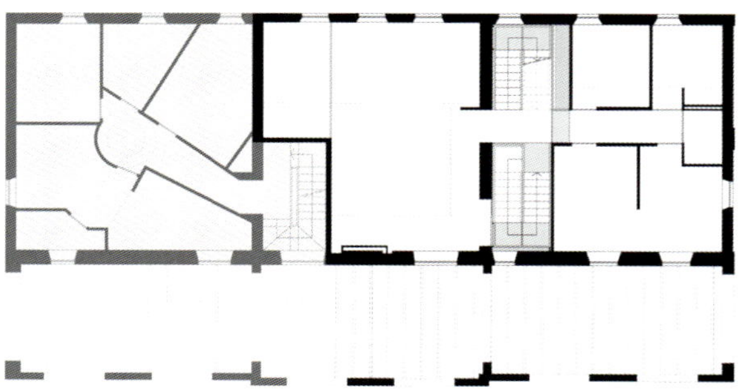

First floor plan

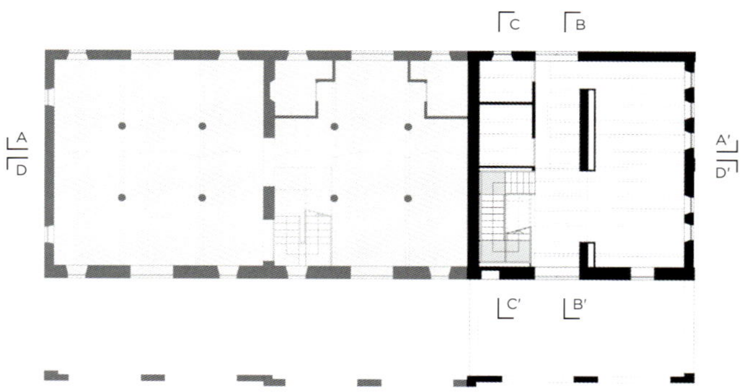

Ground floor plan

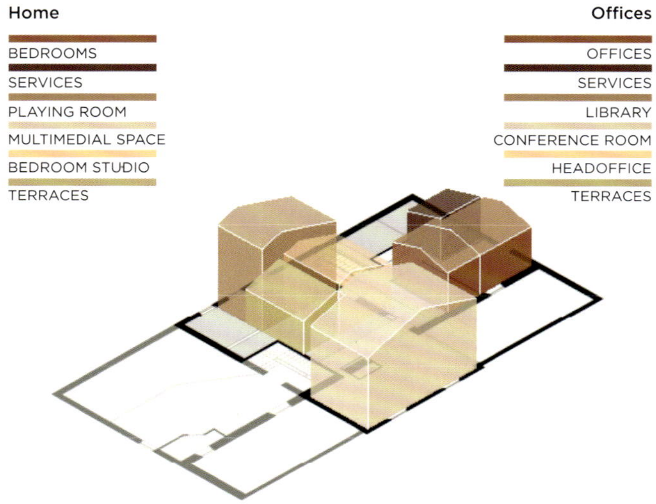

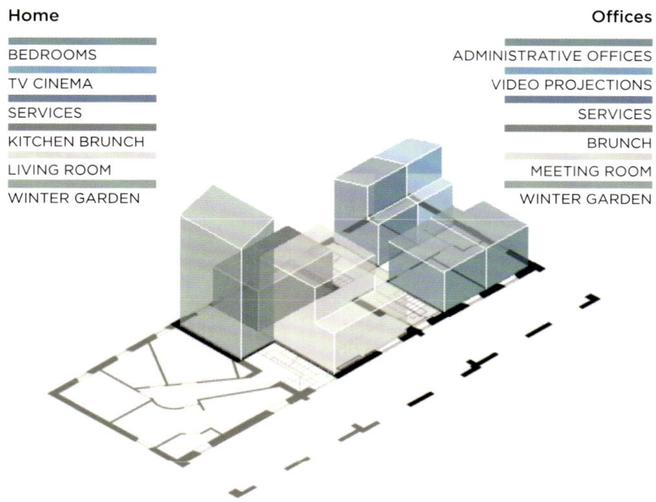

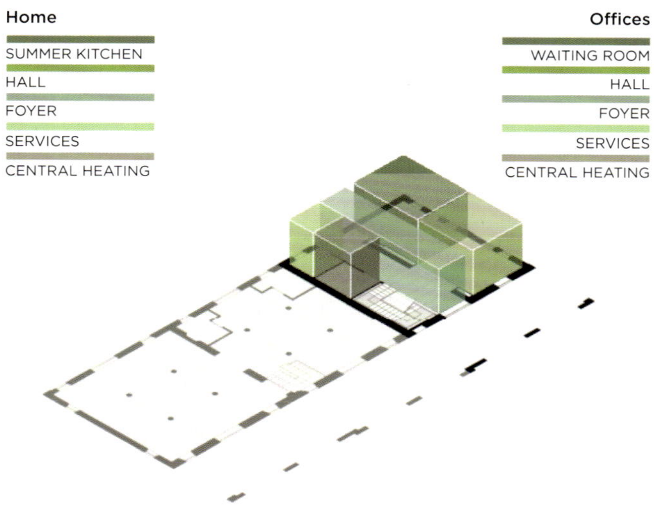

Construction diagrams

NIJI ARCHITECT

Niji Architects First Class Architect Office
An architectural firm co-hosted in 2014 by Masashi Harada and Maiko Taniguchi.
"Building and building the joy and excitement of finding a rainbow in the sky after rain !"
Private houses, apartmens, offices, stores, nurseries, kindergartens, accommodation facilities, medical and welfare facilities, temples and shrines, etc.
Regardless of new construction or renovation, it can correspond to all types of structures such as wooden, steel frame or reinforced concrete.
"We always make proposals considering the ideal form and added value of the architecture."

Niji Architects, erstklassiges Architekturbüro
Ein Architekturbüro, das 2014 gemeinsam von Masashi Harada und Maiko Taniguchi gegründet wurde.
„Bauen und Schaffen mit der Freude und Aufregung, einen Regenbogen nach dem anderen am Himmel zu finden!"
Privathäuser, Wohnhäuser, Büros, Geschäfte, Krippen, Kindergärten, Unterkunftseinrichtungen, medizinische und soziale Einrichtungen, Tempel und Schreine usw.
Wir schlagen Architektur für alle möglichen Zwecke vor, von Privathäusern bis hin zu Wohnungen, Büros, Geschäften, Kindergärten, etc.
Unabhängig davon, ob es sich um einen Neubau oder eine Renovierung handelt, kann sie allen Arten von Bauwerken wie Holz, Stahlrahmen oder Stahlbeton entsprechen.
„Wir machen immer Vorschläge unter Berücksichtigung der idealen Form und des Mehrwerts der Architektur."

Niji Architects Bureau d'architectes de première classe
Un cabinet d'architectes co-organisé en 2014 par Masashi Harada et Maiko Taniguchi.
« Construire et construire la joie et l'excitation de trouver un arc-en-ciel dans le ciel après la pluie ! »
Maisons privées, immeubles d'habitation, bureaux, magasins, crèches, jardins d'enfants, établissements d'hébergement, établissements médicaux et sociaux, temples et sanctuaires, etc.
Nous proposons une architecture pour toutes sortes d'usages, des maisons privées aux appartements, bureaux, magasins, crèches, etc.
Quelle que soit la construction neuve ou la rénovation, elle peut correspondre à tous les types de structures telles que le bois, la charpente métallique ou le béton armé.
« Nous faisons toujours des propositions en tenant compte de la forme idéale et de la valeur ajoutée de l'architecture ».

Niji Architects Oficina de Arquitectura de Primera Clase
Un estudio de arquitectura co-organizado desde 2014 por Masashi Harada y Maiko Taniguchi.
«Construyendo la alegría y la emoción de encontrar un arco iris después de la lluvia».
Casas privadas, apartamentos, oficinas, tiendas, guarderías, jardines de infancia, instalaciones domésticas y médicas, templos y santuarios...
Proponemos arquitectura para todo tipo de tipología, estructura y material (madera, estructuras de acero, hormigón armado...), independientemente de que se trate de una nueva construcción o de una renovación.
«Nuestras propuestas consideran la forma ideal y el valor añadido de la arquitectura».

www.niji-architects.com
info@niji-architects.com

TOWNHOUSE IN TAKABAN

The two-unit three-story rental town house stands in an extremely small lot. Lines derived from legal restrictions and the street gave it a gable form. The two units have the exact same plan. A diagonally placed parting wall and the help of high ceiling gives visitors an impression of spaciousness, masking the small floor area. The form also helps by saving enough floor space for necessary wet areas while providing spacious living areas. Sunlight enters through a large skylight and a wall-length window; light and shadow form different shapes following the diagonal wall and sloped ceiling.

Das zweistöckige bis dreistöckige Mietsstadthaus steht auf einem extrem kleinen Grundstück. Die aus den Beschränkungen im Norden und der Straße abgeleiteten Linien gaben ihm eine Giebelform. Die beiden Einheiten haben genau denselben Plan. Eine diagonal verlaufende Trennwand und eine hohe Decke vermitteln dem Besucher den Eindruck von Weite und verdecken die kleine Grundfläche. Die Form hilft auch, indem sie genügend Bodenfläche für notwendige Nassbereiche spart und gleichzeitig für großzügige Wohnbereiche sorgt. Das Sonnenlicht tritt durch ein großes Oberlicht und ein wandfüllendes Fenster ein; Licht und Schatten bilden verschiedene Formen, die der diagonalen Wand und der schrägen Decke folgen.

La maison de ville, composée de deux unités et trois étages, est située sur un terrain extrêmement petit. Les lignes dérivées des restrictions du Nord et la rue lui ont donné une forme de pignon. Les deux unités ont exactement le même plan. Un mur de séparation placé en diagonale et l'aide d'un haut plafond donne aux visiteurs une impression d'espace, masquant la petite surface au sol. La forme permet également d'économiser suffisamment d'espace au sol pour les zones humides nécessaires tout en offrant des espaces de vie spacieux. La lumière du soleil entre par une grande lucarne et une fenêtre de la longueur d'un mur. La lumière et l'ombre forment des formes différentes suivant la diagonale du mur et le plafond en pente.

La vivienda de dos unidades y tres niveles se encuentra en un terreno de pequeñas dimensiones, donde líneas derivadas de las restricciones de la orientación norte y la calle le dieron una forma de aguilón. Las dos unidades tienen exactamente la misma distribución. Una pared de separación colocada diagonalmente y la ayuda de un techo alto ofrece a los visitantes una impresión de amplitud, enmascarando la pequeña superficie del terreno. Esta forma también ayuda a ahorrar espacio para las áreas húmedas, además de proporcionar zonas de estar más espaciosas. La luz del sol entra a través de un gran tragaluz y una ventana colocada a lo largo de la pared. La luz y la sombra generan diferentes formas imitando a la pared diagonal y el techo inclinado.

LOCATION
Takaban, Meguro-ku, Tokyo, Japan

PHOTOS
© Niji Photo

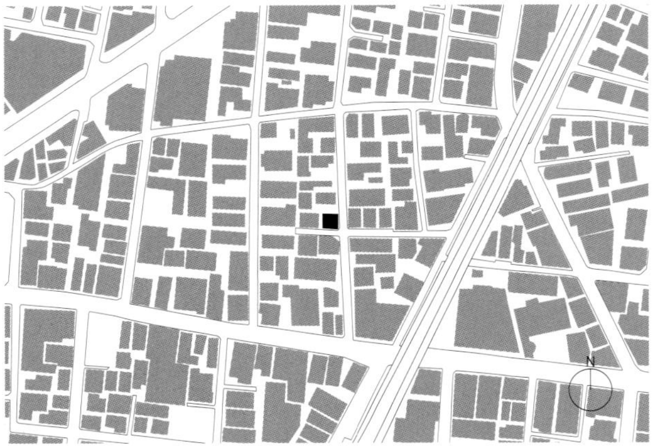

Site plan

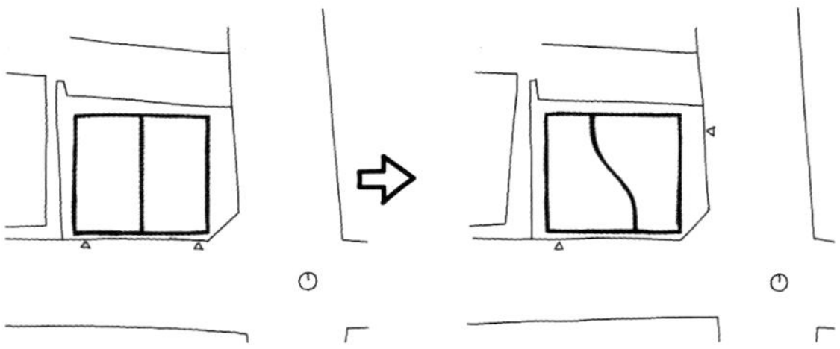

Concept diagram

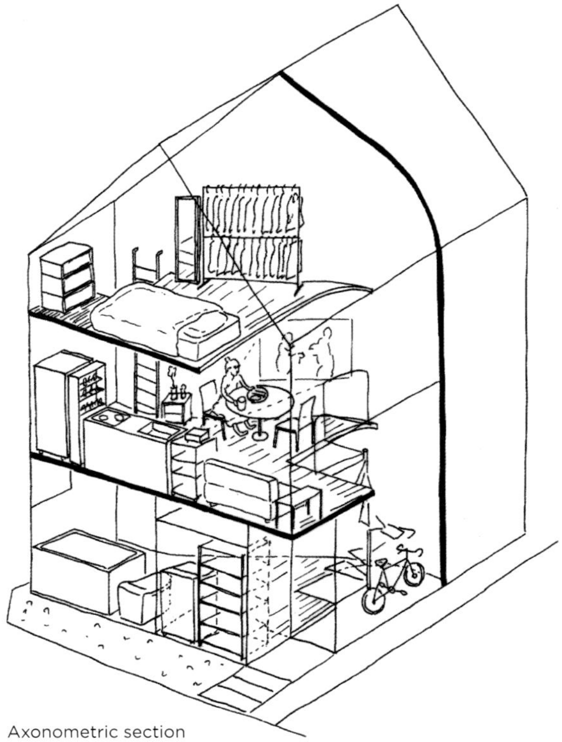

Axonometric section

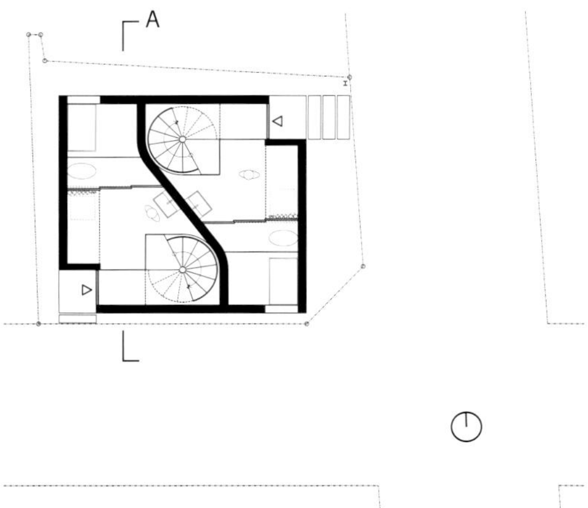

Ground floor plan

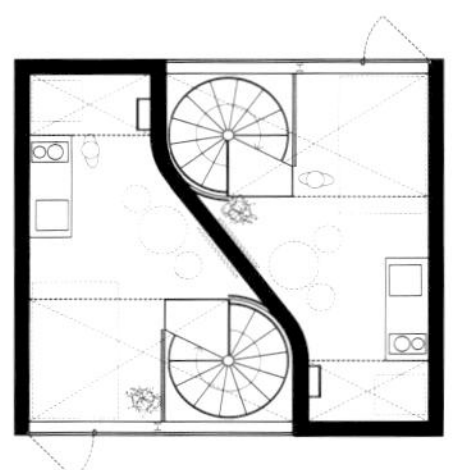

First floor plan

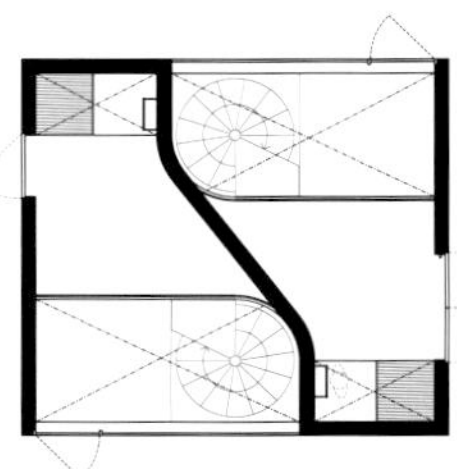

Second floor plan

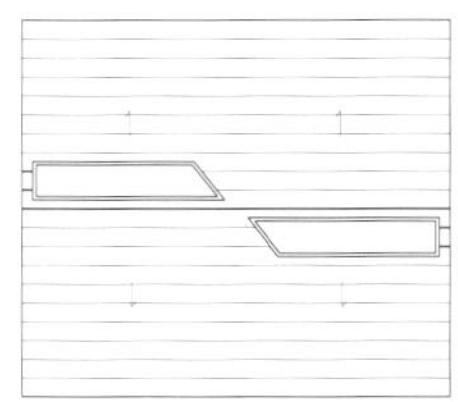

Roof plan

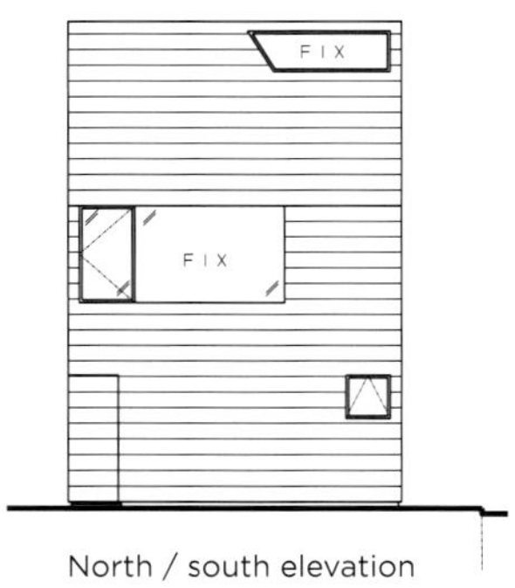

North / south elevation

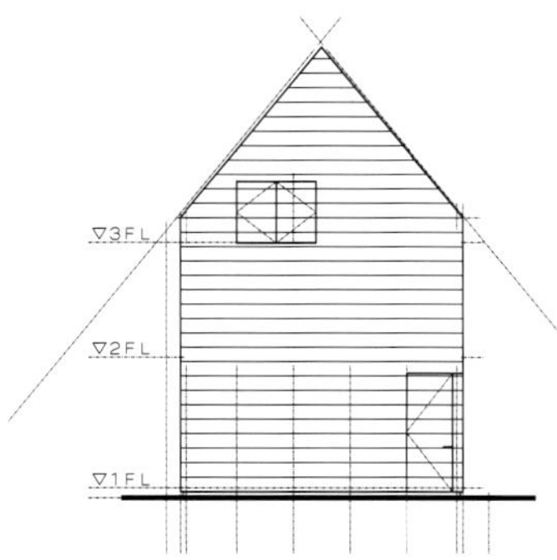

East / west elevation

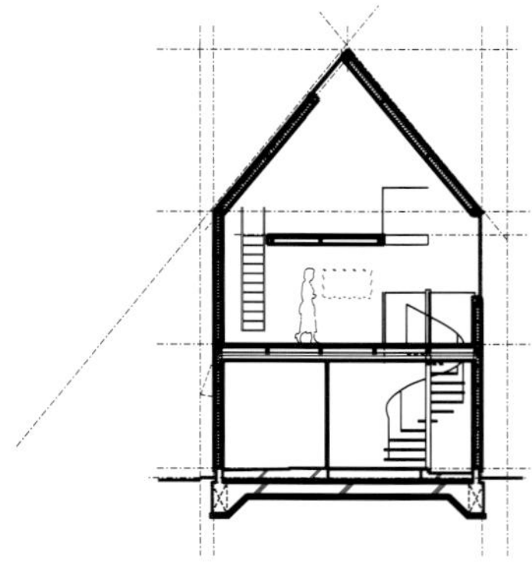

Section A

OBLIQ ARCHITECTUU

JOOST HILLEN

Obliq Architectuur is a young and ambitious office (established and lead by architect Joost Hillen) with a focus on sustainable housing issues for education and day-care, that guarantees thoughtful architecture with a strong attention for detail. Essential in the design process is the realization of clear concepts in close contact with the clients and their needs and wishes. Expertises: architectural design for (re)construction of schools and day-care centers as well as larger apartment buildings and private clients.

http://www.oblq.nl/
info@oblq.nl

Obliq Architectuur ist ein junges und ehrgeiziges Büro (gegründet und geleitet vom Architekten Joost Hillen) mit Schwerpunkt auf nachhaltigem Wohnen für Bildung und Tagespflege, das durchdachte Architektur mit viel Liebe zum Detail garantiert. Wesentlich im Designprozess ist die Umsetzung klarer Konzepte in engem Kontakt mit den Kunden und deren Bedürfnissen und Wünschen. Fachkenntnisse: Architekturentwurf für den (Wieder-) Bau von Schulen und Kindertagesstätten sowie größeren Mehrfamilienhäusern und Privatkunden.

Obliq Architectuur est un bureau jeune et ambitieux (créé et dirigé par l'architecte Joost Hillen) axé sur les questions de logement durable pour l'éducation et la garderie, qui garantit une architecture réfléchie avec une grande attention aux détails. L'essentiel dans le processus de conception est la réalisation de concepts clairs en contact étroit avec les clients et leurs besoins et souhaits. Expertises: conception architecturale pour la (re) construction d'écoles et de crèches ainsi que de grands immeubles d'appartements et clients privés.

Obliq Architectuur es una oficina joven y ambiciosa (establecida y dirigida por el arquitecto Joost Hillen) con un enfoque en temas de vivienda sostenible para la educación y la guardería, que garantiza una arquitectura reflexiva con una gran atención al detalle. Esencial en el proceso de diseño es la realización de conceptos claros en estrecho contacto con los clientes y sus necesidades y deseos. Especialidades: diseño arquitectónico para (re) construcción de escuelas y guarderías, así como edificios de apartamentos más grandes y clientes privados.

THE BLACKSMITH HOUSE

LOCATION
Utrecht, Netherlands

PHOTOS
© Jordi Huisman Photography

An old blacksmith house has been transformed into a modern sustainable home. The workshop with blackened oaken beams, dating back to 1650, and massively thick walls has been turned into a modern living area. By lowering the floor of the living room and raising its roof this area becomes very spacious and is visually separated from the kitchen and dining area. On the first floor, from the master bedroom, doors open onto the roof light and balcony with views over the green roof of the living room and the long garden. Two children rooms on the second floor share a new bathroom in the middle. The old roof trusses dictate and characterize the space.

Ein altes Schmiedehaus wurde in ein modernes, nachhaltiges Haus umgewandelt. Die Werkstatt mit geschwärzten Eichenbalken aus dem Jahr 1650 und massiven, dicken Mauern wurde in einen modernen Wohnbereich verwandelt. Durch das Absenken des Fußbodens des Wohnzimmers und das Anheben des Daches wird dieser Bereich sehr geräumig und ist optisch von der Küche und dem Essbereich getrennt. Im ersten Stock öffnen sich vom Hauptschlafzimmer Türen zum Oberlicht und zum Balkon mit Blick auf das grüne Dach des Wohnzimmers und den langen Garten. Zwei Kinderzimmer im zweiten Stock teilen sich ein neues Badezimmer in der Mitte. Die alten Dachstühle diktieren und charakterisieren den Raum.

Une vieille maison de forgeron a été transformée en une maison moderne et durable. L'atelier aux poutres en chêne noirci, datant de 1650, et aux murs massivement épais a été transformé en un espace de vie moderne. En abaissant le plancher du salon et en élevant son toit, cet espace devient très spacieux et est visuellement séparé de la cuisine et de la salle à manger. Au premier étage, depuis la chambre principale, les portes s'ouvrent sur le toit lumineux, le balcon avec vue sur le toit vert du salon et le long jardin. Deux chambres d'enfants au deuxième étage se partagent une nouvelle salle de bains au milieu. Les anciennes fermes de toit dictent et caractérisent l'espace.

Una vieja herrería se ha transformado en un hogar sostenible. El taller con vigas de roble ennegrecidas, que data de 1650, de paredes muy gruesas, se ha convertido en una vivienda moderna. Tras rebajar el suelo de la sala de estar y subir su techo, esta área se vuelve espaciosa y visualmente separada de la cocina y el comedor. En la primera planta, el dormitorio principal se abre a un balcón con vistas al techo verde de la sala de estar y al jardín. Dos habitaciones para niños en el segundo piso comparten un baño. Las viejas cerchas del techo dictan y caracterizan el espacio.

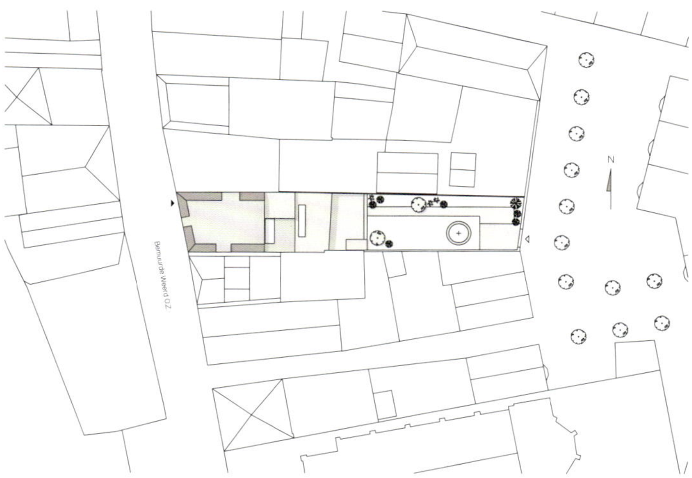

Site plan

Front elevation

Rear elevation

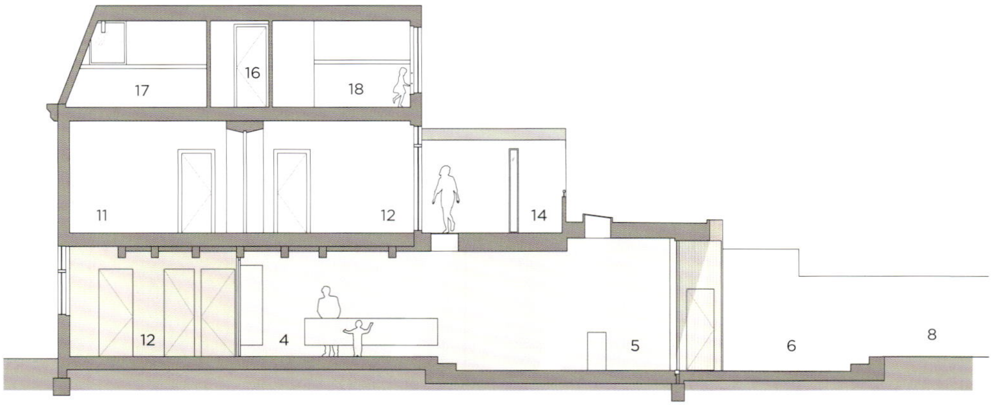

A-A elevation

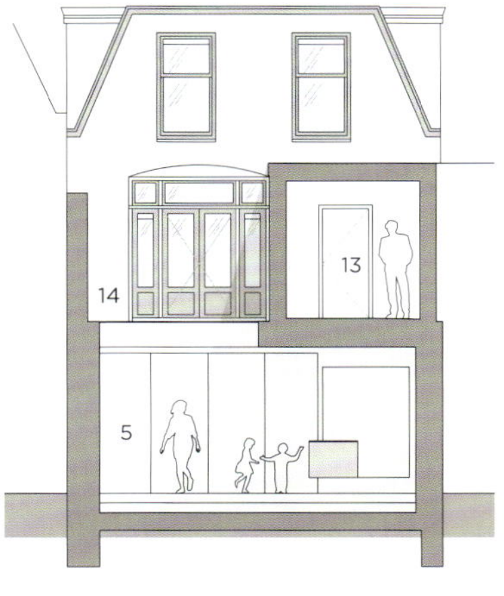

C-C elevation

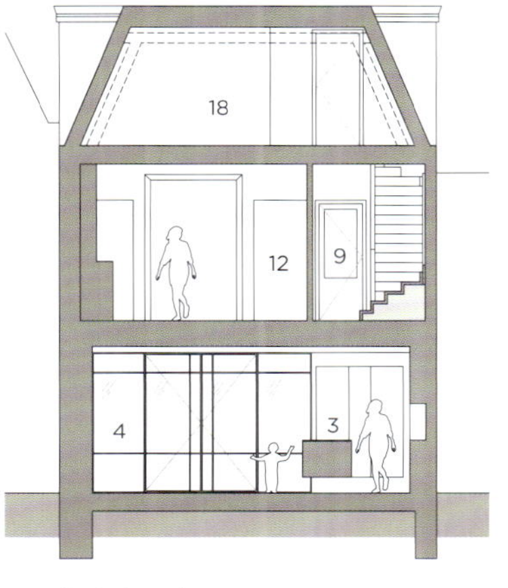

B-B elevation

1. Entrance
2. Play area
3. Kitchen
4. Dining area
5. Living area
6. Patio
7. Heat pump installation
8. Garden
9. Landing 1st floor
10. Guestroom
11. Study / dressing area
12. Master bedroom
13. Bathroom
14. Roof terrace
15. Landing 2nd floor
16. Bathroom
17. Bedroom
18. Bedroom
19. Solar boiler installation

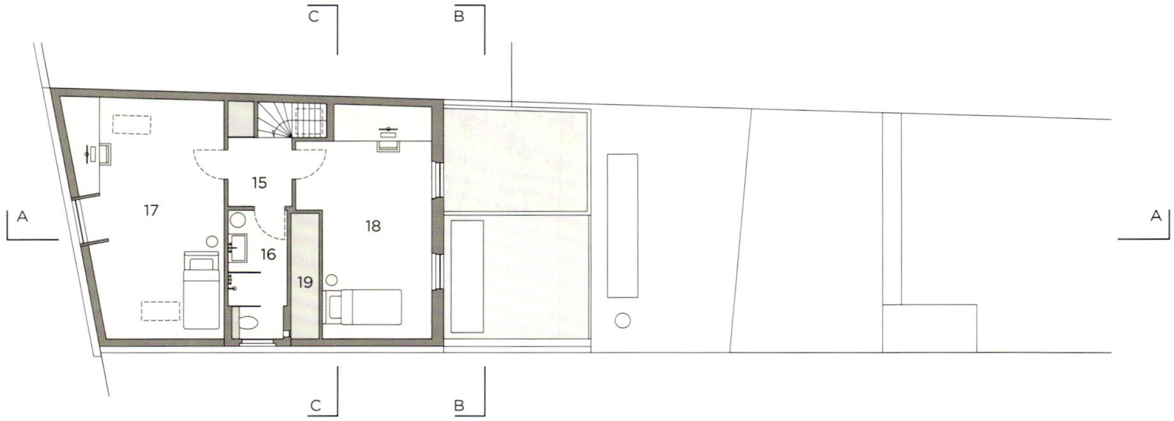

Second floor plan

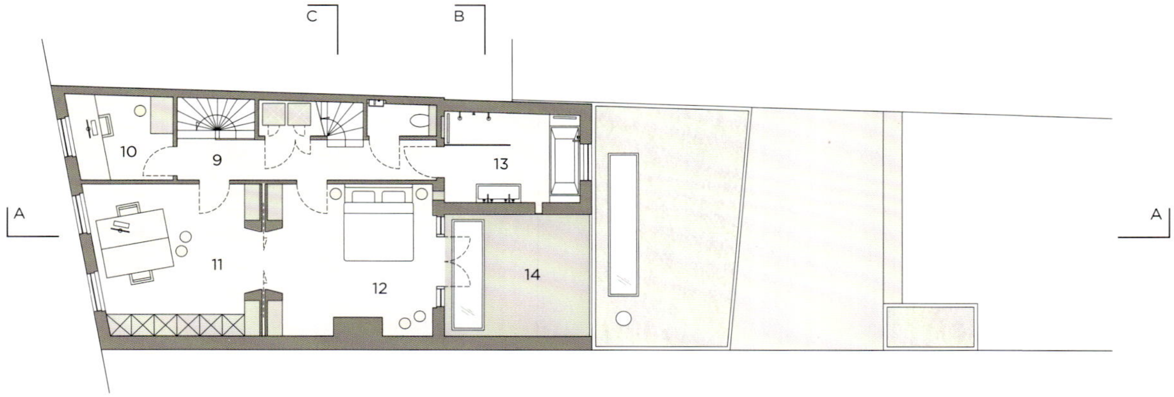

First floor plan

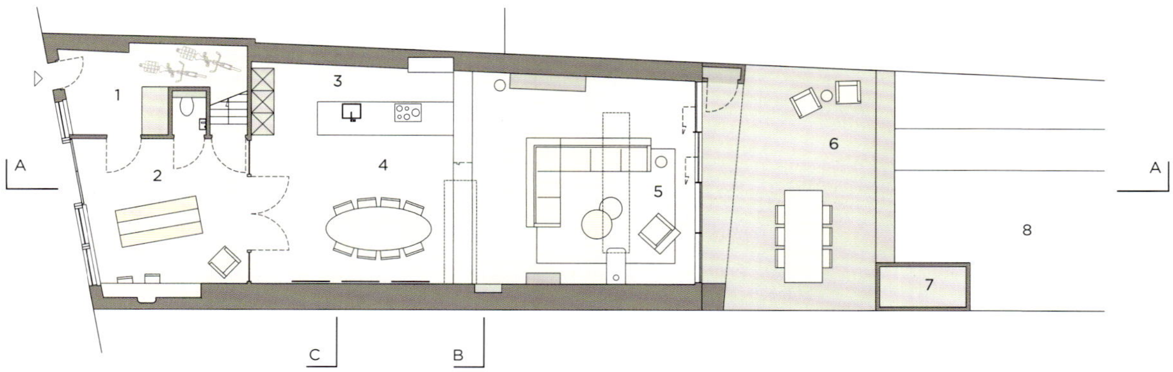

Ground floor plan

1. Entrance
2. Play area
3. Kitchen
4. Dining area
5. Living area
6. Patio
7. Heat pump installation
8. Garden
9. Landing 1st floor
10. Guestroom
11. Study / dressing area
12. Master bedroom
13. Bathroom
14. Roof terrace
15. Landing 2nd floor
16. Bathroom
17. Bedroom
18. Bedroom
19. Solar boiler installation

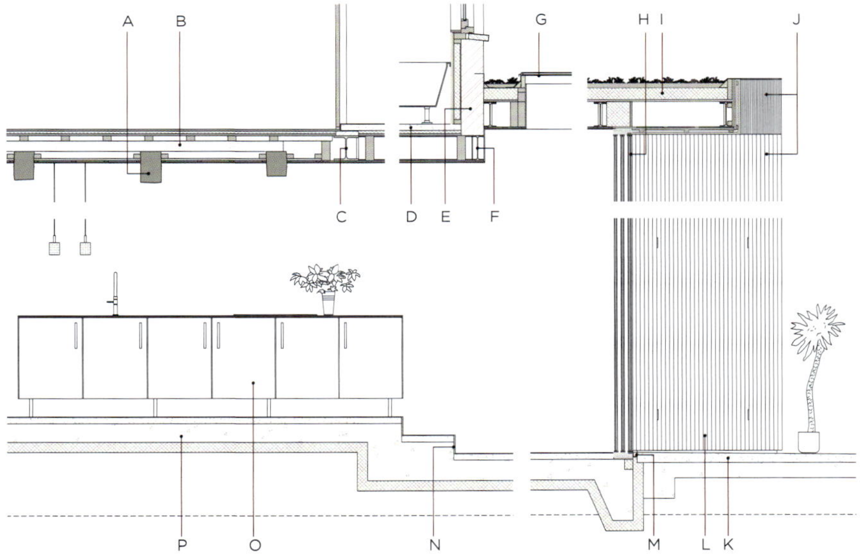

Kitchen elevation

A. Original oaken beams dating back to 1650 - sandblasted
B. Landing first floor specification
- Fishbone parquet flooring
- Underfloor heating in Fermacell fibre boards
- Existing wooden floor built from joists, ledgers and planks
- Original oaken beams with wooden framework and gypsum board with plaster ceiling finish in between
C. Existing steel beam carrying original rear façade
D. Bathroom first floor specification
- DRT screed flooring finish
- Sand/cement screed floor with underfloor heating
- Lewis plates
- Existing floor built from plywood, joists 80 x 240 mm and steel beams
- Gypsum board with plaster ceiling finish
D. Bathroom rear façade specification
- Existing brickwork
- Service cavity layer 20 mm
- Timber studs with insulation
- Wood fibre boards
- Gypsum board with ceramic tiles
F. Existing steel beam carrying rear façade bathroom
G. Heruvent flat roof light 3800 x 800 mm
H. Tudor Pure View aluminum extreme slim sliding door frame 3400 x 5500 mm
I. Living room roof specification
- Green roof module
- Waterproof membrane EPDM
- Insulation 120 mm
- Vapour control barrier
- Roof deck plywood 18 mm
- Steel beams with roof joists 71 x 246 mm
- Gypsum board with plaster ceiling finish
J. Canopy with fraké wood vertical façade cladding 40 x 40 mm
K. Patio floor specification
- Coated sand/cement screed floor
- Concrete slab 150 mm
- Compressed hardcore
L. Storage doors in canopy wall similarly clad with fraké wood
M. Rainwater evacuation
N. 2 long steps from dining room to living room with birch wood risers
O. Floating kitchen with downdraft extractor made by client
P. Living room floor specification
- DRT screed flooring finish
- Sand/cement screed floor with underfloor heating
- 100 mm
- In situ mass concrete slab with reinforcement mesh
- PIR insulation boards 100 mm
- Compressed hardcore

ODOS ARCHITECTS

Office Of David O'Shea - ODOS architects are a Multi-Award winning Architecture established in 2002. Since this time, we have developed a diverse client base and realised a broad range of projects covering a variety of scales and functions.
As a practice, we are wholly interested in the realisation of contemporary architecture, responding to various social and cultural influences by focusing on the latent possibilities inherent in each project.
As designers, we aspire to a simplicity distilled from a core concept, itself a product of both brief and site. In recent years we have grown our practice outside of Ireland, opening offices in both London and New York and currently we are developing a number of projects in the UK, Germany, Malta, Spain, Saudi Arabia and Canada.

www.odosarchitects.com
info@odosarchitects.com

Office Of David O'Shea – Die Architekten von ODOS sind eine mehrfach preisgekröntes Büro, das 2002 gegründet wurde. Seit dieser Zeit haben wir einen breit gefächerten Kundenstamm aufgebaut und eine breite Palette von Projekten mit unterschiedlichen Maßstäben und Funktionen realisiert.
Als Praxis sind wir voll und ganz an der Realisierung zeitgenössischer Architektur interessiert und reagieren auf verschiedene soziale und kulturelle Einflüsse, indem wir uns auf die latenten Möglichkeiten konzentrieren, die jedem Projekt innewohnen.
Als Designer streben wir eine Einfachheit an, die aus einem Kernkonzept destilliert wird, das seinerseits ein Produkt sowohl des Auftrags als auch des Standorts ist. In den letzten Jahren haben wir unser Angebot außerhalb Irlands ausgebaut und Büros sowohl in London als auch in New York eröffnet. Derzeit entwickeln wir eine Reihe von Projekten in Großbritannien, Deutschland, Malta, Spanien, Saudi-Arabien und Kanada.

Office Of David O'Shea - ODOS architects est une agence d'architecture créée en 2002 et récompensée par plusieurs prix. Depuis cette date, nous avons développé une clientèle diversifiée et réalisé un large éventail de projets couvrant une variété d'échelles et de fonctions.
En tant que cabinet, nous sommes entièrement intéressés par la réalisation de l'architecture contemporaine, répondant à diverses influences sociales et culturelles, en nous concentrant sur les possibilités latentes inhérentes à chaque projet.
En tant que designers, nous aspirons à une simplicité distillée à partir d'un concept de base, lui-même produit à la fois du bref et du site. Ces dernières années, nous avons développé notre pratique en dehors de l'Irlande, en ouvrant des bureaux à Londres et à New York. Nous développons actuellement un certain nombre de projets au Royaume-Uni, en Allemagne, à Malte, en Espagne, en Arabie Saoudite et au Canada.

Office of David O'Shea - ODOS Architects es un estudio de arquitectura formada en el año 2002 y ganador de múltiples premios. Desde entonces, hemos desarrollado una diversa base de clientes y realizado una amplia gama de proyectos que cubren una variedad de escalas y funciones.
Como estudio, estamos totalmente interesados en la realización de arquitectura contemporánea, respondiendo a las diversas influencias sociales y culturales, centrándonos en las posibilidades latentes inherentes a cada proyecto.
Como diseñadores, aspiramos a una simplicidad destilada de un concepto central. En los últimos años hemos ampliado nuestro trabajo fuera de Irlanda, abriendo oficinas tanto en Londres como en Nueva York y actualmente estamos desarrollando una serie de proyectos en el Reino Unido, Alemania, Malta, España, Arabia Saudita y Canadá.

707 XZD

PERCY LANE MEWS

The black zinc, curved hat building with stone gables contains three dwellings that have been strategically planned to maximise light and space and benefit from a very carefully considered platter of complementary colours and materials. The curve of the interior roof is built in the double height space linking the kitchen and living spaces. The internal concrete stairwell, with a timber wall, acts not only as a physical connection but also allows natural daylight, reflection and shadow to travel throughout the building in an uninterrupted way.

Das Gebäude mit schwarzem Zink und geschwungenem Hut mit Steingiebeln enthält drei Wohnungen, die strategisch geplant wurden, um Licht und Raum zu maximieren und von einer sehr sorgfältig durchdachten Palette von Komplementärfarben und -materialien zu profitieren. Im Inneren ist die Rundung des Daches in dem doppelt so hohen Raum, der die Küche und die Wohnräume verbindet, erlebbar. Das interne Beton-Treppenhaus mit einer Wand aus Holzrippen dient nicht nur als physischer Verbinder, sondern lässt auch natürliches Tageslicht, Reflexionen und Schatten ungestört durch das Gebäude wandern.

Le bâtiment en zinc noir, à chapeau incurvé et aux pignons en pierre, contient trois logements qui ont été stratégiquement planifiés pour maximiser la lumière et l'espace et bénéficier d'une palette très étudiée de couleurs et de matériaux complémentaires. À l'intérieur, la courbe du toit permet de découvrir l'espace à double hauteur qui relie la cuisine et les espaces de vie. La cage d'escalier interne en béton avec un mur à ailettes en bois agit non seulement comme un lien physique mais permet également à la lumière du jour, aux reflets et aux ombres de circuler dans tout le bâtiment sans interruption.

El propietario quiso renovar esta casa para conseguir un espacio que se adaptara a sus necesidades de forma completa. Los arquitectos propusieron ajustar el espacio interior, atraer la luz natural y añadir un área multiusos sobre el garaje original. El nuevo edificio representa el carácter fuerte y enérgico del propietario, pero a la vez suave y sensible. La vivienda se ha reforzado con una agresiva estructura de acero, pero aún así sigue destilando sensación de ligereza. Unas vasijas de olivo que han sido específicamente diseñadas por artistas de la cerámica y 102 árboles plantados en el jardín realzan su singularidad.

LOCATION
Ballsbridge, Dublin, Ireland

PHOTOS
© Donal Murphy

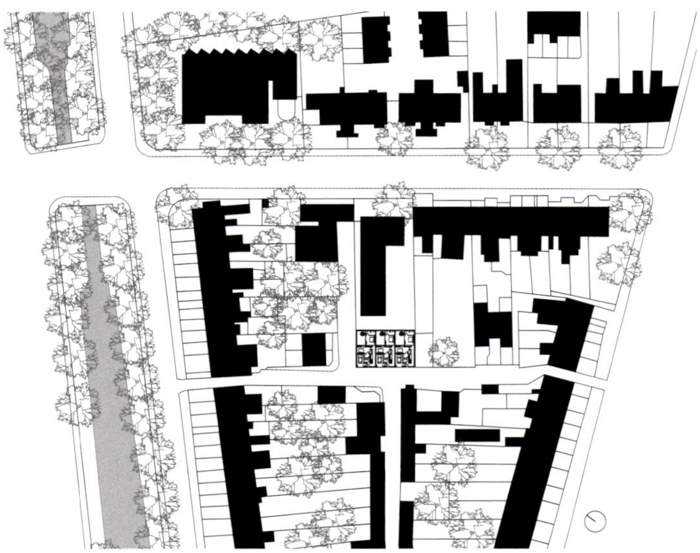

Site plan

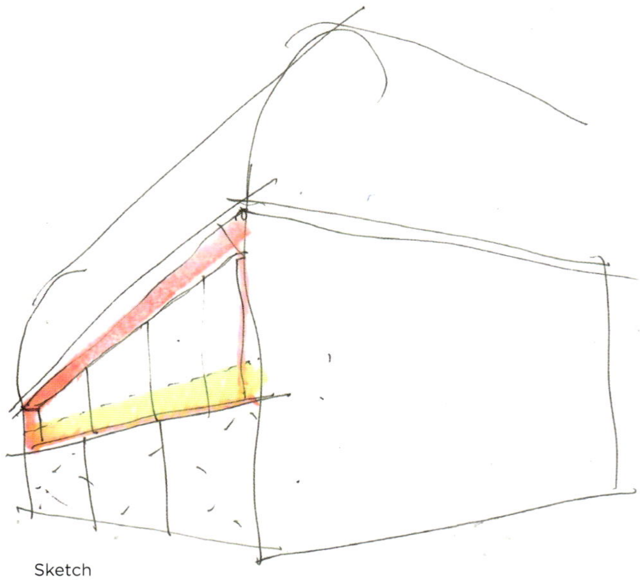

Sketch

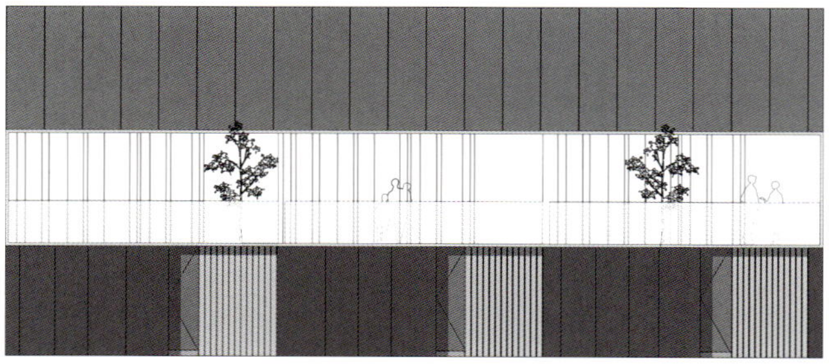

Front elevation

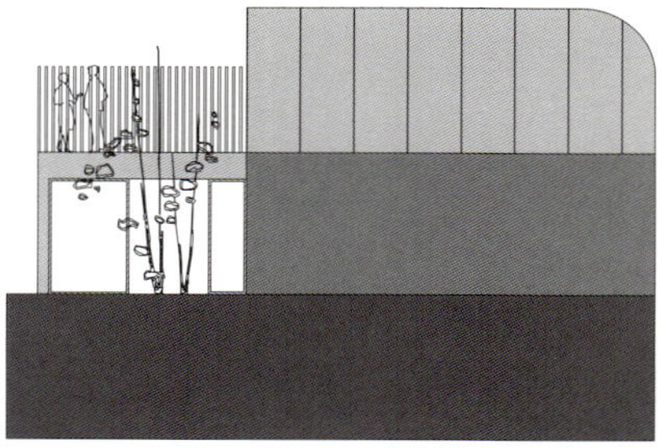

Northwest elevation

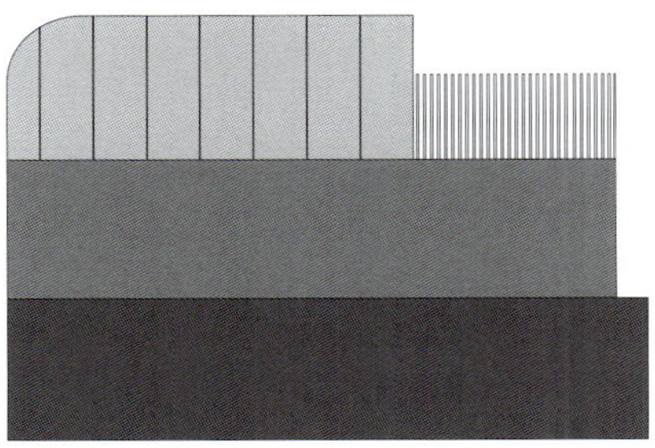

Southeast elevation

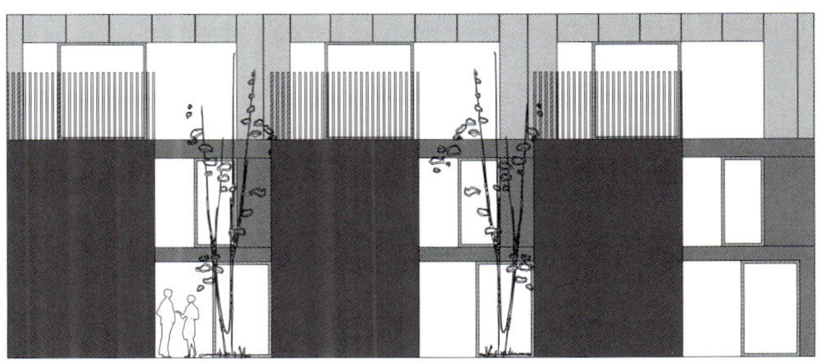

Rear elevation

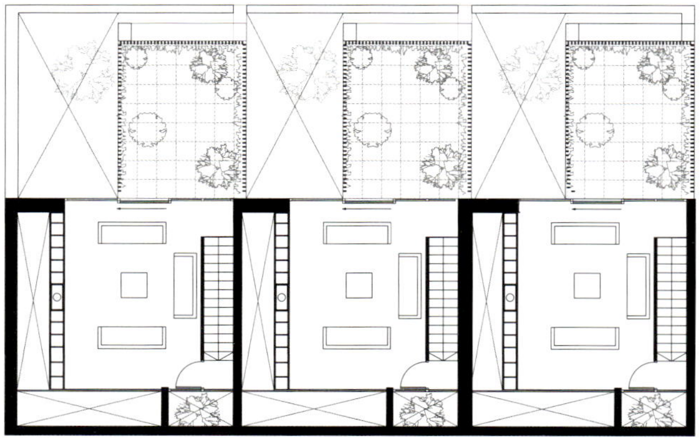

Second floor plan

First floor plan

Ground floor plan

PAULO MARTINS ARCHITECT

Paulo Martins was born in 1979 in Aveiro, Portugal. Principal architect at PAULO MARTINS ARQUITECTURA & DESIGN, he graduated in Architecture in 2003 at ARCA-EUAC, Coimbra, Portugal. Complementing his training, in 2007 he obtained a post-graduation on eco-efficient architecture at Elisava in Barcelona, Spain. Between 2003 and 2008, he collaborated at the Ribas Arquitectes Studio, in Barcelona. After this period, he opened his own studio in Aveiro, where he leads PAULO MARTINS ARQUITECTURA & DESIGN."We are a studio focused on experimental and strategic design, provoking and making the sensorial and emotional experiences part of the process and a goal to be achieved. Through a holistic vision, we view and understand our work as a vehicle responsible for social, political, economical well-being and social equilibrium, assuming this responsibility as an opportunity to reinvent strategies and propose alternatives."

www.paulomartins.com.pt
geral@paulomartins.com.pt

Paulo Martins wurde 1979 in Aveiro, Portugal geboren. Hauptarchitekt bei PAULO MARTINS ARQUITECTURA & DESIGN, 2003 Abschluss in Architektur bei ARCA-EUAC, Coimbra, Portugal. Als Ergänzung zu seiner Ausbildung erhielt er 2007 einen Abschluss in ökoeffizienter Architektur bei Elisava in Barcelona, Spanien. Zwischen 2003 und 2008 arbeitete er im Ribas Arquitectes Studio in Barcelona zusammen. Nach dieser Zeit eröffnete er sein eigenes Studio in Aveiro, wo er PAULO MARTINS ARQUITECTURA & DESIGN leitet. „Wir sind ein Studio, das sich auf experimentelles und strategisches Design konzentriert und die sensorischen und emotionalen Erfahrungen zum Teil des Prozesses und zum Ziel macht erreicht. Durch eine ganzheitliche Vision betrachten und verstehen wir unsere Arbeit als ein Mittel, das für soziales, politisches, wirtschaftliches Wohlergehen und soziales Gleichgewicht verantwortlich ist, und übernehmen diese Verantwortung als Gelegenheit, Strategien neu zu erfinden und Alternativen vorzuschlagen."

Paulo Martins est né en 1979 à Aveiro, au Portugal. Architecte principal chez PAULO MARTINS ARQUITECTURA & DESIGN, il est diplômé en Architecture en 2003 à ARCA-EUAC, Coimbra, Portugal. En complément de sa formation, il a obtenu en 2007 un post-diplôme d'architecture éco-efficace à Elisava à Barcelone, Espagne. Entre 2003 et 2008, il a collaboré au Ribas Arquitectes Studio, à Barcelone. Après cette période, il a ouvert son propre studio à Aveiro, où il dirige PAULO MARTINS ARQUITECTURA & DESIGN. « Nous sommes un studio axé sur le design expérimental et stratégique, provoquant et faisant des expériences sensorielles et émotionnelles une partie du processus et un objectif à atteindre. atteint. À travers une vision holistique, nous considérons et comprenons notre travail comme un véhicule responsable du bien-être social, politique, économique et de l'équilibre social, assumant cette responsabilité comme une opportunité de réinventer des stratégies et de proposer des alternatives. »

Paulo Martins nació en 1979 en Aveiro, Portugal. Arquitecto principal en PAULO MARTINS ARQUITECTURA & DESIGN, se graduó en Arquitectura en 2003 en ARCA-EUAC, Coimbra, Portugal. Complementando su formación, en 2007 obtuvo una postgrado en arquitectura ecoeficiente en Elisava en Barcelona, España. Entre 2003 y 2008, colaboró en el estudio Ribas Arquitectes, en Barcelona. Después de este período, abrió su propio estudio en Aveiro, donde dirige PAULO MARTINS ARQUITECTURA & DISEÑO. «Somos un estudio enfocado en el diseño experimental y estratégico, provocando y haciendo que las experiencias sensoriales y emocionales sean parte del proceso y un objetivo a lograr. A través de una visión holística, vemos y entendemos nuestro trabajo como un vehículo responsable del bienestar social, político, económico y el equilibrio social, asumiendo esta responsabilidad como una oportunidad para reinventar estrategias y proponer alternativas.»

GR HOUSE

Inserted in a terrain of irregular geometry and surrounded by buildings of little architectural value, this house appears as a consequence of its limitations. There is a need for introversion and contemplation which makes the built volume appear inert, imitating nature and its colours. Its forms are irregular and the openings appear in the form of patios and skylights, visible only from higher planes. The social areas of the house are oriented towards the east to enjoy the views and the intimate areas towards the west (street), and separated by an interior patio creating an enriching spatial and visual dynamic.

Eingefügt in ein Gelände mit unregelmäßiger Geometrie und umgeben von Gebäuden von geringem architektonischen Wert, erscheint dieses Haus als Folge seiner Beschränkungen. Es bedarf der Introvertiertheit und des Hermetismus, der das gebaute Volumen träge erscheinen lässt und die Natur und ihre Farben imitiert. Seine Formen sind unregelmäßig und die Öffnungen erscheinen in Form von Terrassen und Oberlichtern, die nur von höheren Ebenen aus sichtbar sind. Die sozialen Bereiche des Hauses sind nach Osten orientiert, um die Aussicht zu genießen, und die intimen Bereiche nach Westen (Straße), die durch einen Innenhof getrennt sind, der eine bereichernde räumliche und visuelle Dynamik erzeugt.

Insérée dans un terrain à géométrie irrégulière et entourée de bâtiments de faible valeur architecturale, cette maison apparaît comme une conséquence de ses limites. Il y a un besoin d'introversion et d'hermétisme, qui fait apparaître le volume construit comme inerte, imitant la nature et ses couleurs. Ses formes sont irrégulières et les ouvertures apparaissent sous forme de patios et de lucarnes, visibles uniquement depuis les plans supérieurs. Les zones sociales de la maison sont orientées vers l'est pour profiter des vues et les zones intimes vers l'ouest (rue) et séparées par un patio intérieur créant une dynamique spatiale et visuelle enrichissante.

Insertada en un terreno de geometría irregular y rodeada de construcciones de poco valor arquitectónico, esta casa aparece como consecuencia de sus limitaciones. Existe una necesidad de introversión y hermetismo, que hace que el volumen construido parezca inerte, imitando la naturaleza, sus colores. Sus formas son irregulares y las aberturas aparecen en forma de patios y tragaluces, visibles solo desde planos superiores. Las áreas sociales de la casa se encuentran orientadas hacia el este para disfrutar de las vistas y las áreas íntimas hacia el oeste (calle), y separadas por un patio interior creando una dinámica espacial y visual enriquecedora.

LOCATION
Aveiro, Portugal

PHOTOS
© Its. Ivo Tavares Studio

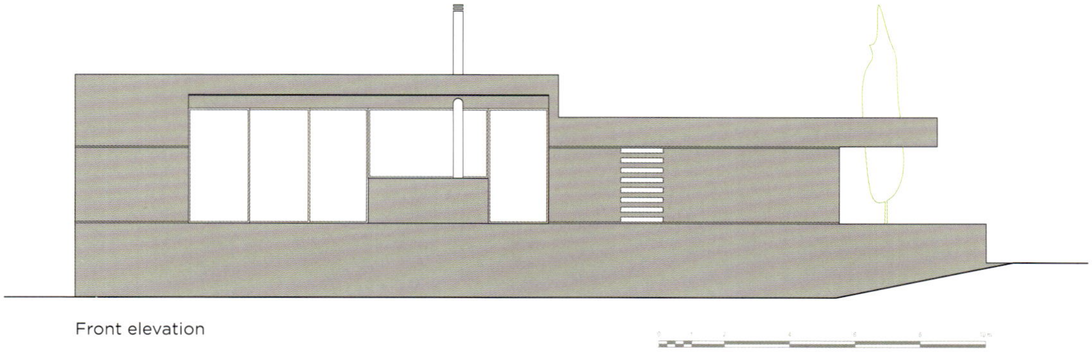

Front elevation

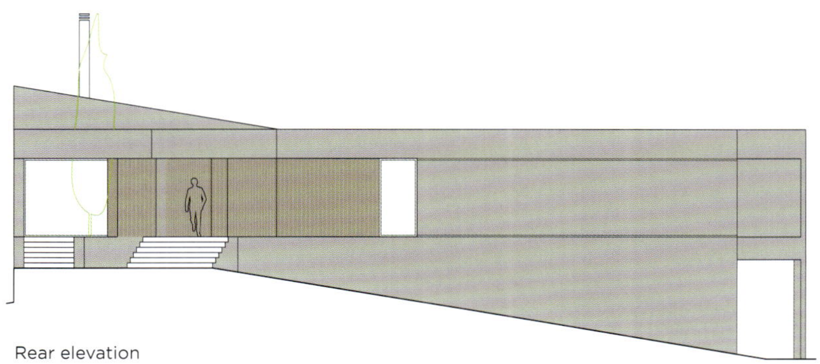

Rear elevation

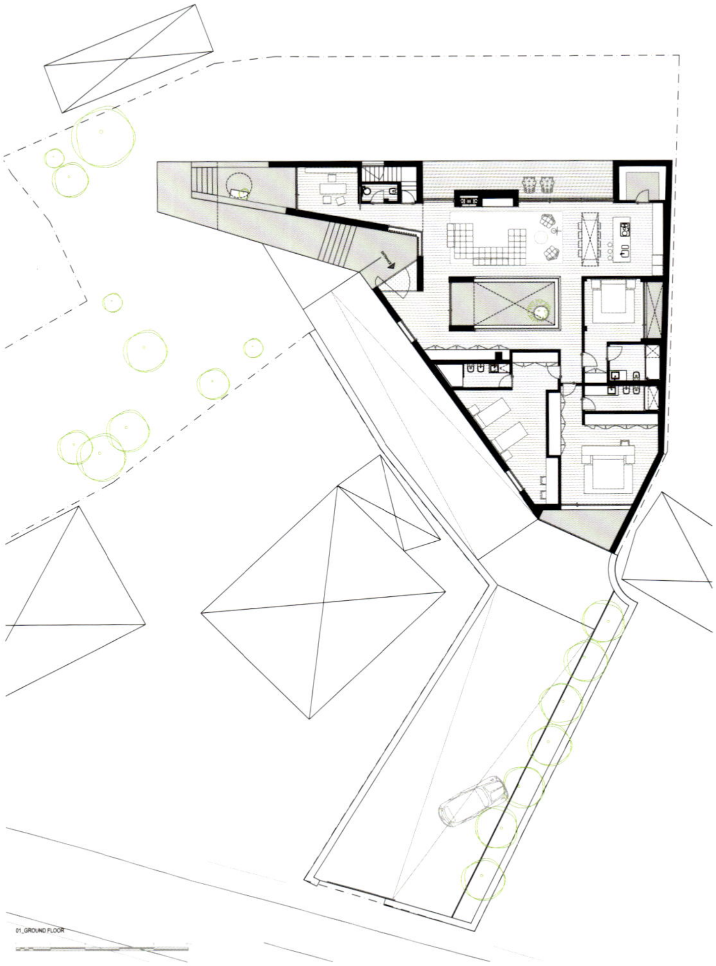

Floor plan

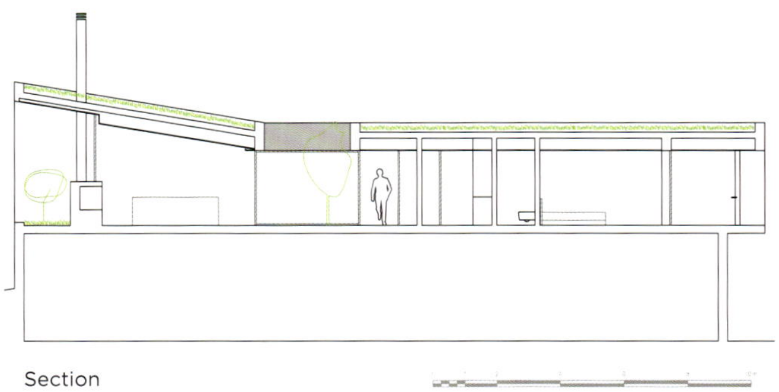

Section

RENATO D'ETTORR ARCHITECTS

Born in Italy, moved to Australia with his family in the 1960's, studied architecture at the University of Technology, Sydney. In 1984 Renato lived in Sardinia investigating many architectural sites around the mediterranean islands. He later worked for Pier Luigi Nervi and Paolo Portoghesi in Roma and Harry Seidler and Romaldo Giurgola in Sydney.
Our object is to create an architecture that is evocative, that attempts a sense of place and beauty, satisfies the human need for textural and tactile expressions, calms or stimulates the senses with light and shade, space and materiality, whilst reducing complexity to achieve clarity and simplicity thus emphasising the ephemeral elements that good architecture can generate.

www.dettorrearchitects.com.au
info@dettorrearchitects.com.au

Geboren in Italien, zog Renato D'Ettore mit seiner Familie in den 1960er Jahren nach Australien und studierte Architektur an der Technischen Universität in Sydney. Im Jahr 1984 lebte Renato auf Sardinien und untersuchte viele architektonische Stätten rund um die Mittelmeerinseln. Später arbeitete er für Pier Luigi Nervi und Paolo Portoghesi in Rom und Harry Seidler und Romaldo Giurgola in Sydney.
Unser Ziel ist es, eine Architektur zu schaffen, die evokativ ist, einen Sinn für den Ort und die Schönheit hat, das menschliche Bedürfnis nach strukturellen und taktilen Ausdrucksformen befriedigt, die Sinne mit Licht und Schatten, Raum und Materialität beruhigt oder anregt und gleichzeitig die Komplexität reduziert, um Klarheit und Einfachheit zu erreichen und so die flüchtigen Elemente hervorzuheben, die gute Architektur erzeugen kann.

Né en Italie, il s'est installé en Australie avec sa famille dans les années 1960 et a étudié l'architecture à l'université de technologie de Sydney. En 1984, Renato a vécu en Sardaigne où il a étudié de nombreux sites architecturaux autour des îles méditerranéennes. Il a ensuite travaillé pour Pier Luigi Nervi et Paolo Portoghesi à Rome et pour Harry Seidler et Romaldo Giurgola à Sydney.
Notre objectif est de créer une architecture qui soit évocatrice. Celle-ci tente de créer un sens du lieu et de la beauté, satisfait le besoin humain d'expressions texturales et tactiles et calme ou stimule les sens par la lumière et l'ombre, l'espace et la matérialité. Cela se fait tout en réduisant la complexité pour atteindre la clarté et la simplicité, soulignant ainsi les éléments éphémères qu'une bonne architecture peut générer.

Nacido en Italia, se mudó a Australia con su familia en los años 60. Allí estudió arquitectura en la Universidad de Tecnología de Sídney. En 1984 Renato vivió en Cerdeña investigando lugares de interés arquitectónico alrededor de las islas del Mediterráneo. Más tarde trabajó para Pier Luigi Nervi y Paolo Portoghesi en Roma y Harry Seidler y Romaldo Giurgola en Sídney.
Su objetivo es crear una arquitectura que sea evocadora, que intente dar sentido al lugar y que satisfaga la necesidad humana de gozar de expresiones texturales y táctiles. Una arquitectura que calme o estimule los sentidos a través de la luz y las sombras, del espacio y la materialidad, y que al mismo tiempo reduzca la complejidad para lograr de esta forma claridad y simplicidad, enfatizando así los elementos efímeros que la buena arquitectura puede generar.

ITALIANATE HOUSE

LOCATION
Surry Hills, Sydney, New South Wales, Australia

PHOTOS
© Justin Alexander

This is a large addition and alterations project restoring an existing heritage-listed 1890s three story, "Victorian-Italian style Terrace House with Carriageway" into a modern home. The underlying challenge was to translate the current 1990's office fit-out into a contemporary residence, honouring the historic style with its charming features, while living in up to date well-being.This are new spaces of silence and contemplation, through calming and restrained aesthetics that will serve the young family well into the 21st Century.

Es handelt sich um ein großes An- und Umbauprojekt, mit dem ein bestehendes, unter Denkmalschutz stehendes dreistöckiges „viktorianisches Terrassenhaus im italienischen Stil mit Fahrbahn" aus den 1890er Jahren in ein mutiges, modernes Haus umgewandelt wird. Die zugrunde liegende Herausforderung bestand darin, die heutige Büroausstattung der 1990er Jahre in ein modernes Wohnhaus zu übersetzen, das den historischen Stil mit seinen charmanten Merkmalen ehrt und gleichzeitig in modernem Komfort lebt. Es sind Räume der Stille und Kontemplation, die durch eine ruhige und zurückhaltende Ästhetik der jungen Familie bis weit ins 21. Jahrhundert hinein dienen werden.

Il s'agit d'un vaste projet d'agrandissement et de modification visant à restaurer une maison de trois étages des années 1890. Elle est classée au patrimoine mondial : « maison en terrasse de style victorien à l'italienne avec une chaussée ». L'objectif est d'en faire une maison moderne et courageuse. Le défi sous-jacent était de traduire l'aménagement actuel des bureaux des années 1990 en une résidence contemporaine, en honorant le style historique avec ses caractéristiques charmantes, tout en vivant dans un confort moderne. Ce sont des espaces de silence et de contemplation, à travers une esthétique apaisante et sobre, qui serviront à la jeune famille pendant une bonne partie du XXIe siècle.

Este es un gran proyecto de adición y rehabilitación de un edificio protegido de tres pisos de la década de 1890. Una «casa adosada victoriana» de estilo italiano se ha convertido en un hogar valiente y moderno. El desafío subyacente consistió en convertir una oficina de los años 90 del siglo XIX en una residencia contemporánea, honrando el estilo histórico pero sin renunciar al bienestar actual. Son espacios de silencio y contemplación a través de una estética tranquila y sobria que servirá a la joven familia hasta bien entrado el siglo XXI.

ARNE JACOBSEN

Sections

Street elevation

Stable front elevation

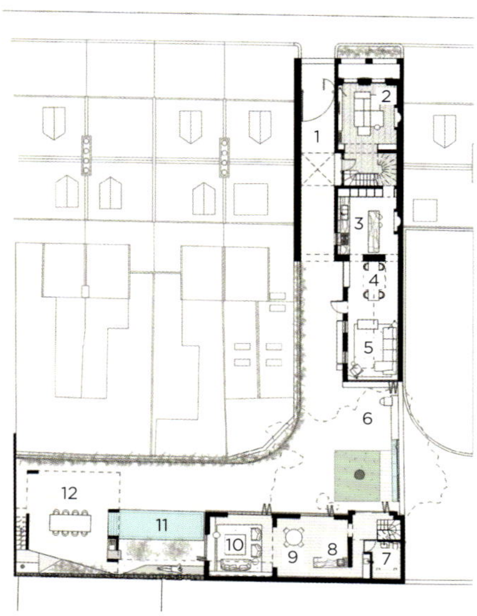

Ground floor plan

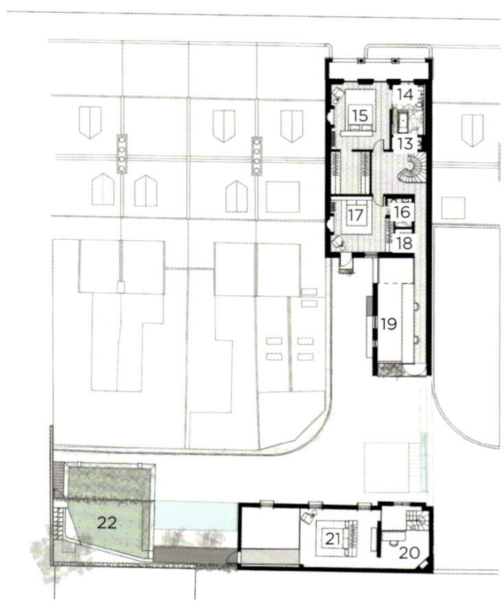

First floor plan

Second floor plan

1. Carriage way
2. Living room
3. Kitchen
4. Dining
5. Family room
6. Courtyard
7. Bathroom
8. Kitchen
9. Dining
10. Pool side lounge
11. Pool
12. Outdoor dining
13. Guest powder room
14. Master ensuite
15. Master bedroom
16. Ensuite 2
17. Bedroom 2
18. Linen
19. Study
20. Study
21. Bedroom 4
22. Roof garden
23. Lounge room
24. Laundry
25. Ensuite 3
26. Bedroom 3
27. Kitchenette
28. Conservatory

SEIDLER GROUP

Seidler Group has built a reputation for excellence in the luxury home market. Innovation, technology and uncompromising craftsmanship are combined to perfect the lifestyle you desire; our focus is on your future. We achieve a flawless result by generating the ultimate fusion of design brilliance with the highest levels of construction excellence.
We offer a fully integrated design that embraces every aspect of interior design, landscaping and recreational activities, drawing these essential factors together to form one complete functional family living center. Our vision is to inspire our clients and the design industry, to constantly develop innovative techniques and set ourselves apart, allowing a modern movement and progression for Seidler Group.

Die Seidler-Gruppe hat sich auf dem Markt für Luxusimmobilien einen hervorragenden Ruf erworben. Innovation, Technologie und kompromisslose Handwerkskunst werden kombiniert, um den von Ihnen gewünschten Lebensstil zu perfektionieren. Unser Fokus liegt auf Ihrer Zukunft. Wir erzielen ein makelloses Ergebnis, indem wir die ultimative Verschmelzung von Designbrillanz mit höchster baulicher Exzellenz erzeugen.
Wir bieten ein vollständig integriertes Design, das jeden Aspekt der Innenarchitektur, der Landschaftsgestaltung und der Freizeitaktivitäten umfasst und diese wesentlichen Faktoren zu einem voll funktionsfähigen Familienwohnzentrum zusammenführt. Unsere Vision ist es, unsere Kunden und die Designindustrie zu inspirieren, ständig innovative Techniken zu entwickeln, und uns von anderen abzuheben, um eine moderne Bewegung und Weiterentwicklung der Seidler-Gruppe zu ermöglichen.

Le groupe Seidler s'est forgé une réputation d'excellence sur le marché des maisons de luxe. L'innovation, la technologie et un savoir-faire sans compromis sont combinés pour perfectionner le style de vie que vous souhaitez. Notre objectif est de vous aider à construire votre avenir. Nous obtenons un résultat sans faille en générant la fusion ultime de la brillance du design avec les plus hauts niveaux d'excellence de la construction.
Nous proposons une conception totalement intégrée qui englobe tous les aspects de la décoration intérieure, de l'aménagement paysager et des activités de loisirs, en rassemblant ces facteurs essentiels pour former un centre de vie familiale fonctionnel et complet. Notre vision est d'inspirer nos clients et l'industrie du design, de constamment développer des techniques innovantes et de nous démarquer. Cela permet un mouvement et une progression moderne pour le groupe Seidler.

El Grupo Seidler ha construido una reputación excelente en el mercado de casas de lujo. La innovación, la tecnología y la artesanía inflexible se combinan para perfeccionar el estilo de vida deseado por el cliente, enfocándonos en su futuro. Logramos un resultado impecable fusionando la brillantez en el diseño con los más altos niveles de excelencia en la construcción.
Ofrecemos un diseño totalmente integrado que abarca todos los aspectos del diseño interior, el paisajismo y las actividades recreativas, uniendo estos factores esenciales para formar un completo y funcional centro de vida familiar. Nuestra visión es inspirar a nuestros clientes y a la industria del diseño, para desarrollar constantemente técnicas innovadoras y diferenciadoras, permitiendo un movimiento moderno y progresista.

www.seidlergroup.com.au
enquiry@seidlergroup.com.au

86

THE SHADE HOME

This project is a marriage of old and new. The existing home iconic textured render influenced the use of materially to provide a seamless transition honouring the heritage character, we emphasised a delineation between period and current architecture by using the entry space as a junction of old and new. The interior spaces praise the unique architectural style, flowing harmoniously from the outside in. Inspiration was drawn directly from the raw materials and sophisticated shapes of the building to create an internal space that reflected it emotionally.

Diese neue Stadtwohnung in einem Vorort der mittelgroßen Stadt Gent hat eine bereichernde Beziehung zu ihrer Umgebung. Die großzügigen Vorder- und Rückfassaden treten durch die verschiedenen Außenbereiche in einen Dialog mit der Straße, der durch das teilweise Zurückziehen der Fassade entsteht. Dadurch entsteht ein faszinierendes Spiel von positiven und negativen Räumen. Als sogenanntes „durchleuchtetes Haus" konzipiert, sind die verschiedenen Wohnräume auch vertikal durch Hohlräume und Oberlichter miteinander verbunden. Das vertikale/gestapelte Wohnen wird daher als räumlich befreiend erlebt.

Ce projet est un mariage d'ancien et de nouveau. Le rendu texturé iconique des maisons existantes a influencé l'utilisation des matériaux pour assurer une transition en douceur de l'ancien au nouveau. En collaboration avec nos architectes du patrimoine, nous avons mis l'accent sur la délimitation entre l'architecture d'époque et l'architecture actuelle. Pour ce faire, nous avons utilisé l'espace d'entrée comme un point de jonction entre l'ancien et le nouveau. La collaboration avec Mim Design a permis à l'espace intérieur de faire l'éloge du style architectural unique, qui s'écoule harmonieusement de l'extérieur vers l'intérieur. L'inspiration a été directement tirée des matériaux bruts et des formes sophistiquées du bâtiment pour créer un espace intérieur qui le reflète avec émotion.

Este proyecto es un matrimonio entre lo viejo y lo nuevo. La textura icónica de las casas existentes influyó en el uso de material para proporcionar una transición perfecta de lo viejo a lo nuevo. Colaborando con nuestros arquitectos especialistas en Patrimonio, enfatizamos una delineación entre la arquitectura de época y la actual usando el espacio de entrada como una unión de lo antiguo y de lo moderno. La colaboración con Mim Design permitió que el espacio interior alabara el estilo arquitectónico único, fluyendo armoniosamente de fuera a dentro. La inspiración se extrajo directamente de las materias primas y de las formas sofisticadas del edificio para acabar creando un espacio interior que lo reflejara emocionalmente.

LOCATION
Kew, Victoria, Australia

PHOTOS
© Peter Clarke Photo

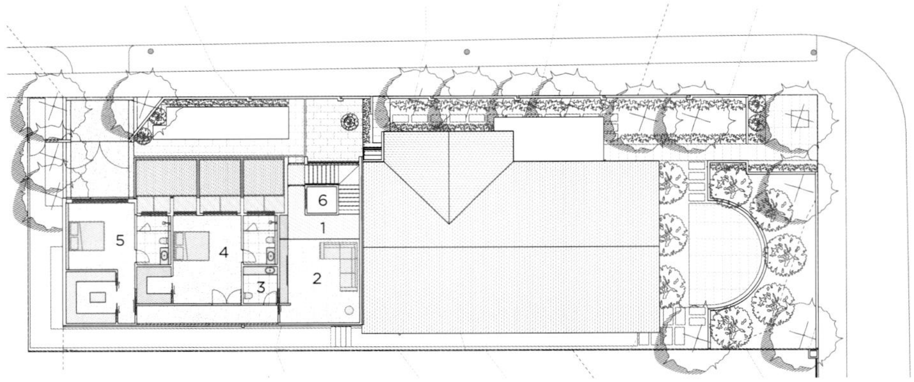

First floor plan

0 1 2 3 5m

1. Landing
2. Rumpus
3. Powder
4. Bedroom suite 2
5. Bedroom suite 3
6. Lift

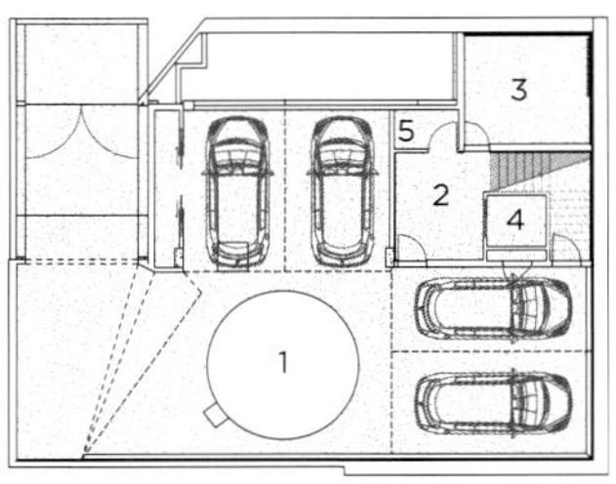

Ground floor plan

1. Garage
2. Lobby
3. Gym
4. Lift
5. Store

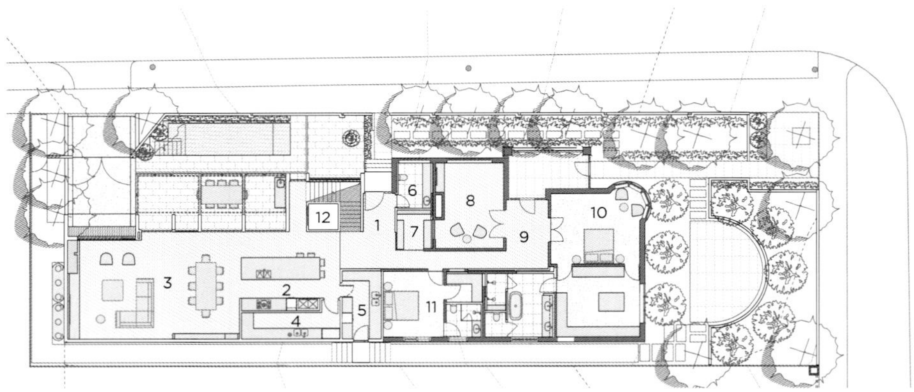

Ground floor plan

1. Family entry
2. Kitchen
3. Living / dining
4. Butlers
5. Laundry
6. Powder
7. Wine
8. Den
9. Guest entry
10. Master suite
11. Bedroom suite 1
12. Lift

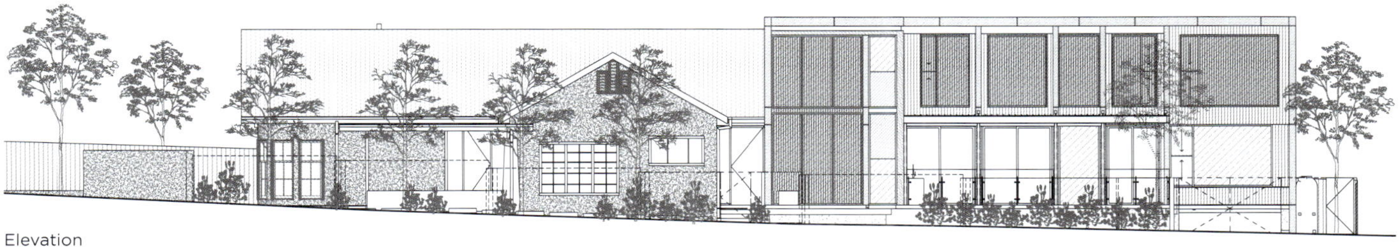

Elevation

SHOGO ARATANI ARCHITECT & ASSOCIATES

Philosophy: experience recorded in the heart. We want to create a space that can be remembered in the hearts of such residents.
Create your own place: there are spaces that can be described in several ways, such as a comfortable living room and a relaxing Japanese-style room, but this is not the only part. Every beautiful design has a reason. As with the word functional beauty, the forms that have been carved based on rationality are beautiful.
Basically housing: we believe that the basis of all spaces is the indispensable one, the basic space used.

www.ararchitect.com
info@ararchitect.com

Philosophie: im Herzen festgehaltene Erfahrung. Wir wollen einen Raum schaffen, der in den Herzen seiner Bewohner bewahrt werden kann.
Schaffen Sie Ihren eigenen Ort: Es gibt Räume, die auf verschiedene Weise beschrieben werden können, wie zum Beispiel „gemütliches Wohnzimmer" und ein „entspannender Raum im japanischen Stil", aber das ist nicht das Einzige: Jede schöne Gestaltung hat einen Grund. Wie es der Begriff „funktionelle Schönheit" zum Ausdruckt bringt, sind Formen, die auf der Grundlage der Rationalität geschnitzt wurden, schön.
So auch beim Wohnen: Wir glauben, dass die Grundlage aller Räume das Unverzichtbare ist, der grundlegende Raum, der genutzt wird.

Philosophie : l'expérience enregistrée dans le cœur. Nous voulons créer un espace qui puisse être mémorisé dans le cœur de ces résidents.
Créer son propre lieu : il existe des espaces qui peuvent être décrits de plusieurs façons, comme un salon confortable et une chambre relaxante de style japonais, mais ce n'est pas la seule partie. Tout beau design a une raison d'être. Comme pour le mot «beauté fonctionnelle», les formes qui ont été sculptées sur la base de la rationalité sont belles.
Fondamentalement, le logement : nous pensons que la base de tous les espaces est l'indispensable, l'espace de base utilisé.

La filosofía del estudio son las experiencias registradas en el corazón. Queremos crear un espacio que pueda ser recordado en los corazones de los residentes.
Crear su propio lugar: hay espacios que pueden ser descritos de varias maneras, como un cómodo salón o una relajante habitación de estilo japonés, pero esta no es la única parte de su concepción de la arquitectura; cada diseño hermoso tiene un motivo. Al igual que la expresión «belleza funcional», las formas que se han tallado basadas en la racionalidad son también hermosas.
Creemos que la base de todos los espacios de vivienda debe ser la indispensable, el espacio básico a utilizar.

HOUSE IN TAKATSUKI

The architectural program for this project was to rebuild a house in a residential community. On this property, the longer sides of the lot were particularly exposed to nearby houses.
We responded by bringing the edges of the building right up to the setback lines and including a buffer zone on the inner side of the exterior walls, distancing the living spaces from adjoining properties. The core living spaces are covered by a single large roof with skylights running all along its length. This roof admits an even sunlight to the entire house, including the main room, kitchen, studio, and even the bathrooms.

Das architektonische Programm für dieses Projekt bestand darin, ein Haus in einer Wohnunterabteilung wiederaufzubauen.
Auf diesem Grundstück waren die längeren Seiten des Grundstücks besonders den Nachbarhäusern ausgesetzt. Wir reagierten darauf, indem wir die Gebäudekanten bis an die Rückzugslinien heranführten und eine Pufferzone an der Innenseite der Außenwände einbauten, wodurch die Wohnräume von den Nachbargrundstücken entfernt wurden. Die Hauptwohnräume sind von einem einzigen großen Dach mit Oberlichtern über die gesamte Länge bedeckt, die eine gleichmäßige Sonneneinstrahlung in das gesamte Haus, einschließlich des Hauptraums, der Küche, des Arbeitszimmers und sogar der Badezimmer ermöglichen.

Le programme architectural de ce projet consistait à reconstruire une maison dans un lotissement résidentiel.
Sur cette propriété, les côtés les plus longs du lot étaient particulièrement exposés aux maisons voisines. Nous avons réagi en amenant les bords du bâtiment jusqu'aux lignes de retrait et en incluant une zone tampon sur le côté intérieur des murs extérieurs. Cela a permis d'éloigner les espaces de vie des propriétés voisines. Les principaux espaces de vie sont couverts par un seul grand toit avec des lucarnes sur toute sa longueur qui laissent passer une lumière solaire uniforme dans toute la maison, y compris la pièce principale, la cuisine, le bureau et même les salles de bain.

El programa arquitectónico de este proyecto consistió en reconstruir una casa ubicada en una urbanización residencial.
Los lados más largos de la propiedad estaban particularmente expuestos a las casas vecinas. Respondimos llevando los bordes del edificio hasta las líneas de separación e incluyendo una zona de respeto en el lado interior de los muros exteriores, distanciando así los espacios de vida de las propiedades vecinas. El núcleo de los espacios interiores está cubierto por un único y gran techo con tragaluces que permiten gozar de luz solar uniforme en toda la casa, incluyendo la habitación principal, la cocina, el estudio e incluso los baños.

LOCATION
Takatsuki-city, Osaka, Japan

PHOTOS
© Shigeo Ogawa

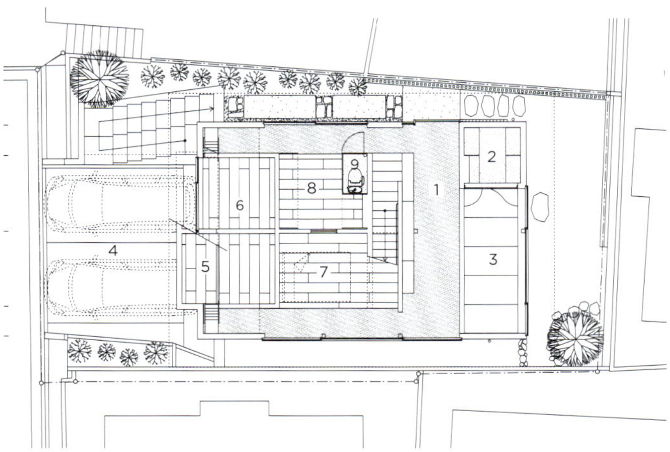

Ground floor plan

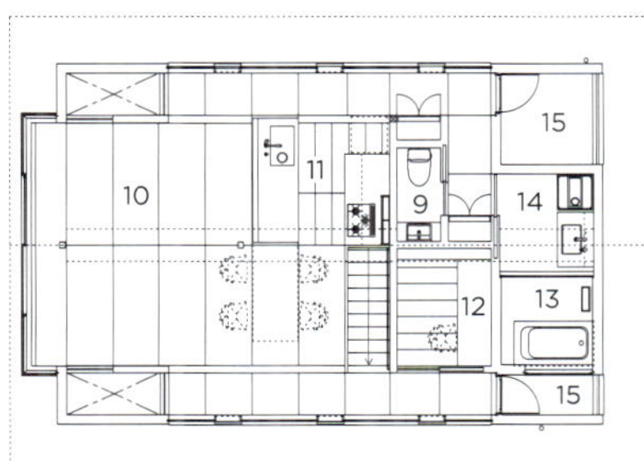

First floor plan

1. Entrance
2. Storage
3. Tatami room
4. Cartport
5. Loft
6. Children's room
7. Bedroom
8. Closet
9. Toilet
10. Living room
11. Kitchen
12. Study room
13. Bathroom
14. Lavatory
15. Balcony

HOUSE IN HYOGO

This property has three levels due to the relationship between the roads on the west and north sides and the neighbour lot. Three floor levels, adjusted to each height, were individually made. The west-side volume in the lowest part of the site has an entrance and a guestroom. The southeast body, in the highest part, accommodates the more private spaces. The third one connects them through a garage that is accessible from the north side, and a living space.

Dieses Grundstück hat drei Ebenen aufgrund der Beziehung zwischen den Straßen auf der West- und Nordseite und dem benachbarten Grundstück. Die drei Stockwerke, die an jede Höhe angepasst sind, wurden individuell angefertigt. Durch deren Verbindung wurde der gesamte Raum konstituiert. Das westseitige Volumen im untersten Teil des Grundstücks hat einen Eingang und ein Gästezimmer, und das südöstliche Volumen im höchsten Teil verfügt über private Räume wie ein Schlafzimmer. Das dritte Volumen verbindet sie miteinander und verfügt zudem über eine Garage, die von der Nordseite aus zugänglich ist, und einen Wohnraum, der das Zentrum des Wohnens darstellt.

Ce lot a trois niveaux en raison de la relation entre les routes des côtés ouest et nord et le lot voisin. Trois niveaux de plancher, ajustés à chaque hauteur, ont été réalisés individuellement. En les reliant entre eux, l'espace entier a été constitué. Le volume du côté ouest, dans la partie la plus basse du site, comporte une entrée et une chambre d'amis. Le volume sud-est, dans la partie la plus haute, comporte des espaces privés tels qu'une chambre à coucher. Le troisième volume les relie et possède également un garage qui est accessible du côté nord et un espace de vie qui est le centre de l'habitation.

Este terreno tiene tres niveles consecuencia de la relación entre las carreteras de los lados oeste y norte y la propiedad vecina. Los tres niveles, ajustados a cada altura, fueron construidos de forma individual y, conectándolos, se logró completar todo el espacio. El volumen del lado oeste en la parte más baja de la propiedad tiene una entrada y un cuarto de huéspedes. El volumen del lado sureste, en la parte más alta, presenta los espacios de carácter más privados, como el dormitorio. El tercer volumen conecta con los otros dos y acoge un garaje al que se accede de desde el lado norte, y una sala de estar que se ha convertido en el centro de reunión familiar.

LOCATION
Hazetsuka-cho, Nishinomiya Hyogo, Japan

PHOTOS
© Shigeo Ogawa

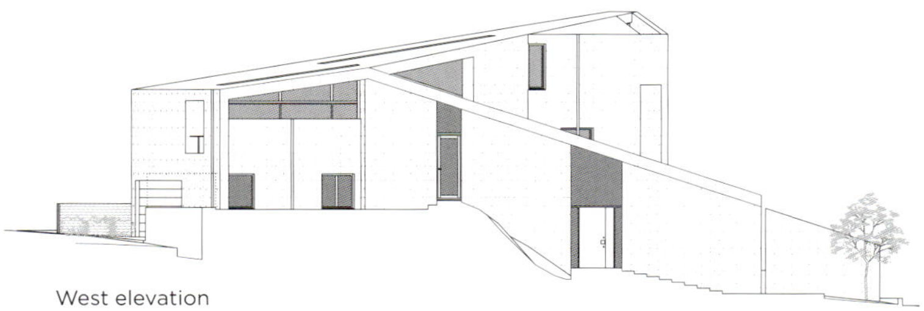

West elevation

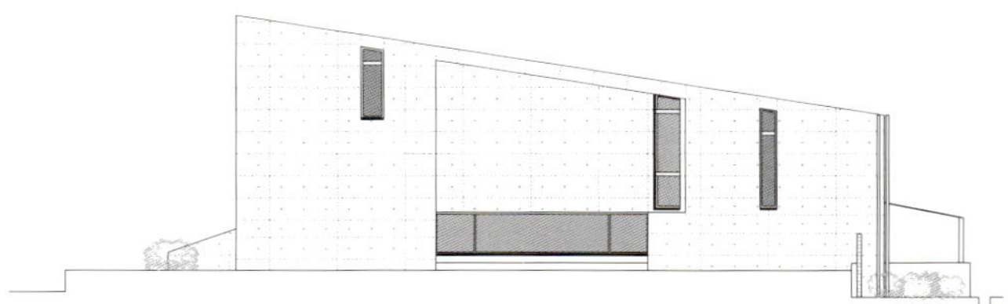

East elevation

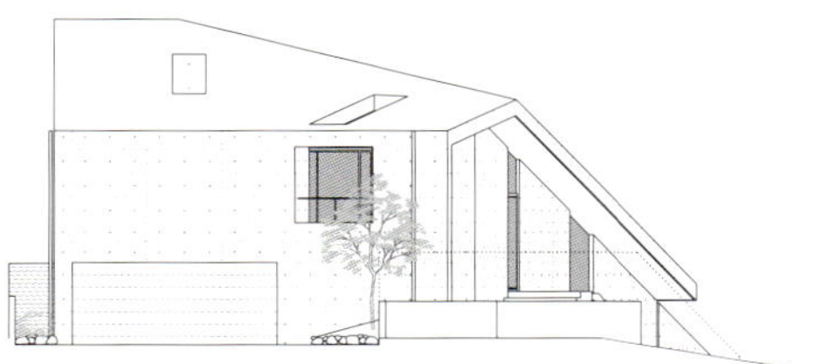

North elevation

South elevation

Sections

1. Hall
2. Tatami room
3. Storage
4. Terrace
5. Bathroom
6. Lavatory
7. Utility
8. SCL
9. Kitchen
10. Dining room
11. Living room
12. Bedroom
13. Master bedroom
14. Garage
15. WCL

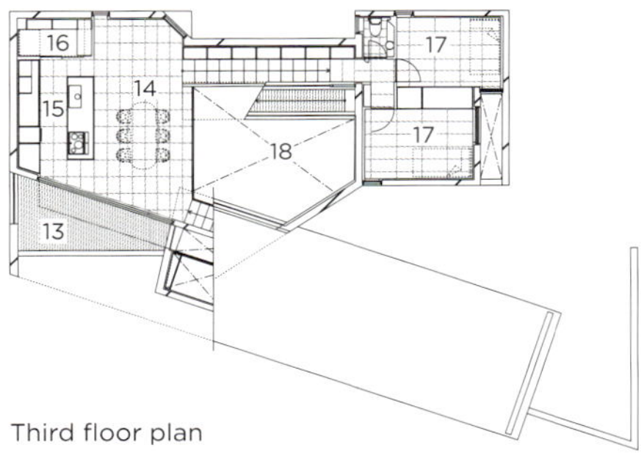

Third floor plan

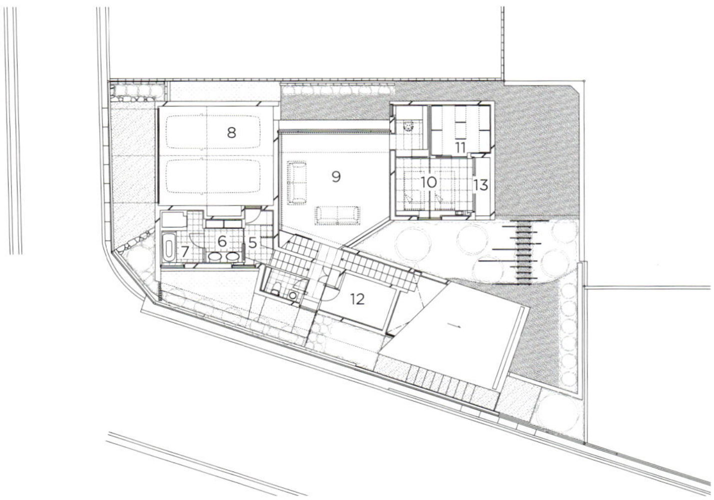

Second floor plan

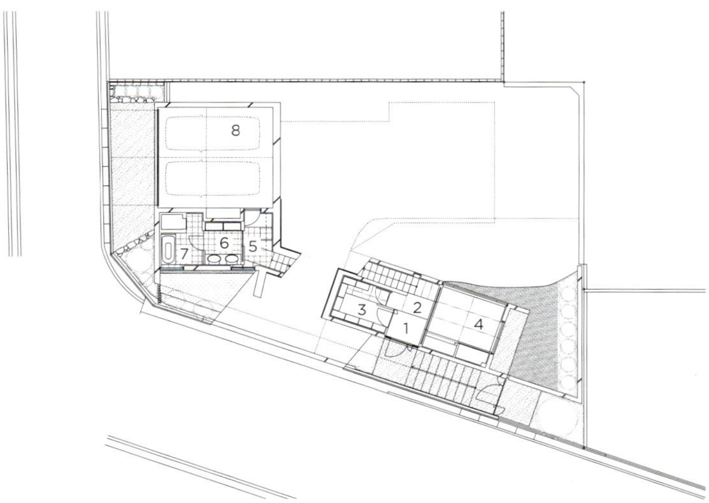

Ground floor plan

1. Entrance
2. Hall
3. SCL
4. Tatami room
5. Utility
6. Lavatory
7. Bathroom
8. Garage
9. Living room
10. Master bedroom
11. WCL
12. Storage
13. Terrace
14. Dining room
15. Kitchen
16. Pantry
17. Bedroom
18. Void

STUDIO MK27

Studio MK27 located in São Paulo was founded in the late 70's by architect Marcio Kogan and today is comprised of 30 architects and various collaborators worldwide. The architects of the team, great admirers of the Brazilian modernism generation, seek to fulfill the task of rethinking and giving continuity to this iconic architectural movement.
Kogan is an honorary member of the American Institute of Architecture, Professor at Escola da Cidade in São Paulo and Politecnico di Milano, and considered by Época magazine as one of the 100 Most Influential persons in Brazil, he is also part of "Wallpaper's 150 Famous for 15 Years."
Since 2001, when he started a co-creation and cooperative work system at the office, Studio MK27 has won more than 250 national and international awards.

www.studiomk27.com
info@studiomk27.com.br

Das Studio MK27 mit Sitz in São Paulo wurde Ende der 70er Jahre vom Architekten Marcio Kogan gegründet und besteht heute aus 30 Architekten und verschiedenen Mitarbeitern weltweit. Die Architekten des Teams, große Bewunderer der brasilianischen Modernismus-Generation, versuchen die Aufgabe zu erfüllen, diese ikonische Architekturbewegung neu zu überdenken und ihr Kontinuität zu verleihen.
Kogan ist Ehrenmitglied des American Institute of Architecture, Professor an der Escola da Cidade in São Paulo und am Politecnico di Milano, und wird von der Zeitschrift Época als eine der 100 einflussreichsten Personen Brasiliens betrachtet. Er ist Teil von „Wallpaper's 150 Famous for 15 Years".
Seit 2001, als er im Büro ein System der Co-Kreation und kooperativen Arbeit begann, hat das Studio MK27 mehr als 250 nationale und internationale Preise gewonnen.

Le Studio MK27 situé à São Paulo a été fondé à la fin des années 70 par l'architecte Marcio Kogan et compte aujourd'hui 30 architectes et divers collaborateurs dans le monde entier. Les architectes de l'équipe, grands admirateurs de la génération du modernisme brésilien, cherchent à remplir la tâche de repenser et de donner une continuité à ce mouvement architectural emblématique.
Kogan est membre honoraire de l'Institut américain d'architecture, professeur à l'Escola da Cidade de São Paulo et au Politecnico di Milano et il est considéré par le magazine Época comme l'une des 100 personnes les plus influentes du Brésil. Il fait partie du groupe « Wallpaper's 150 Famous for 15 Years ».
Depuis 2001, date à laquelle il a lancé un système de co-création et de travail coopératif au bureau, le Studio MK27 a remporté plus de 250 prix nationaux et internationaux.

El Studio MK27, situado en São Paulo, fue fundado a finales de los años 70 por el arquitecto Marcio Kogan y hoy en día está compuesto por 30 arquitectos y varios colaboradores en todo el mundo. Los arquitectos del equipo, grandes admiradores de la generación del modernismo brasileño, buscan cumplir la tarea de repensar y dar continuidad a este icónico movimiento arquitectónico.
Kogan es miembro honorario del American Institute of Architects, profesor de la Escola da Cidade de São Paulo y del Politécnico de Milán, y considerado por la revista Época como una de las 100 personas más influyentes de Brasil. Ha formado parte de la revista «Wallpaper's 150 Famous for 15 Years».
Desde 2001, año en que inició un sistema de trabajo cooperativo y de co-creación en la oficina, el Studio MK27 ha ganado más de 250 premios nacionales e internacionales.

CASA B+B

LOCATION
São Paulo, Brazil

PHOTOS
© Fernando Guerra

The arrival to the house, the access to the living area, is done through an architectural path, by means of an open ramp protected by the sides, a clear influence of Brazilian modernism. This zone of the house creates a sensation of warmth and comfort, in an open space, without any structural interference for the arrangement of the furniture. The bedrooms are located on the ground floor in direct relation to the garden. The wooden elements of the façade of this floor allow the internal control of sunlight and providing a great thermal performance.

Die Ankunft zum Haus - der Zugang zum Sozialbereich - erfolgt über einen architektonischen Weg, mittels einer offenen, seitlich geschützten Rampe, ein deutlicher Einfluss der brasilianischen Moderne. Der soziale Bereich des Hauses schafft ein Gefühl von Wärme und Behaglichkeit, in einem offenen Raum, ohne strukturelle Eingriffe für die Anordnung der Möbel. Die Schlafzimmer befinden sich im Erdgeschoss in direkter Beziehung zum Garten. Die hölzernen Elemente der Fassade dieses Stockwerks ermöglichen die interne Kontrolle des Sonnenlichts und bieten daher eine große thermische Leistung.

Pour arriver à la maison - soit accéder à l'espace social, on chemine à travers des éléments architecturaux au moyen d'une rampe ouverte protégée sur les côtés ; on distingue une nette influence du modernisme brésilien. L'espace social de la maison crée une sensation de chaleur et de confort ; c'est un lieu ouvert, sans aucune interférence structurelle au niveau de l'agencement des meubles. Les chambres sont situées au rez-de-chaussée, reliées directement au jardin. Les éléments en bois de la façade de cet étage permettent le contrôle interne de la lumière du soleil et offrent donc une excellente performance thermique.

La llegada a la casa -el acceso al área social- se realiza a través de una trayectoria arquitectónica, por medio de una rampa abierta protegida por los laterales, clara influencia del modernismo brasileño. El área social de la vivenda crea una sensación de calidez y confort, en un espacio abierto, sin ninguna interferencia estructural para la disposición de los muebles. Los dormitorios se encuentran en la planta baja en relación directa con el jardín. Los elementos de madera de la fachada de este piso permiten el control interno de la luz solar y, por ello, proporcionan un gran rendimiento térmico.

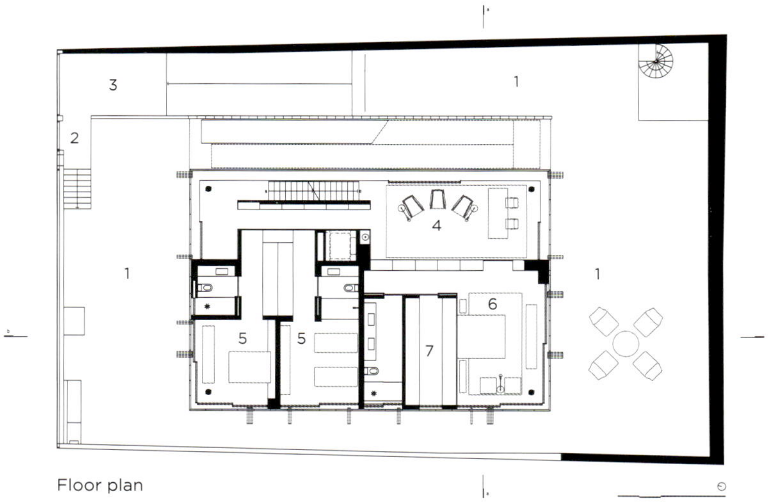

Floor plan

1. Garden
2. Pedestrian access
3. Car access
4. Office
5. En suite bedroom
6. En suite master bedroom
7. Walk-in closet

TCA
THIER+CURRAN ARCHITECTS

Established in 2005 in Hamilton, Ontario, TCA | Thier + Curran Architects is a full-service design firm that is busy, dynamic, and ambitious. Our work is decidedly contemporary, yet respectful of context and history. Our buildings are thoughtful and engaging, transcending the ordinary.

Our diverse portfolio is founded on two constant principles: a highly collaborative design approach, and a recognition that buildings and sites themselves collaborate in the making of places. We aim to create architecture that is expressive and participatory, architecture that responds to the human needs of habitation; and that draws on alliances with context, landscape, the arts, and the rhythms of human activity. The results are thoughtful and engaging buildings that create memorable and meaningful places.

www.tcarch.ca
curran@tcarch.ca

TCA | Thier + Curran Architects wurde 2005 in Hamilton, Ontario, gegründet. TCA | Thier + Curran Architects ist ein Full-Service-Designbüro, das vielbeschäftigt, dynamisch und ehrgeizig ist. Unsere Arbeit ist entschieden zeitgenössisch, respektiert jedoch den Kontext und die Geschichte. Unsere Gebäude sind nicht nur durchdacht und ansprechend, sondern gehen auch über das Gewöhnliche hinaus.

Unser vielfältiges Portfolio basiert auf zwei beständigen Prinzipien: einem hochgradig kooperativen Designansatz und der Erkenntnis, dass Gebäude und Orte selbst an der Gestaltung mitwirken. Unser Ziel ist es, eine Architektur zu schaffen, die ausdrucksstark und partizipatorisch ist, eine Architektur, die auf die menschlichen Bedürfnisse des Wohnens reagiert und die sich auf Allianzen mit dem Kontext, der Landschaft, den Künsten und den Rhythmen menschlicher Aktivitäten stützt. Das Ergebnis sind durchdachte und ansprechende Gebäude, die denkwürdige und bedeutungsvolle Orte schaffen.

Créé en 2005 à Hamilton, Ontario, TCA | Thier + Curran Architects est un bureau d'études complet très actif, dynamique et ambitieux. Notre travail est résolument contemporain, tout en respectant le contexte et l'histoire. Nos bâtiments sont réfléchis et attrayants. Ils transcendent l'ordinaire.

Notre portefeuille diversifié est fondé sur deux principes constants : une approche de conception hautement collaborative et la reconnaissance du fait que les bâtiments et les sites eux-mêmes collaborent à la création de lieux. Notre objectif est de créer une architecture expressive et participative, une architecture qui répond aux besoins humains en matière d'habitation et qui s'appuie sur des alliances avec le contexte, le paysage, les arts et les rythmes de l'activité humaine. Il en résulte des bâtiments réfléchis et attrayants qui créent des lieux mémorables et significatifs.

Establecida en 2005 en Hamilton, Ontario, TCA | Thier + Curran Architects es una empresa dinámica y ambiciosa que ofrece servicios completos de diseño. Nuestro trabajo es decididamente contemporáneo, pero respetuoso con el contexto y la historia. Nuestros edificios son reflexivos y atractivos, trascienden lo ordinario.

Nuestros proyectos se basan en dos principios constantes: un enfoque de diseño altamente colaborativo y el reconocimiento de que los edificios y los propios lugares participan en la creación. Nuestro objetivo es crear una arquitectura expresiva, una arquitectura que responda a las necesidades humanas de vivienda y que se base en alianzas con el contexto, el paisaje, las artes y los ritmos modernos. Los resultados son edificios pen-

THE RESERVOIR DOGS TOWNHOUSE LOFTS

This project consists of the reuse of a 1910 industrial building into three large loft style houses, trying to preserve its original essence both inside and outside. The modern facade is a fusion of the original elements, purely industrial, with modern steel, large glass windows and corrugated metal cladding. Inside, the houses are bright and spacious, with very high ceilings, beams and columns. Generous windows, in addition to light, provide cross ventilation and multiple skylights facilitate natural heat ventilation in summer.

Dieses Projekt besteht aus der Wiederverwendung eines Industriegebäudes aus dem Jahr 1910 in drei großen Häusern im *Loft*-Stil, wobei versucht wird, sein ursprüngliches Wesen sowohl innen als auch außen so weit wie möglich zu erhalten. Die moderne Fassade ist eine Verschmelzung der ursprünglichen, rein industriellen Elemente mit modernem Stahl, großen Glasfenstern und Wellblechverkleidung. Im Inneren sind die Häuser hell und geräumig, mit sehr hohen Decken, Balken und Säulen. Großzügige Fenster sorgen neben dem Licht für eine Querlüftung und mehrere Oberlichter erleichtern die natürliche Belüftung im Sommer.

Ce projet consiste en la réutilisation d'un bâtiment industriel de 1910 dans trois grandes maisons de style *loft*, en essayant de préserver autant que possible son essence originale à l'intérieur comme à l'extérieur. La façade moderne est une fusion des éléments originaux, purement industriels, avec l'acier moderne, les grandes fenêtres en verre et le revêtement en métal ondulé. A l'intérieur, les maisons sont claires et spacieuses ; avec des plafonds, des poutres et des colonnes très hauts. En plus de la lumière, de généreuses fenêtres assurent une ventilation transversale et de multiples lucarnes facilitent la ventilation naturelle de la chaleur en été.

Este proyecto consiste en la reutilización de un edificio industrial de 1910 en tres grandes viviendas estilo *loft* intentando preservar al máximo su esencia original tanto en el interior como en el exterior. La moderna fachada es una fusión de los elementos originales, puramente industriales, con moderno acero, grandes ventanales de vidrio y revestimiento de metal corrugado. En su interior, las viviendas son luminosas y espaciosas, de techos muy altos, con vigas y columnas. Generosas ventanas, además de luz, proporcionan ventilación cruzada y múltiples claraboyas facilitan la ventilación de calor natural en verano.

LOCATION
Hamilton, Ontario, Canada

PHOTOS
© Industyous Photography

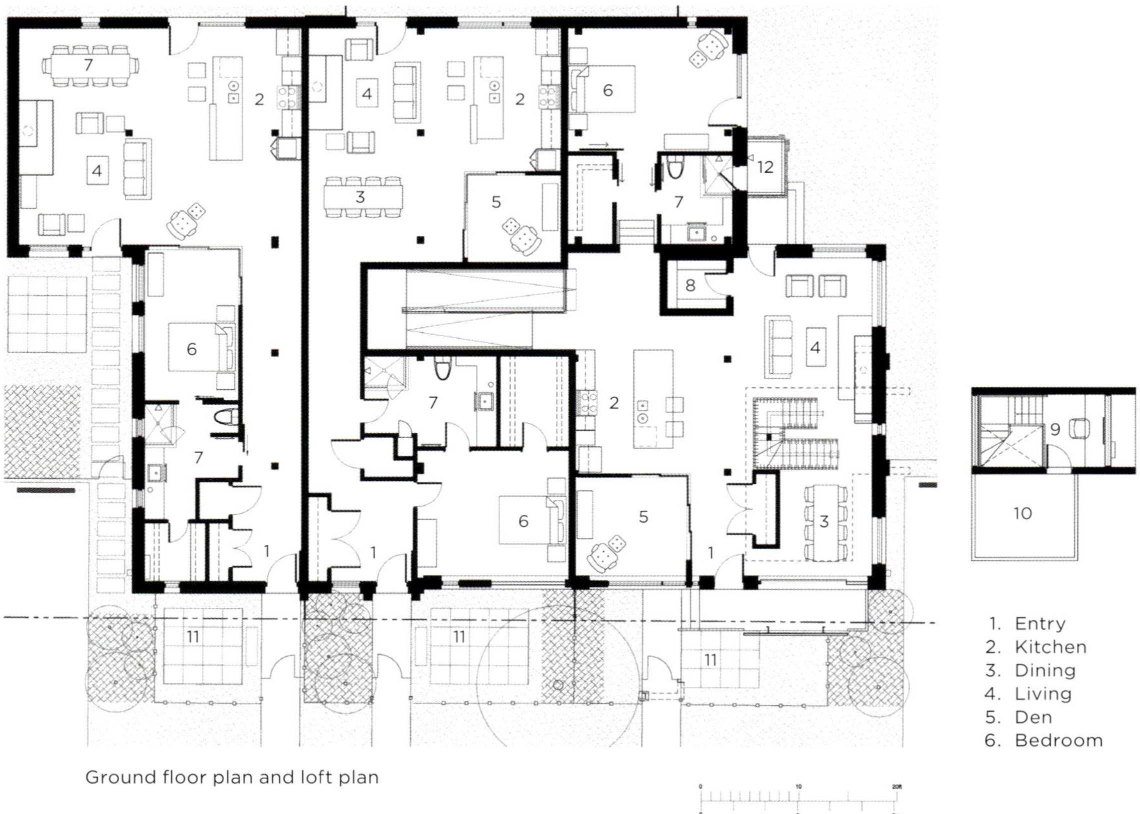

1. Entry
2. Kitchen
3. Dining
4. Living
5. Den
6. Bedroom
7. Washroom
8. Wine cellar
9. Loft
10. Roof deck
11. Garden terrace
12. Outdoor shower

Ground floor plan and loft plan

TAILLANDIER ARCHITECTES ASSOCIÉS

Founded in 1993 by Pierre-Louis Taillandier, Taillandier Architectes Associés (TAA) is an architecture and urban planning agency. TAA is an organization that works with private and public partners. TAA's people give their best to develop architectural solutions to improve the experience. Independently of the project, the answer must improve the quality of life of the user and the direct environment. To achieve this goal, the approach must be well-designed and well-constructed.
Each project solves equations that combine program, user, and environmental specifications. To achieve an architectural and urban solution, Pierre-Louis Taillandier established a rational and efficient methodology divided into five dimensions: contextual, intellectual, technical, financial, and sensitive. The associates and affiliates bring together about 90 collaborators.

www.starchitectes.com
agence@starchitectes.com
Leroy@starchitectes.com

Taillandier Architectes Associés (TAA) wurde 1993 von Pierre-Louis Taillandier gegründet und ist ein Architektur- und Stadtplanungsbüro. TAA ist eine Organisation, die mit privaten und öffentlichen Partnern arbeitet. Die Menschen bei TAA geben ihr Bestes, um architektonische Lösungen zu entwickeln, die das Erlebnis unabhängig vom Projekt verbessern sollen. Das Ergebnis muss der Lebensqualität der Nutzer und der direkten Umgebung dienen. Um dieses Ziel zu erreichen, muss der Ansatz gut konzipiert und aufgebaut sein.
Jedes Projekt löst Gleichungen, die Programm-, Benutzer- und Umweltspezifikationen kombinieren. Um eine architektonische und urbane Lösung zu erreichen, entwickelte Pierre-Louis Taillandier eine rationale und effiziente Methodik, die in fünf Dimensionen unterteilt ist: kontextuell, intellektuell, technisch, finanziell und sensibel. Die Associates und Affiliates bringen etwa neunzig Mitarbeiter zusammen.

Fondée en 1993 par Pierre-Louis Taillandier, Taillandier Architectes Associés (TAA) est une agence d'architecture et d'urbanisme. TAA est une organisation qui travaille avec des partenaires privés et publics. Le personnel de TAA fait de son mieux pour développer des solutions architecturales afin d'améliorer l'expérience indépendamment du projet, la réponse doit améliorer la qualité de vie de l'utilisateur et l'environnement direct. Pour atteindre cet objectif, l'approche doit être bien conçue et bien construite.
Chaque projet résout des équations qui combinent les spécifications du programme, de l'utilisateur et de l'environnement. Pour parvenir à une solution architecturale et urbaine, Pierre-Louis Taillandier a établi une méthodologie rationnelle et efficace divisée en cinq dimensions : contextuelle, intellectuelle, technique, financière et sensible. Les Associés et affiliés rassemblent environ quatre-vingt-dix collaborateurs.

Fundada en 1993 por Pierre-Louis Taillandier, Taillandier Architectes Associés (TAA) es una agencia de arquitectura y urbanismo. TAA es una organización que trabaja con socios privados y públicos. Las personas de TAA dan lo mejor de sí para desarrollar soluciones arquitectónicas para mejorar la experiencia independientemente del proyecto, la respuesta debe mejorar la calidad de vida del usuario y el entorno directo. Para alcanzar este objetivo, el enfoque debe estar bien diseñado y bien construido.
Cada proyecto resuelve ecuaciones que combinan el programa, el usuario y las especificaciones ambientales. Para lograr una solución arquitectónica y urbana, Pierre-Louis Taillandier estableció una metodología racional y eficiente dividida en cinco dimensiones: contextual, intelectual, técnica, financiera y sensible. Los Asociados y afiliados reúnen a unos noventa colaboradores.

METAMORPHOSIS OF A TOULOUSE WOMAN

The aim of the project is to create a new family home while preserving only the existing historic façade of this house type called the "Toulousaine" in harmony with the urban sequence of the street. The new house is divided in two zones. The sleeping areas occupy the upper two floors, while the living and dining areas link the street level in the front to the lower garden level in the back. Resolutely contemporary, the rear façade is the exterior expression of the dual design intended by the architect for this renovation. Radical is also the layout of the garden, designed as a "grassy void" with a swimming pool.

Ziel des Projekts ist es, ein neues Einfamilienhaus zu schaffen und dabei nur die bestehende historische Fassade dieses Haustyps, der „Toulousaine" genannt wird, in Harmonie mit der urbanen Abfolge der Straße zu erhalten. Das neue Haus ist in zwei Zonen unterteilt. Die Schlafbereiche nehmen die beiden oberen Stockwerke ein, während die Wohn- und Essbereiche die Straßenebene im vorderen Teil mit dem unteren Gartengeschoss im hinteren Teil verbinden. Die entschieden zeitgenössische hintere Fassade ist der äußere Ausdruck des vom Architekten für diese Renovierung vorgesehenen doppelten Entwurfs. Ebenso radikal ist die Gestaltung des Gartens, der als „grasbewachsene Leere" mit einem Schwimmbad konzipiert ist.

L'objectif du projet est de créer une nouvelle maison familiale en conservant uniquement la façade historique existante de ce type de maisons, appelées «Toulousaines», en harmonie avec la séquence urbaine de la rue. La nouvelle maison est divisée en deux zones. Les chambres à coucher occupent les deux étages supérieurs, tandis que le salon et la salle à manger relient le niveau de la rue à l'avant au niveau inférieur du jardin à l'arrière. Résolument contemporaine, la façade arrière est l'expression extérieure de la double conception voulue par l'architecte pour cette rénovation. L'aménagement du jardin est tout aussi radical et a été conçu comme un «vide herbeux» avec une piscine.

El objetivo del proyecto es crear un nuevo hogar familiar conservando sólo la fachada histórica existente de este tipo de casa llamada «Toulousaine» en armonía con la secuencia urbana de la calle. La nueva casa está dividida en dos zonas. Las zonas de dormitorio ocupan las dos plantas superiores, mientras que las zonas de estar y de comedor unen el nivel de la calle en la parte delantera con el nivel inferior del jardín en la parte trasera. Absolutamente contemporánea, la fachada trasera es la expresión del doble diseño previsto por el arquitecto para esta renovación. Igual de radical es la disposición del jardín, que está diseñado a partir de un espacio de hierba con piscina.

LOCATION
Toulouse, France

PHOTOS
© Luc Boegly

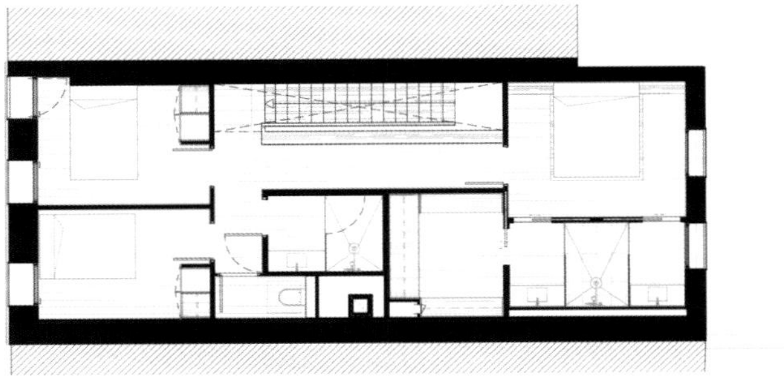

Second floor plan

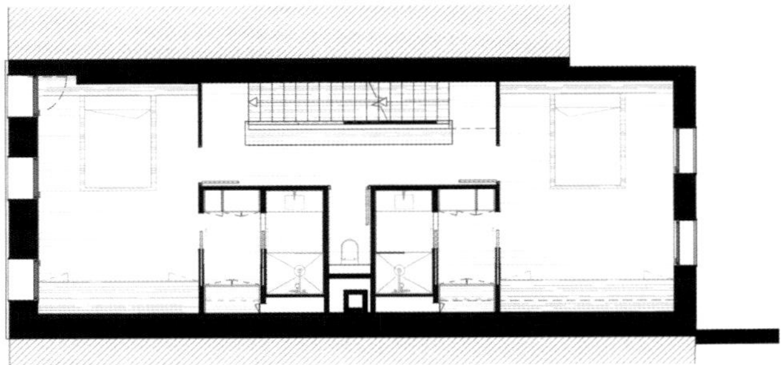

First floor plan

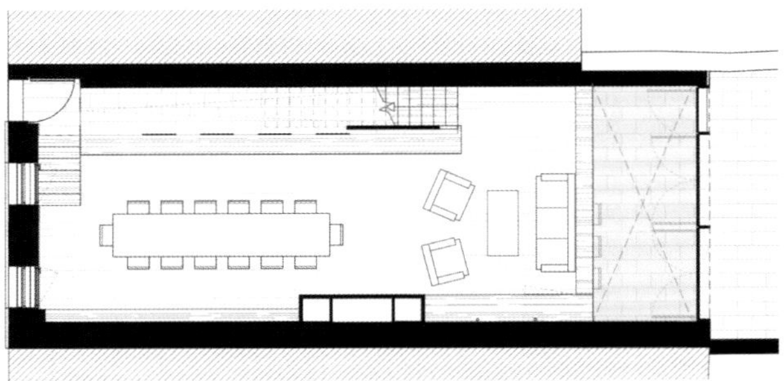

Ground floor plan

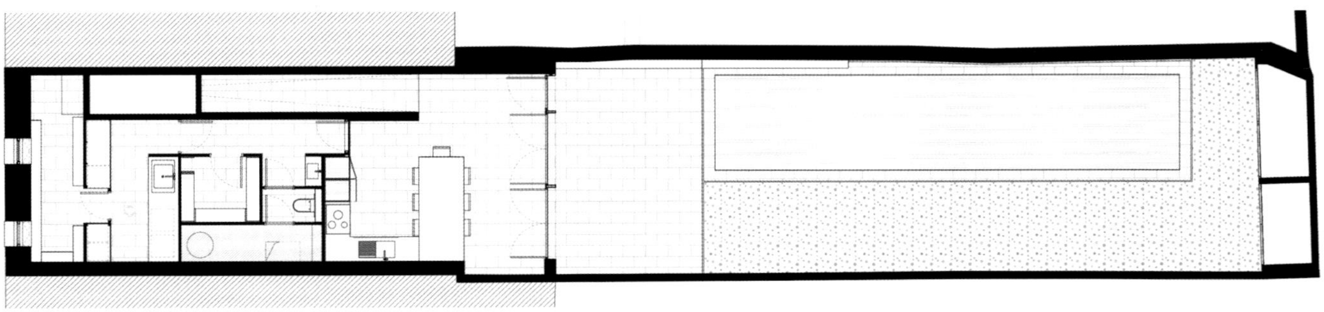

Garden plan

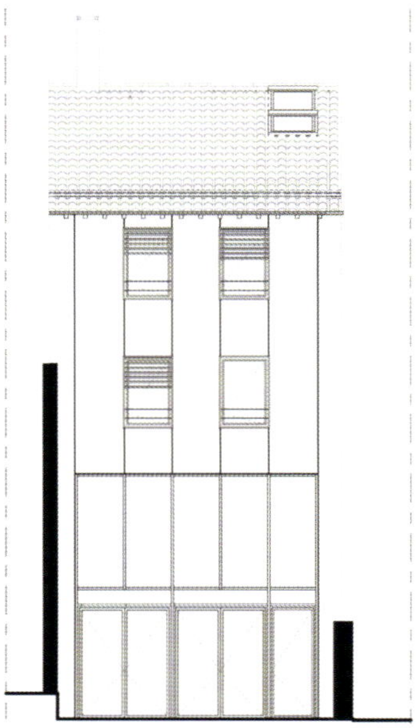

East elevation

West elevation

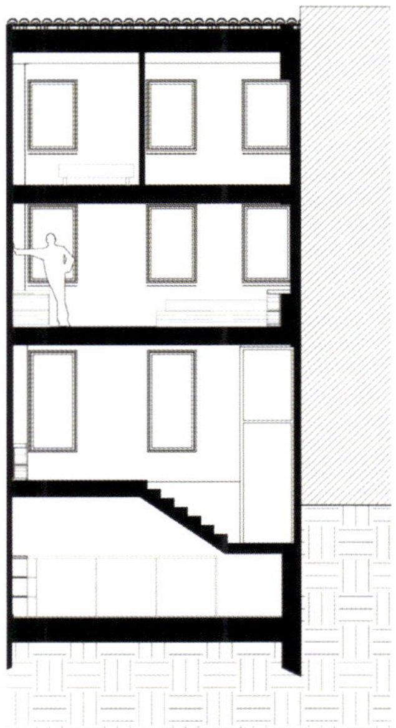

Transversal section

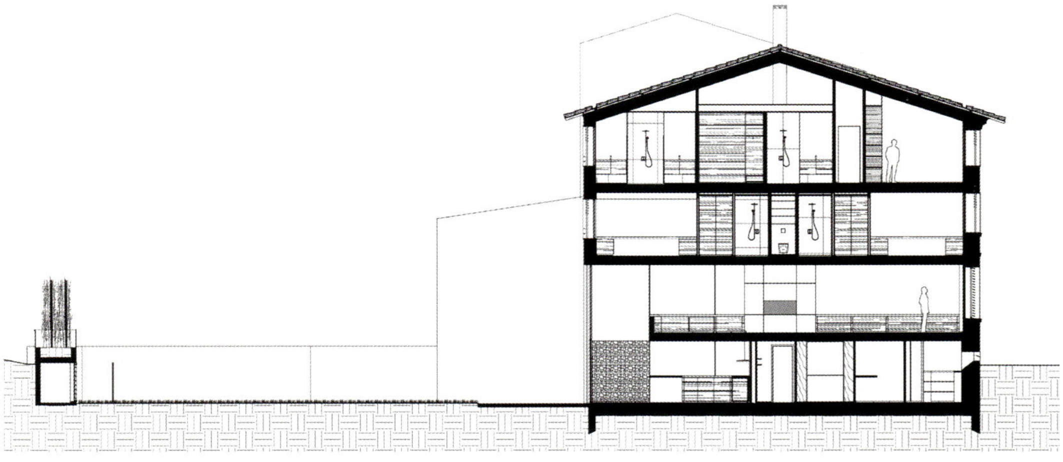

Longitudinal section

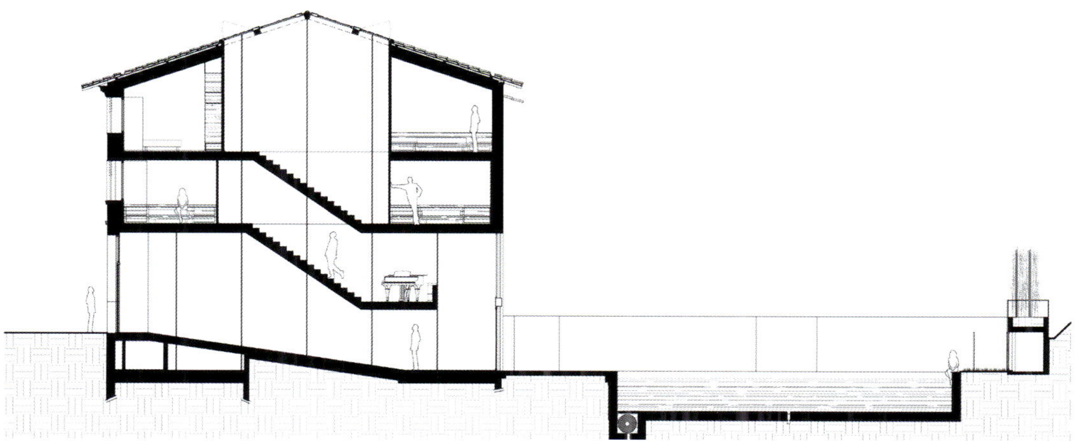

Longitudinal section

TAKATINA

Takatina is a NY-based multi-disciplinary design consultancy led by Takaaki and Christina Kawabata. Since 2003, we have completed projects reimagining the old and creating exquisite new designs.
It is our mutually held belief that design has the potential to enhance the quiet pleasures of life. With every built gesture we strive to materialize that aspiration.
Guided by our client and the site program, rather than by fashion or trends, our goal is to formulate a simple, unique solution each time.
We admire timeless design with pure and tactile materials. We focus on function, quality and detail. Above all, we want each of our creations to last, and be loved, whether you're entering for the first time, or waking up there every day.

www.takatina.com
info@takatina.com

Takatina ist ein in NY ansässiges multidisziplinäres Designberatungsunternehmen unter der Leitung von Takaaki und Christina Kawabata. Seit 2003 haben wir Projekte abgeschlossen, bei denen wir das Alte neu erfinden und exquisite neue Designs schaffen.
Es ist unsere gemeinsame Überzeugung, dass Design das Potenzial hat, die stillen Freuden des Lebens zu steigern. Mit Bauwerk streben wir danach, diese Überzeugung zu verwirklichen.
Geleitet von unserem Kunden und dem Standortprogramm, nicht von Mode oder Trends, ist es unser Ziel, jedes Mal eine einfache, einzigartige Lösung zu formulieren.
Wir bewundern zeitloses Design mit reinen und taktilen Materialien. Wir konzentrieren uns auf Funktion, Qualität und Details. Vor allem wollen wir, dass jede unserer Kreationen Bestand hat und geliebt wird, ob man sie zum ersten Mal betritt oder jeden Tag dort aufwacht.

Takatina est un cabinet de conseil en design multidisciplinaire basé à New York et dirigé par Takaaki et Christina Kawabata. Depuis 2003, nous avons mené à bien des projets qui réimaginent l'ancien et créent de nouveaux designs exquis.
Nous sommes tous convaincus que le design a le potentiel d'améliorer les plaisirs tranquilles de la vie. Avec chaque geste construit, nous nous efforçons de matérialiser cette aspiration.
Guidés par notre client et le programme du site, plutôt que par la mode ou les tendances, notre objectif est de formuler une solution simple et unique à chaque fois.
Nous admirons le design intemporel avec des matériaux purs et tactiles. Nous mettons l'accent sur la fonction, la qualité et le détail. Par-dessus tout, nous voulons que chacune de nos créations dure et soit aimée, que vous y entriez pour la première fois ou que vous vous y réveilliez chaque jour.

Takatina es una consultora de diseño multidisciplinar con sede en Nueva York, dirigida por Takaaki y Christina Kawabata. Desde 2003 hemos completado proyectos re imaginando lo antiguo y creando nuevos y exquisitos diseños.
Creemos que el diseño tiene el potencial de mejorar los placeres de la vida. Con cada gesto construido nos esforzamos por materializar esa aspiración.
Guiados por nuestro cliente y el programa del lugar y más que por la moda o las tendencias, nuestro objetivo es formular una solución simple y única en cada ocasión.
Admiramos el diseño atemporal con materiales puro. Nos centramos en la función, la calidad y el detalle. Por encima de todo, queremos que cada una de nuestras creaciones dure y sea amada, tanto al entrar en ella por primera vez como si el cliente se despierta cada día allí.

BLACK BOX HOUSE

The main concept of this house was to reject this outside scenery while creating an introspective micro cosmos filled with natural light and wind. Due to the adjacent north side street descending and zoning restriction, the windows ´s arrangement was gathered mainly at this side to disperse a soft glow throughout the day without any window treatment for privacy. Large sliding door connects the main living area to a garden terrace that creates a buffer zone to the neighbours. The black industrial Galvanium panel was erected to cover this simple volume without any ornamentation to meet the budget and client's affection for machine-like aesthetics.

Die Ablehnung der äußeren Szenerie und die Schaffung eines introspektiven Mikrokosmos, der mit natürlichem Licht und Wind gefüllt ist, wurde zum Hauptkonzept dieses Hauses. Aufgrund der angrenzenden, nach Norden hin abfallenden Straße und der Beschränkung durch die Parzelleneinteilung wurde die Fensterung hauptsächlich auf dieser Seite angebracht, um tagsüber einen sanften Schein zu verbreiten, ohne dass die Privatsphäre durch die Fenster beeinträchtigt würde. Eine große Schiebetür verbindet den Hauptwohnbereich mit einer Gartenterrasse, die eine Pufferzone zu den Nachbarn bildet. Das schwarze Industriegalvanium-Paneel wurde errichtet, um dieses einfache Volumen ohne jegliche Verzierung zu bedecken und um dem Budget und der Vorliebe des Kunden für maschinenähnliche Ästhetik gerecht zu werden.

Rejeter ce paysage extérieur tout en créant un microcosme introspectif rempli de lumière naturelle et de vent est devenu le concept principal de cette maison. En raison de la descente de la rue adjacente du côté nord et des restrictions de zonage, la fenestration a été rassemblée principalement de ce côté. Cela permet de disperser une douce lueur tout au long de la journée sans aucun traitement des fenêtres pour l'intimité. Une grande porte coulissante relie la zone de séjour principale à une terrasse de jardin qui crée une zone tampon pour les voisins. Le panneau de galvanium industriel noir a été érigé pour couvrir ce simple volume sans aucune ornementation pour répondre au budget et à l'affection du client pour l'esthétique machinale.

Rechazar este escenario exterior mientras se crea un microcosmos introspectivo lleno de luz natural y aire se convirtió en el concepto principal de esta casa. Debido al descenso de la calle adyacente del lado norte y a la restricción urbanística de la zona, la ventanas se reunieron principalmente en este lado de la casa para iluminar suavemente el interior a lo largo del día sin ningún tratamiento especial para conseguir privacidad. Una gran puerta corrediza conecta la zona principal de la vivienda con una terraza junto al jardín. El panel de galvanizado industrial negro fue erigido como cubrimiento de este simple volumen sin ningún tipo de adorno para cumplir con el presupuesto y complacer el afecto del cliente por la estética industrial.

LOCATION
Kanagawa, Japan

PHOTOS
© Mikiko Kikuyama

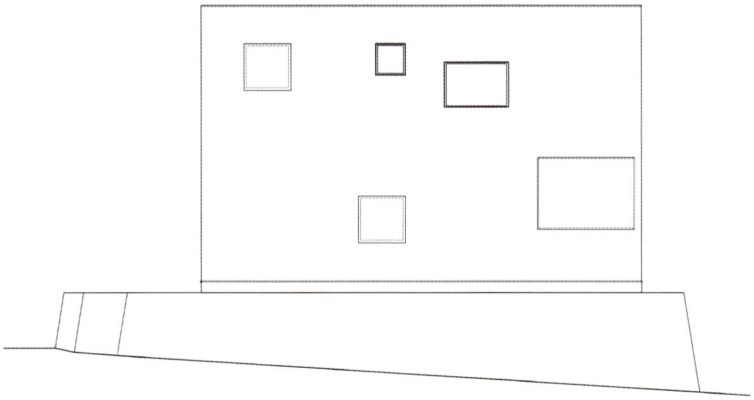

North elevation

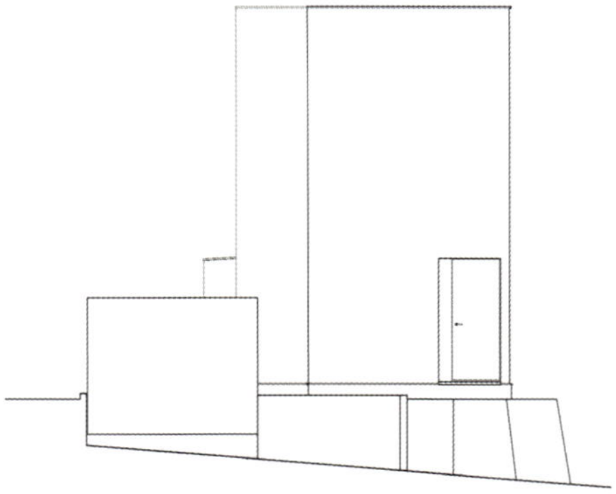

East elevation

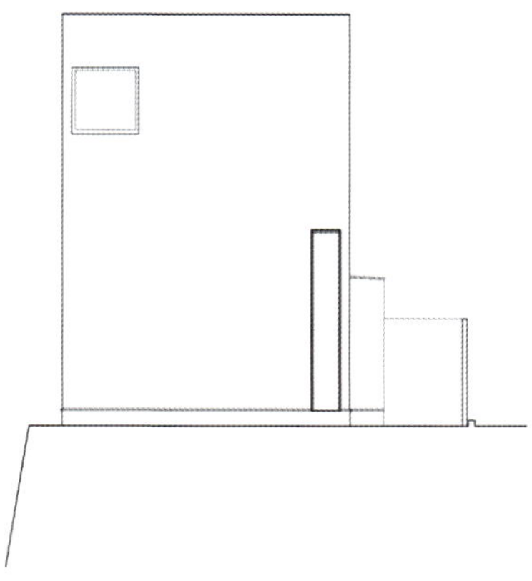

West elevation

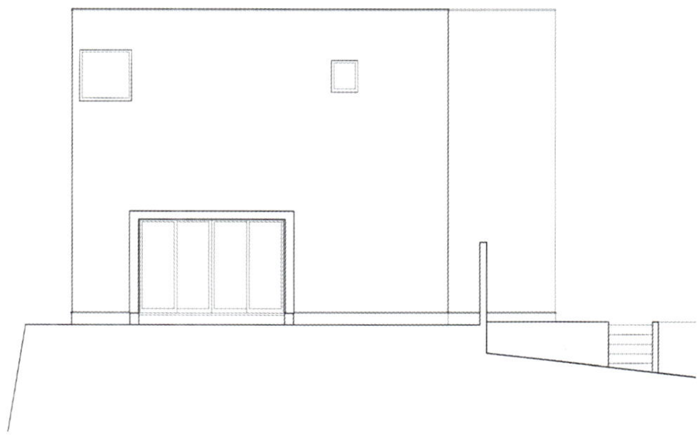

South elevation

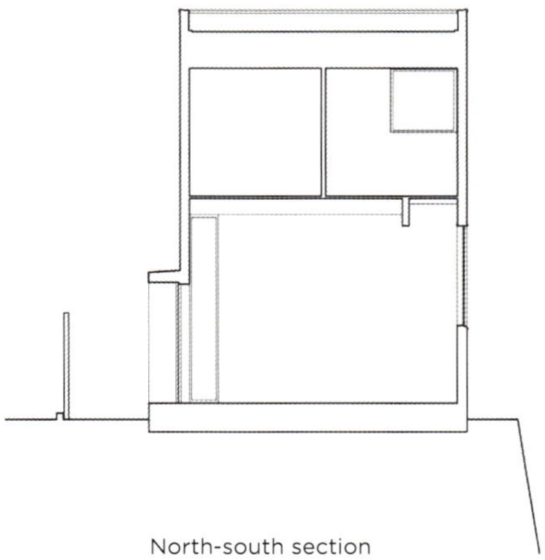

North-south section

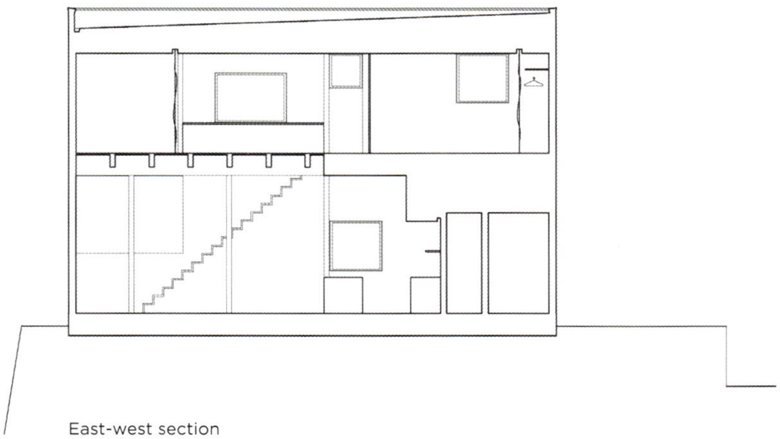

East-west section

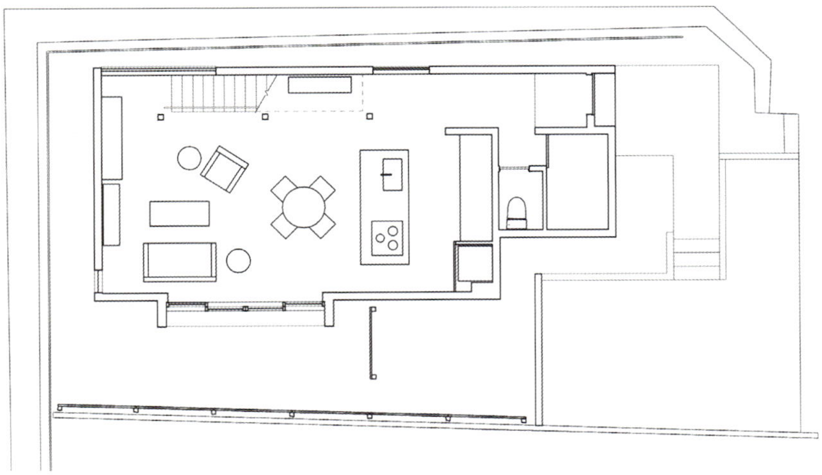

Ground floor plan

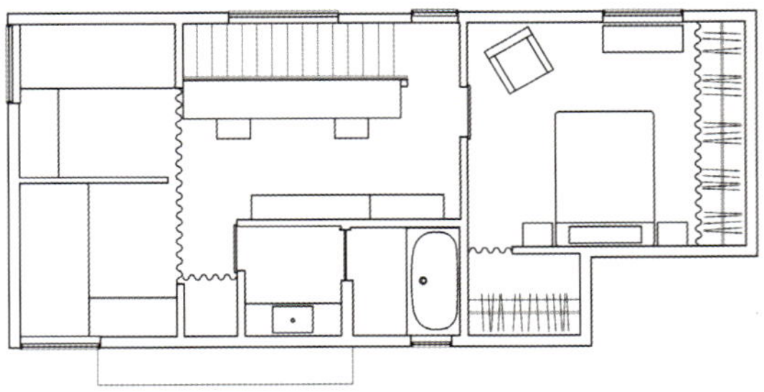

First floor plan

WESPI DE MEURON ROMEO ARCHITECTS

WESPI DE MEURON ROMEO ARCHITECTS is an architectural practice based in Zurich, Switzerland, led by Markus Wespi, Jérôme De Meuron and Luca Romeo since 2012.
Markus Wespi (1957), self-taught, Collaborated with André M. Studer, Zurich 1975-82; Ernst E. Anderegg, Meiringen 1983; Fred Cramer, Zumikon 1983; Franc S. Bridges, Lugano 1983. Own office in Caviano and Zurigo since 1984.
Jérôme De Meuron (Münsingen, 1971). He study at the professional school in Burgdorf 1993-96; architectural practice in Ghana (Africa) 1996-97.
Luca Romeo (Locarno, 1984). He study at the vocational school of Lugano-Trevano 2003-06; collaboration with Sergio Cattaneo, Bellinzona 2000-03 and 2006-11.

WESPI DE MEURON ROMEO ARCHITECTS ist ein Architekturbüro mit Sitz in Zürich, Schweiz, das seit 2012 von Markus Wespi, Jérôme De Meuron und Luca Romeo geleitet wird.
Markus Wespi (*1957), Autodidakt, Zusammenarbeit mit André M. Studer, Zürich 1975–82; Ernst E. Anderegg, Meiringen 1983; Fred Cramer, Zumikon 1983; Franc S. Bridges, Lugano 1983. Seit 1984 eigene Büros in Caviano und Zürich.
Jérôme De Meuron (*1971, Münsingen). Studium an der Berufsschule in Burgdorf 1993–96; Architekturbüro in Ghana (Afrika) 1996–97.
Luca Romeo (*1984, Locarno). Studium an der Berufsschule Lugano-Trevano 2003–06; Zusammenarbeit mit Sergio Cattaneo, Bellinzona 2000–03 und 2006–11.

www.wdmra.ch
info@wdmra.ch

WESPI DE MEURON ROMEO ARCHITECTS est un cabinet d'architecture basé à Zurich, en Suisse, dirigé par Markus Wespi, Jérôme De Meuron et Luca Romeo depuis 2012.
Markus Wespi (1957), autodidacte, a collaboré avec André M. Studer, Zurich 1975-82 ; Ernst E. Anderegg, Meiringen 1983 ; Fred Cramer, Zumikon 1983 ; Franc S. Bridges, Lugano 1983. Propre bureau à Caviano et Zurigo depuis 1984.
Jérôme De Meuron (Münsingen, 1971). Il a étudié à l'école professionnelle de Burgdorf 1993-96 ; cabinet d'architecture au Ghana (Afrique) 1996-97.
Luca Romeo (Locarno, 1984). Il a étudié à l'école professionnelle de Lugano-Trevano 2003-06 ; collaboration avec Sergio Cattaneo, Bellinzona 2000-03 et 2006-11.

WESPI DE MEURON ROMEO ARCHITECTS es un estudio de arquitectura con sede en Zurich, Suiza, dirigido por Markus Wespi, Jérôme De Meuron y Luca Romeo desde 2012.
Markus Wespi (1957), autodidacta, colaboró con André M. Studer, Zurich (1975-82), Ernst E. Anderegg, Meiringen (1983), Fred Cramer, Zumikon (1983) y Franc S. Bridges, Lugano (1983) hasta que abrió oficina propia en Caviano y Zurigo en 1984.
Jérôme De Meuron (Münsingen, 1971) estudió en la escuela profesional de Burgdorf de 1993 a 1996 y trabajó en un estudio de arquitectura en Ghana (África) de 1996 a 1997.
Luca Romeo (Locarno, 1984) estudió en la escuela profesional de Lugano-Trevano (2003-06). Colaboró con Sergio Cattaneo, Bellinzona en 2000-2003 y 2006-2011.

RENOVATION BRICKHOUSE IN FELDBERG

This is a project of renovation using existing traditional rural constructions methods and materials; a discourse between the historical massive raw masonry and the supplementary materials like concrete, wood, glass and steel as well as the furniture installations in black MDF. The interior layout was made according to the existing construction. The only substantial intervention was to remove the ceiling above the dining room. It allows visible connections from several points and brings more light inside without adding new windows (it was not allowed to modify the façade). The quite small space becomes now an important extension.

Es handelt sich um ein Renovierungsprojekt unter Verwendung bestehender traditioneller ländlicher Bauweisen und Materialien. Das Projekt ist ein Diskurs zwischen dem historischen massiven Rohmauerwerk und den ergänzenden Materialien wie Beton, Holz, Glas und Stahl sowie den Möbelinstallationen aus schwarzem MDF. Die Inneneinrichtung wurde in Anlehnung an die bestehende Struktur vorgenommen. Der einzige wesentliche Eingriff war die Entfernung der Decke über dem Esszimmer. Sie ermöglicht sichtbare Verbindungen von mehreren Punkten aus und bringt mehr Licht ins Innere, ohne neue Fenster hinzuzufügen (die Fassade durfte nicht verändert werden), und der recht kleine Raum wird zu einer wichtigen Erweiterung.

Il s'agit d'un projet de rénovation utilisant les méthodes et les matériaux de construction ruraux traditionnels existants. Le projet est un discours entre la maçonnerie brute massive historique et les matériaux supplémentaires comme le béton, le bois, le verre et l'acier ainsi que les installations de meubles en MDF noir. L'aménagement intérieur a été réalisé en fonction de la structure existante. La seule intervention substantielle a été de supprimer le plafond au-dessus de la salle à manger. Il permet des connexions visibles de plusieurs points et apporte plus de lumière à l'intérieur sans ajouter de nouvelles fenêtres (il n'était pas permis de modifier la façade). L'espace assez restreint devient une extension importante.

Se trata de un proyecto de renovación utilizando métodos y materiales tradicionales de la construcción rural. El diseño es un discurso entre la masiva mampostería histórica y los materiales complementarios como el hormigón, la madera, el vidrio y el acero, así como las instalaciones de mobiliario en MDF negro. La distribución interior se hizo de acuerdo con la estructura existente. La única intervención sustancial fue eliminar el techo sobre el comedor, lo que permite conexiones visibles desde varios puntos y aporta más luz en el interior sin tener que añadir nuevas ventanas ni modificar la fachada (no estaba permitido). El espacio, bastante reducido de tamaño, se ha convertido en una importante extensión del volumen principal.

LOCATION
Feldberg, Germany

PHOTOS
© Mecklenburg-Vorpommern

Site plan

Ground floor plan

First floor plan

1. Courtyard
2. Storage room
3. Entrance
4. Entrance
5. Garden Place
6. Garden
7. Hall
8. Wardrobe
9. Corridor
10. Storage
11. Workshop
12. Cellar
13. Technical / store room
14. Kitchen
15. Dining room
16. Bedrooms
17. Bathroom
18. Entrance / cloakroom
19. Stairs to the attic
20. Bathroom
21. Corridor
22. Bedroom
23. Studio
24. Outdoor dining room
25. Living room

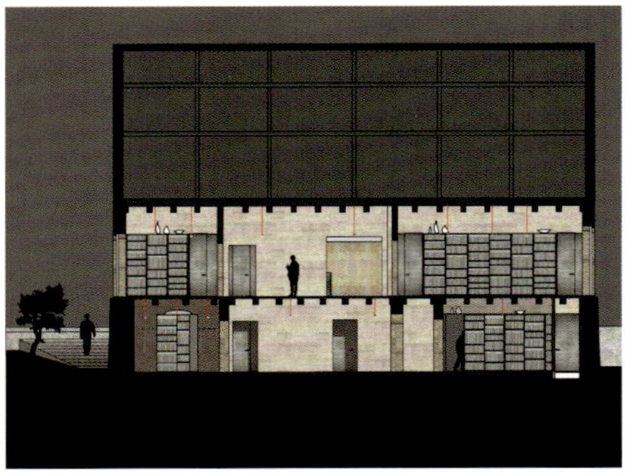

A-A section

E-E section

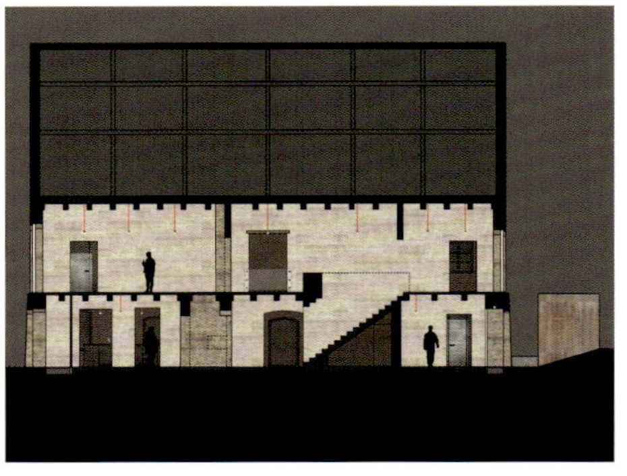

B-B section

F-F section

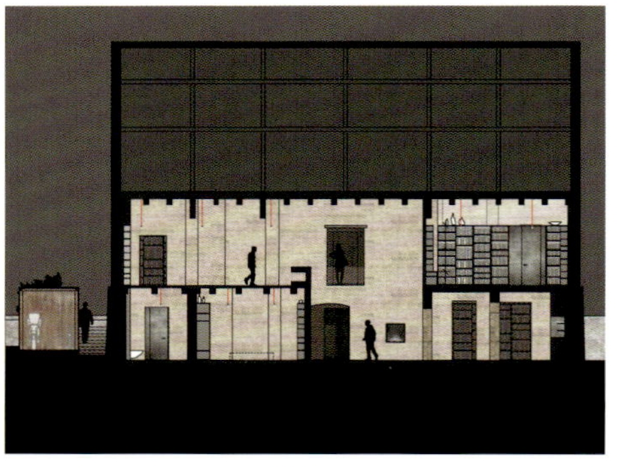

C-C section

G-G section

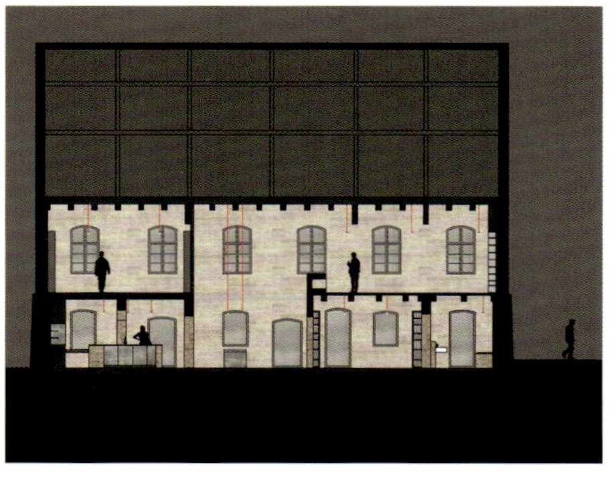

D-D section

H-H section

WUTOPIA LAB

Wutopia Lab is located in Shanghai. Founded by the famous architect YU Ting in 2013 and designer MIN Erni. We think all the hard training, thinking and design process should be presented with a relaxed gesture in the end.
If the world is not good enough, let us create a better one. Through magical realism, Wutopia Lab , a cutting edge architecture studio, is aiming to create miracles in daily life based on GLOCALIZATION.

www.wutopialab.com
project1@wutopia.work

Das Wutopia-Labor befindet sich in Shanghai. Es wurde 2013 von dem berühmten Architekten YU Ting und die Designer MIN Erni gegründet. Wir denken, dass der harte Trainings-, Denk- und Designprozess am Ende mit einer entspannten Geste präsentiert werden sollte.
Wenn die Welt nicht gut genug ist, lasst uns eine bessere Welt schaffen. Durch magischen Realismus will das Wutopia Lab in Shanghai als innovatives Architekturstudio auf der Grundlage der GLOCALISIERUNG Wunder im täglichen Leben schaffen.

Le laboratoire Wutopia est situé à Shanghai. Il a été fondé par le célèbre architecte YU Ting en 2013 et la designer MIN Erni. Nous pensons que tout le processus d'entraînement, de réflexion et de conception doit être présenté avec un geste détendu à la fin.
Si le monde n'est pas assez bon, créons-en un meilleur. Grâce à un réalisme magique, le Wutopia Lab, en tant que studio d'architecture de pointe, vise à créer des miracles dans la vie quotidienne en se basant sur la GLOCALISATION.

El Laboratorio Wutopia se encuentra en Shanghai. Fue fundado por el famoso arquitecto YU Ting en 2013 y la diseñadora MIN Erni.
«Creemos que todo el duro proceso de preparación, pensamiento y diseño debe ser presentado con un gesto relajado. Si el mundo no es lo suficientemente bueno, creemos uno mejor». A través del realismo mágico, el Laboratorio Wutopia, como un estudio de arquitectura de vanguardia, tiene como objetivo crear milagros en la vida diaria basados en la GLOCALIZACIÓN.

HIS HOUSE AND HER HOUSE: URBAN VILLAGE RENOVATION

LOCATION
Shenzhen, China

PHOTOS
© CreatAR Images (AI Qing)

"His House and Her House", is a conceptual installation result of the transformation of two small buildings in an urban slum of Shenzhen into a conversation about the contrasting roles of men and women in the kitchen and how this is reflected in dietary habits. Using blue as an allusion to the masculine traits of perseverance and crudeness, and pink for the feminine virtues of sensitivity and refinement, the project is also a playful metaphor for the complimentary forces that power urban rejuvenation.

„Sein Haus und ihr Haus" ist eine konzeptuelle Installation, die zwei kleine Gebäude in einem städtischen Slum von Shenzhen in ein Gespräch über die gegensätzlichen Rollen von Männern und Frauen in der Küche und darüber, wie sich dies in den Ernährungsgewohnheiten widerspiegelt, verwandelt hat. Mit Blau als Anspielung auf die männlichen Züge von Beharrlichkeit und Rohheit und Rosa für die weiblichen Tugenden von Sensibilität und Raffinesse ist das Projekt auch eine spielerische Metapher für die komplementären Kräfte, die die städtische Verjüngung vorantreiben.

« His House and Her House », est une installation conceptuelle qui a transformé deux petits bâtiments d'un bidonville de Shenzhen en une conversation sur les rôles contrastés des hommes et des femmes dans la cuisine et sur la manière dont cela se reflète dans les habitudes alimentaires. Utilisant le bleu comme allusion aux traits masculins de la persévérance et de la grossièreté et le rose pour les vertus féminines de la sensibilité et du raffinement, le projet est aussi une métaphore ludique des forces complémentaires qui alimentent le rajeunissement urbain

«His House and Her House» es una instalación conceptual consecuencia de la transformación de dos pequeños edificios en un barrio marginal urbano de Shenzhen, en una conversación sobre los roles de hombres y mujeres en la cocina y cómo esto se refleja en los hábitos alimenticios. Utilizando el azul como una alusión a los rasgos masculinos de perseverancia y rudeza, y el rosa para las virtudes femeninas de sensibilidad y refinamiento, el proyecto es también una metáfora lúdica de las fuerzas complementarias que impulsan el rejuvenecimiento urbano.

Elevation

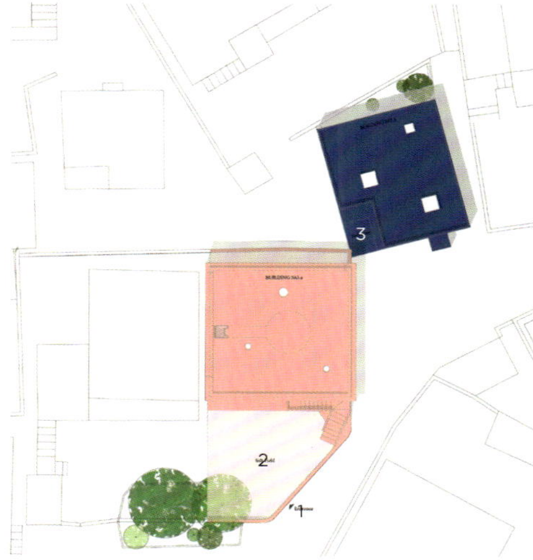

Master plan

1. Entry
2. Salt field
3. Barbecue

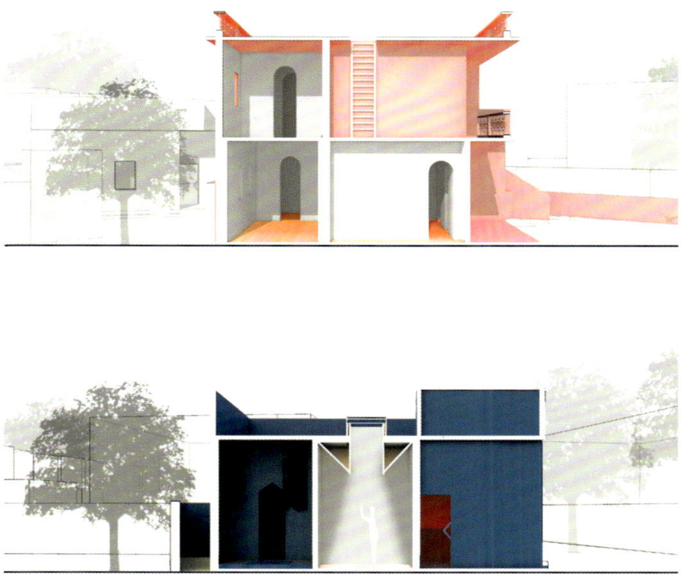

Sections

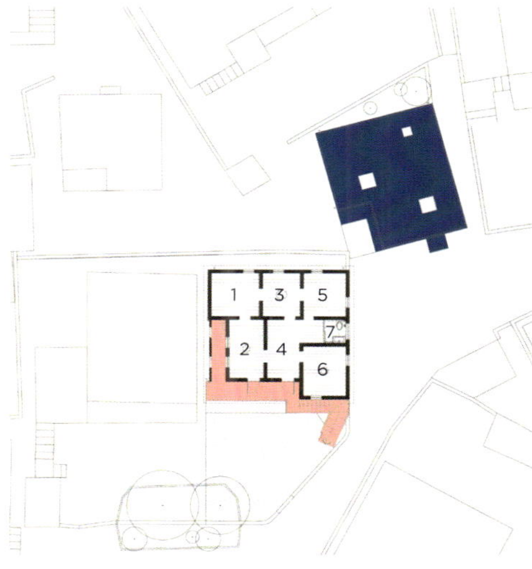

Second floor plan

1. Occidental blending
2. Orient blending
3. Orient ikebana
4. Occidental ikebana
5. Occidental vegetarian diet
6. Orient tonic diet
7. Rest room

First floor plan

1. Entry
2. Salt field
3. Green house
4. Occidental afternoon tea
5. Orient afternoon tea
6. Orient bakery
7. Occidental bakery
8. Rest
9. Rest room
10. Meat
11. Liquor
12. Meditation
13. Barbecue

FRAMEWORK: FROM HOME SPACE TO CITY PLACE
FROM LEISURE TIME TO THIRD PLACE

Contemporary architecture, intended as scientific and theoretical research, reflects on the ways in which built spaces correspond to existing places and their inhabitants. Architecture doesn't research on the image in itself (self-referential architecture), it researches on the space as a generator of well-being. To do this, architecture focuses on the concepts of density, efficiency and flexibility, as they appear in the book and it links city and houses.

In the projects selected and presented in the book, all or some of these priorities and concepts emerge to establish a building framework that links the spatial to the experiential, superimposing principles of the organization of work and living spaces and going to configure a sort of third place (in the definition of Ray Oldenburg, The Great Good Place), which allows the inhabitants to live a continuity of approach between home, work and leisure. (01)

The house is increasingly moving towards a place of physical and mental well-being that also incorporates work or productive activity. The interiors are therefore being transformed into spaces with variable use, which with some few adjustments and changings, are continually reconfigured and modified in relation to people's day life.

The versatility allows the use and configuration of the space as a home and as an office, mixing the characters of the respective uses and innovating the compositional dynamics of the two types of space. This configures spaces with variable density inside a latent structure, able to preserve the principles of organization and flows, and at the same time open to different uses.

The workspace tries to bring back some of the characteristics of the house in its informality and continuity. moving from the logic of the dedicated and divided single spaces, to the open space. up to the assembly in a single space of multiple open and perceptively continuous places. If purely productive spaces already established this practice of openness, the nature of office work has been revolutionized by technologies that allow working in mobile conditions. (02)

The flexibility of internal spaces, hence, outlines the possibility of configuring the offices as independent clusters with distribution and separation structures coherent to the plan layout or as a single building capable to diversify the internal offices in relation to their activities and needs, transferring to the spaces a possible typological variability: from block to network, from cellular to plate. (03)

The role of the project, which would seem to be diminished by the need to correspond to these variables, becomes more and more significant. since the physical place is an essential condition for being "in mobility", transforming, for example, the office into a social condenser, whose organization makes possible better and richer forms of collaboration and interaction. (04)

This ultimately distinguishes the office from the home: the best possible performance in terms of connectivity and virtual community. Furthermore, in the offices there are spaces dedicated to culture and leisure, very similar to those of the home, which can increase the employee's involvement and promote loyalty to the company.

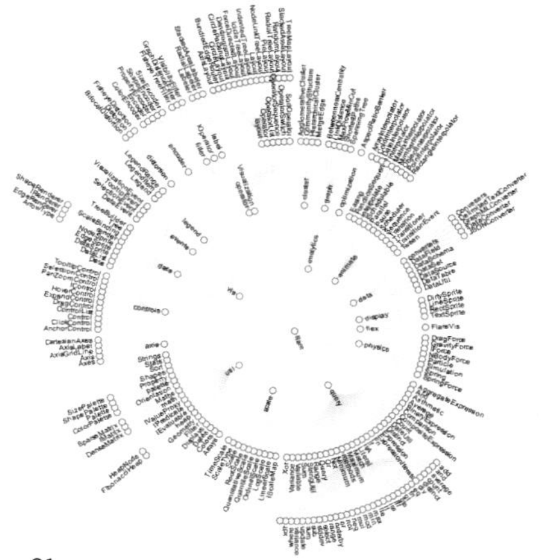

01

D3 Radial Tree Example Diagram – Architecture

D3 stands for Data-Driven Documents. It is an open-source JavaScript library developed by Mike Bostock to create custom interactive data visualizations in the web browser using SVG, HTML and CSS. With the massive amount of data being generated today, communicating this information is getting difficult.

D3 Radialer Baum Beispieldiagramm – Architektur

D3 steht für datengesteuerte Dokumente. Es handelt sich um eine Open-Source-JavaScript-Bibliothek, die von Mike Bostock entwickelt wurde, um benutzerdefinierte interaktive Datenvisualisierungen im Webbrowser unter Verwendung von SVG, HTML und CSS zu erstellen. Bei der enormen Datenmenge, die heute erzeugt wird, wird die Kommunikation dieser Informationen immer schwieriger.

D3 Exemple de diagramme de l'arbre radial - Architecture

D3 est l'acronyme de Data-Driven Documents. Il s'agit d'une bibliothèque JavaScript open-source développée par Mike Bostock pour créer des visualisations de données interactives personnalisées dans le navigateur web en utilisant SVG, HTML et CSS. Avec la quantité massive de données qui sont générées aujourd'hui, la communication de ces informations devient difficile.

D3 Diagrama de ejemplo de árbol radial – Arquitectura

D3 son las siglas de Data-Driven Documents. Es una biblioteca de JavaScript de código abierto desarrollada por Mike Bostock para crear visualizaciones de datos interactivos personalizados en el navegador web usando SVG, HTML y CSS. Con la enorme cantidad de datos que se generan hoy en día, comunicar esta información se está volviendo difícil.

Free time is in fact the main actor in people's lives today, if we think it as a time dedicated to their individual personal identity. The increasingly marked individualism of our society is in fact the basic unit from which to proceed in order to design any kind of space, if you want it to correspond to the contemporary "interactive man".

Thus, if Architecture wants to constitute itself as the engine of man's evolution, has to turn its procedural and compositional gaze to the concept of time, a concept that the contemporary virtual and technological world has made syncopated: an instantaneous shortened time, which structures fragments and not sequences, which has more to do with the idea of free time than with the idea of structured time of work, because in the fragment we find forms of immediate and absolute freedom. (05)

Precisely for this reason the concept of free time has a lot to do with the spatial concept of "third place" (Ray Oldenburg), able to produce a network of physical-perceptual and cultural-creative relationships capable of configuring multiple real and virtual places.

This multiplicity of spaces is the latent structure to be designed to obtain a real and not only virtual correspondence between man and physical place, between human experience (always more virtual and free in economic and time terms) and experience of the place (always less physical and more expensive in economic and time terms). Architecture has to think of man constantly on the move and the net, in real physical perceptive terms and virtual intellectual sensorial terms.

From this new concept of architecture new dynamics emerge, to be applied to the design of public spaces, which can survive as places of meeting, sharing and heritage only if they intercept and create a network of physical-perceptual and cultural-creative relationships that can configure multiple real and virtual places. (06)

In this system of coordinates the public space must be able to interpret multiple identities (virtual and real) in order to correspond to the largest number of users and to be conceived as real for all. So in a process of eternal comeback, architecture must return to think and research about the home to be able to configure public spaces: those common to all, in which everyone bears their individual identity and must unfold it.

Today it isn't possible to configure the city, without rethinking the house, because only inside the house, conceived as the minimum living unit, the people could unfold their lifetime, in physical connection with the others: family members, relatives or friends. (07)

The house, therefore, becomes a place of excellence for the experimentation of architecture and from it can emerge the decisive characteristics able to configure all the other private and public spaces, which will increasingly be places of mediation and activation of virtual and real mixed social practices.

Christian Gasparini
NAT Office

02

Collaborative Innovation Network. Office

Collaborative innovation is a process in which multiple players (within and outside an organization) contribute towards creating and developing new products, services, policies, processes, or business solutions. It might include the involvement of customers, suppliers and multiple stakeholders such as agencies and consultants.

Gemeinsames Innovationsnetzwerk. Büro

Kollaborative Innovation ist ein Prozess, bei dem mehrere Akteure (innerhalb und außerhalb einer Organisation) zur Schaffung und Entwicklung neuer Produkte, Dienstleistungen, Richtlinien, Prozesse oder Geschäftslösungen beitragen. Sie kann die Beteiligung von Kunden, Lieferanten und mehreren Interessengruppen wie Agenturen und Beratern umfassen.

Réseau d'innovation collaborative. Bureau

L'innovation collaborative est un processus dans lequel de multiples acteurs (à l'intérieur et à l'extérieur d'un organisme) contribuent à la création et au développement de nouveaux produits, services, processus, ou de nouvelles politiques ou solutions commerciales. Elle peut inclure la participation de clients, de fournisseurs et de multiples parties prenantes telles que des agences et des consultants.

Red de Innovación Colaborativa. Oficina

La innovación en colaboración es un proceso en el que múltiples actores (dentro y fuera de una organización) contribuyen a crear y desarrollar nuevos productos, servicios, políticas, procesos o soluciones comerciales. Puede incluir la participación de clientes, proveedores y múltiples interesados, como organismos y consultores.

RAHMENWERK: VOM WOHNRAUM ZUM STADTPLATZ VON DER FREIZEIT ZUM DRITTEN PLATZ

Zeitgenössische Architektur, die als wissenschaftliche und theoretische Forschung gedacht ist, reflektiert die Art und Weise, wie gebaute Räume mit bestehenden Orten und ihren Bewohnern korrespondieren. Architektur erforscht nicht das Bild an sich (selbstreferentielle Architektur), sondern den Raum als Generator des Wohlbefindens. Dabei konzentriert sich die Architektur auf die Konzepte der Dichte, Effizienz und Flexibilität, wie sie im Buch erscheinen, und verbindet Stadt und Häuser.

In den ausgewählten und im Buch vorgestellten Projekten tauchen alle oder einige dieser Prioritäten und Konzepte auf, um einen Gebäuderahmen zu schaffen, der das Räumliche mit den erfahrbaren, sich überlagernden Prinzipien der Organisation von Arbeits- und Lebensräumen verbindet und eine Art dritten Ort (in der Definition von Ray Oldenburg, The Great Good Place) konfiguriert, der es den Bewohnern erlaubt, eine Kontinuität der Annäherung zwischen Heim, Arbeit und Freizeit zu leben. (01)

Das Haus bewegt sich immer mehr in Richtung eines Ortes des körperlichen und geistigen Wohlbefindens, der auch Arbeit oder produktive Tätigkeit einschließt. Die Innenräume verwandeln sich daher in Räume mit variabler Nutzung, die mit wenigen Anpassungen und Veränderungen immer wieder neu konfiguriert und in Bezug auf das Alltagsleben der Menschen verändert werden.

Die Vielseitigkeit ermöglicht die Nutzung und Konfiguration des Raumes als Wohnung und als Büro, wobei die Charakteristika der jeweiligen Nutzungen vermischt und die kompositorische Dynamik der beiden Raumtypen erneuert werden. Dadurch werden Räume mit variabler Dichte innerhalb einer latenten Struktur konfiguriert, die in der Lage sind, die Prinzipien der Organisation und der Flüsse zu bewahren und gleichzeitig offen für verschiedene Nutzungen sind.

Der Arbeitsraum versucht, einige der Charakteristika des Hauses in seiner Informalität und Kontinuität wiederzugeben, indem er sich von der Logik der dedizierten und geteilten Einzelräume zum offenen Raum hin bewegt. bis hin zur Montage in einem einzigen Raum mit mehreren offenen und wahrnehmbaren, kontinuierlichen Orten. Wenn rein produktive Räume diese Praxis der Offenheit bereits etabliert haben, so wurde die Natur der Büroarbeit durch Technologien revolutioniert, die ein Arbeiten unter mobilen Bedingungen ermöglichen. (02)

Die Flexibilität der Innenräume bietet daher die Möglichkeit, die Büros als unabhängige Cluster mit Verteilungs- und Trennungsstrukturen zu konfigurieren, die mit dem Planlayout kohärent sind, oder als ein einziges Gebäude, das in der Lage ist, die Innenbüros in Bezug auf ihre Aktivitäten und Bedürfnisse zu diversifizieren, wobei auf die Räume eine mögliche typologische Variabilität übertragen wird: vom Block zum Netz, von der Zelle zum Teller. (03)

Die Rolle des Projekts, die durch die Notwendigkeit, diesen Variablen zu entsprechen, geschmälert zu werden scheint, gewinnt immer mehr an Bedeutung, denn der physische Ort ist eine wesentliche Voraussetzung, um „in Bewegung" zu sein, indem er zum Beispiel das Büro in einen sozialen Kondensator verwandelt, dessen Organisation bessere und reichere Formen der Zusammenarbeit und Interaktion ermöglicht. (04)

Dies unterscheidet letztlich das Büro vom reinen Heim: die bestmögliche Leistung in Bezug auf Konnektivität und virtuelle Gemeinschaft. Darüber hinaus gibt es in den Büros Räume für Kultur und Freizeit, die denen des Hauses sehr ähnlich sind, was die Beteiligung der Mitarbeiter erhöhen und die Loyalität zum Unternehmen fördern kann.

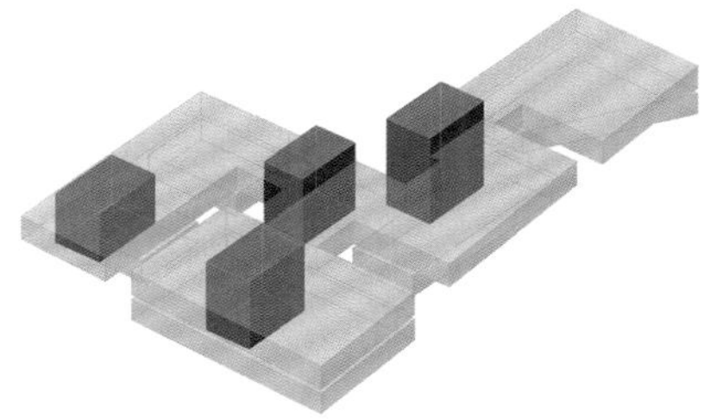

03

LHSM NAT Office - Typological Variability

Selected project - New Liuni Haedquarters Milan - 2 Steps National Competition - First Floor Clusters' Office

LHSM NAT Office - Typologische Variabilität

Ausgewähltes Projekt - Neues Liuni-Haedquarter in Mailand - 2 Schritte nationaler Wettbewerb - Büro der Cluster im ersten Stock

LHSM NAT Office - Variabilité typologique

Projet sélectionné - Nouveau siège de Liuni à Milan - Concours national en 2 étapes - Condensateur social du rez-de-chaussée

LHSM NAT Office - Variabilidad tipológica

Proyecto seleccionado - Nueva sede de Liuni Milán - Concurso Nacional 2 Pasos - Oficina de Clusters del primer piso

Die Freizeit ist in der Tat der Hauptdarsteller im Leben der Menschen von heute, wenn man sie als eine Zeit betrachtet, die ihrer individuellen persönlichen Identität gewidmet ist. Der immer stärker ausgeprägte Individualismus unserer Gesellschaft ist tatsächlich die Grundeinheit, von der man ausgeht, um jede Art von Raum zu gestalten, wenn man will, dass er dem zeitgenössischen „interaktiven Menschen" entspricht.

Wenn die Architektur sich also als Motor der Entwicklung des Menschen konstituieren will, muss sie ihren prozessualen und kompositorischen Blick auf den Begriff der Zeit richten, einen Begriff, den die heutige virtuelle und technologische Welt synkopiert hat: eine augenblicklich verkürzte Zeit, die Fragmente und nicht Sequenzen strukturiert, was mehr mit der Idee der freien Zeit als mit der Idee der strukturierten Arbeitszeit zu tun hat, denn in dem Fragment finden wir Formen der unmittelbaren und absoluten Freiheit. (05)

Genau aus diesem Grund hat der Begriff der Freizeit viel mit dem räumlichen Konzept des „dritten Ortes" (Ray Oldenburg) zu tun, der in der Lage ist, ein Netzwerk von physisch-perzeptiven und kulturell-kreativen Beziehungen herzustellen, das in der Lage ist, mehrere reale und virtuelle Orte zu konfigurieren.

Diese Vielzahl von Räumen ist die latente Struktur, die entworfen werden muss, um eine reale und nicht nur virtuelle Korrespondenz zwischen Mensch und physischem Ort, zwischen menschlicher Erfahrung (immer virtueller und freier in wirtschaftlicher und zeitlicher Hinsicht) und der Erfahrung des Ortes (immer weniger physisch und teurer in wirtschaftlicher und zeitlicher Hinsicht) zu erhalten. Die Architektur muss an den ständig in Bewegung befindlichen Menschen und das Netz denken, in realer physischer Wahrnehmung und virtueller intellektueller Sinneserfahrung.

Aus diesem neuen Konzept der Architektur entsteht eine neue Dynamik, die auf die Gestaltung öffentlicher Räume angewendet werden muss, die als Orte der Begegnung, des Austauschs und des Erbes nur dann überleben können, wenn sie ein Netzwerk von physisch-perzeptiven und kulturell-kreativen Beziehungen abfangen und schaffen, das mehrere reale und virtuelle Orte konfigurieren kann. (06)

In diesem Koordinatensystem muss der öffentliche Raum in der Lage sein, mehrere Identitäten (virtuelle und reale) zu interpretieren, um der größten Anzahl von Nutzern zu entsprechen und als real für alle konzipiert zu werden. In einem Prozess des ewigen Comebacks muss die Architektur also zum Nachdenken und Forschen über das Zuhause zurückkehren, um öffentliche Räume zu gestalten: jene, die allen gemeinsam sind, in denen jeder seine individuelle Identität trägt und diese entfalten muss.

Heute ist es nicht mehr möglich, die Stadt zu gestalten, ohne das Haus neu zu überdenken, denn nur im Inneren des Hauses, das als minimale Wohneinheit konzipiert ist, können die Menschen ihr Leben entfalten, in physischer Verbindung mit den anderen: Familienmitgliedern, Verwandten oder Freunden. (07)

Das Haus wird so zu einem exzellenten Ort für das Experimentieren mit Architektur und kann daraus die entscheidenden Merkmale hervorbringen, die alle anderen privaten und öffentlichen Räume gestalten können, die zunehmend zu Orten der Vermittlung und Aktivierung virtueller und realer gemischter sozialer Praktiken werden.

Christian Gasparini
NAT Office

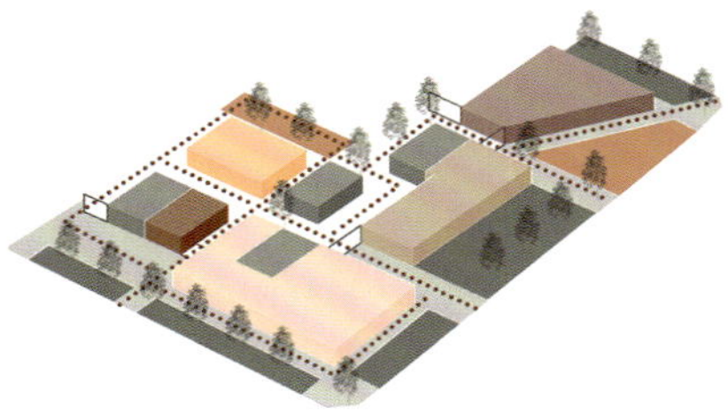

04

LHSM NAT Office - Social Condenser

Selected project - New Liuni Haedquarters Milan - 2 Steps National Competition - Ground Floor Social Condenser

LHSM NAT Office - Sozialer Kondensator

Ausgewähltes Projekt - Neues Liuni-Haedquarter in Mailand - 2 Schritte nationaler Wettbewerb - Sozialkondensator im Erdgeschoss

LHSM NAT Office - Condensateur social

Projet sélectionné - Nouveau siège de Liuni à Milan - Concours national en 2 étapes - Condensateur social du rez-de-chaussée

LHSM NAT Office - Condensador Social

Proyecto seleccionado - Nueva sede de Liuni Milán - Concurso Nacional 2 Pasos - Condensador social de la planta baja

CADRE : DE LA MAISON À LA VILLE DES LOISIRS À LA TROISIÈME PLACE

L'architecture contemporaine, conçue comme une recherche scientifique et théorique, réfléchit sur la manière dont les espaces construits correspondent aux lieux existants et à leurs habitants. L'architecture ne recherche pas sur l'image en soi (architecture autoréférentielle), elle recherche sur l'espace en tant que générateur de bien-être. Pour ce faire, l'architecture se concentre sur les concepts de densité, d'efficacité et de flexibilité, tels qu'ils apparaissent dans le livre et elle relie la ville et les maisons.

Dans les projets sélectionnés et présentés dans le livre, tout ou partie de ces priorités et concepts émergent pour établir un cadre de construction qui relie le spatial à l'expérientiel, superposant les principes de l'organisation du travail et des espaces de vie et allant configurer une sorte de troisième lieu (dans la définition de Ray Oldenburg, The Great Good Place), qui permet aux habitants de vivre une continuité d'approche entre le domicile, le travail et les loisirs. (01)

La maison s'oriente de plus en plus vers un lieu de bien-être physique et mental qui intègre également le travail ou l'activité productive. Les intérieurs se transforment donc en espaces à usage variable, qui, avec quelques ajustements et changements, sont continuellement reconfigurés et modifiés en fonction de la vie quotidienne des personnes.

La polyvalence permet d'utiliser et de configurer l'espace comme une maison ou comme un bureau, mélangeant les caractères des fonctions respectives et innovant la dynamique de composition des deux types d'espace. Cela permet de configurer des espaces à densité variable à l'intérieur d'une structure latente, capable de préserver les principes d'organisation et de flux, tout en restant ouverte à différents usages.

L'espace de travail tente de ramener certaines des caractéristiques de la maison à leur informalité et leur continuité. On passe ainsi de la logique des espaces uniques dédiés et divisés à l'espace ouvert, et ce jusqu'à l'assemblage dans un seul espace de multiples lieux ouverts et perceptivement continus. Si les espaces purement productifs ont déjà établi cette pratique d'ouverture, la nature des activités de bureau a été révolutionnée par les technologies qui permettent de travailler dans des conditions mobiles. (02)

La flexibilité des espaces internes permet donc de configurer les bureaux comme des groupes indépendants dotés de structures de distribution et de séparation cohérentes avec le plan d'aménagement, ou comme un unique bâtiment capable de diversifier les espaces internes en fonction des activités et des besoins, en transférant dans les espaces une éventuelle variabilité typologique : du bloc au réseau, du cellulaire à l'assiette. (03)

Le rôle du projet, qui semble être diminué par la nécessité de correspondre à ces variables, devient de plus en plus significatif. En effet, le lieu physique est une condition essentielle pour être « en mobilité », transformant par exemple le bureau en un condensateur social, dont l'organisation permet des formes de collaboration et d'interaction meilleures et plus riches. (04)

C'est ce qui distingue finalement le bureau de la maison : on y cherche la meilleure performance possible en termes de connectivité et de communauté virtuelle. En outre, les bureaux disposent d'espaces dédiés à la culture et aux loisirs, très semblables à ceux de la maison, ce qui peut accroître l'implication du salarié et favoriser sa fidélité à l'entreprise.

Le temps libre est en effet le principal élément de la vie des gens aujourd'hui, si l'on considère qu'il s'agit d'un temps consacré à leur identité personnelle ; l'individualisme de plus en plus marqué de notre société est l'unité de base à partir de laquelle il faut procéder pour concevoir tout type d'espace, si l'on veut qu'il corresponde à l'« homme interactif » contemporain.

Ainsi, si l'Architecture veut se constituer comme moteur de l'évolution de l'homme, elle doit tourner un regard procédural et compositionnel vers le concept de temps, concept que le monde virtuel et technologique contemporain a rendu syncopé : un temps instantané raccourci, qui structure des fragments et non des séquences, qui a plus à voir avec l'idée de temps libre qu'avec l'idée de temps structuré de travail. En effet, dans le fragment, on trouve des formes de liberté immédiate et absolue. (05)

C'est précisément pour cette raison que le concept de temps libre a beaucoup à voir avec le concept spatial de « troisième lieu » (Ray Oldenburg), potentiellement producteur d'un réseau de relations physiques-perceptuelles et culturelles-créatives capables de configurer de multiples lieux réels et virtuels.

Cette multiplicité d'espaces est une structure latente à concevoir pour obtenir une correspondance réelle, et pas seulement virtuelle entre l'homme et le lieu physique, entre l'expérience humaine (toujours plus virtuelle et libre en termes économiques et temporels) et l'expérience du lieu (toujours moins physique et plus coûteuse en termes économiques et temporels). L'architecture doit avoir à cœur l'homme constamment en mouvement et en réseau, en termes de perception physique réelle et en termes sensoriels, intellectuels et virtuels.

De ce nouveau concept d'architecture émerge une nouvelle dynamique à appliquer à la conception des espaces publics, qui ne peuvent survivre en tant que lieux de rencontre, de partage et de patrimoine que s'ils interceptent et créent un réseau de relations physiques-perceptives et culturelles-créatives capables de configurer de multiples lieux réels et virtuels. (06)

Dans ce système de coordonnées, l'espace public doit pouvoir interpréter des identités multiples (virtuelles et réelles) afin de correspondre au plus grand nombre d'utilisateurs et d'être conçu comme réel pour tous. Ainsi, dans un processus d'éternel retour, l'architecture doit revenir à la réflexion et à la recherche sur le foyer afin de pouvoir configurer des espaces publics : ceux qui sont communs à tous, dans lesquels chacun porte son identité individuelle et doit la déployer.

Aujourd'hui, il n'est pas possible de configurer la ville sans repenser au foyer, car ce n'est qu'à l'intérieur du foyer, conçu comme unité de vie minimale, que les gens peuvent déployer leur vie en lien physique avec les autres : membres de la famille, parents ou amis. (07)

Le foyer devient donc un lieu d'excellence pour l'expérimentation de l'architecture ; de là peuvent émerger les caractéristiques décisives capables de configurer tous les autres espaces privés et publics, qui seront de plus en plus des lieux de médiation et d'activation de pratiques sociales mixtes, virtuelles et réelles.

Christian Gasparini
NAT Office

05

La Piazza – Alberto Giacometti – City

Four men stride across a wide plaza, each moving toward the center, yet none apparently directed toward an encounter with one another. A single woman stands isolated and motionless near the center. The featureless figures exist independently within their haphazardly grouped unity, their multiple, nonconverging paths suggesting individual ambitions and absorptions.

La Piazza – Alberto Giacometti – Stadt

Vier Männer schreiten über einen breiten Platz, jeder bewegt sich auf die Mitte zu, aber keiner scheint auf eine Begegnung miteinander ausgerichtet zu sein. Eine einzelne Frau steht isoliert und bewegungslos in der Nähe des Zentrums. Die gesichtslosen Figuren existieren unabhängig voneinander in ihrer zufällig gruppierten Einheit, ihre vielfältigen, nicht konvergierenden Wege lassen individuelle Ambitionen und Absorptionen vermuten.

La Piazza - Alberto Giacometti - Ville

Quatre hommes traversent une grande place, chacun se déplaçant vers le centre, mais aucun ne semble dirigé vers une rencontre avec l'autre. Une femme seule se tient isolée et immobile près du centre. Les figures sans traits existent indépendamment dans une unité groupée de façon aléatoire, leurs chemins multiples et non convergents suggérant des ambitions et des absorptions individuelles.

La Piazza - Alberto Giacometti - Ciudad

Cuatro hombres atraviesan una amplia plaza, cada uno moviéndose hacia el centro, pero ninguno aparentemente dirigido hacia un encuentro con el otro. Una mujer soltera está aislada e inmóvil cerca del centro. Las figuras sin rasgos existen independientemente dentro de su unidad agrupada al azar, sus múltiples caminos no convergentes sugieren ambiciones y absorciones individuales.

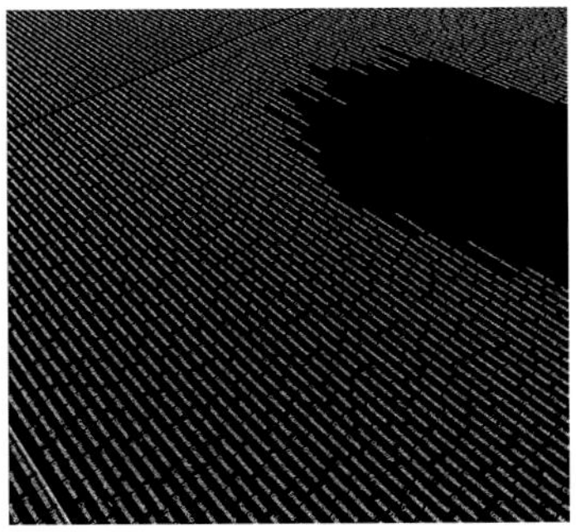

06

Names' Space. Chris Demattè
City / Houses
Der Raum der Namen
(Mauthausen 2018)
[20180206|24]

Raum der Namen. Chris Demattè
Stadt / Häuser
Der Raum der Namen
(Mauthausen 2018)
[20180206|24]

L'espace des noms - Chris Demattè
Ville / Maisons
Der Raum der Namen
(Mauthausen 2018)
[20180206|24]

El espacio de los nombres. Chris Demattè
Ciudad / Vivienda
Der Raum der Namen
(Mauthausen 2018)
[20180206|24]

MARCO: DEL ESPACIO DOMÉSTICO AL URBANO DEL TIEMPO LIBRE AL TERCER LUGAR

La arquitectura contemporánea, entendida como investigación científica y teórica, reflexiona sobre las formas en que los espacios construidos se corresponden con los lugares existentes y sus habitantes. La arquitectura no investiga sobre la imagen en sí misma (arquitectura autorreferencial), investiga sobre el espacio como generador de bienestar. Para ello, la arquitectura se centra en los conceptos de densidad, eficiencia y flexibilidad, tal y como aparecen en el libro, vinculando la ciudad y las casas.

En los proyectos seleccionados y presentados, todas o algunas de estas prioridades y conceptos emergen para establecer un marco de construcción que vincula lo espacial con lo vivencial, superponiendo principios de organización de los espacios de trabajo y de vida, configurando una especie de tercer lugar (en la definición de Ray Oldenburg, The Great Good Place), que permite a los habitantes vivir una continuidad de enfoque entre el hogar, el trabajo y el ocio. (01)

La casa se está desplazando cada vez más hacia un lugar de bienestar físico y mental que también incorpora el trabajo o la actividad productiva. Por lo tanto, los interiores se están transformando en espacios de uso variable, que con algunos pocos ajustes y cambios, se reconfiguran y modifican continuamente en relación con la vida cotidiana de cada uno.

La versatilidad permite el uso y la configuración del espacio como hogar y como oficina, mezclando las características de los respectivos usos e innovando la dinámica compositiva de los dos tipos de espacio. Esto configura espacios de densidad variable dentro de una estructura latente, capaz de preservar los principios de organización y flujos, y al mismo tiempo abiertos a diferentes usos.

El espacio de trabajo trata de recuperar algunas de las características de la casa en su informalidad y continuidad, pasando de la lógica de los espacios individuales y divididos, al espacio abierto, llegando hasta el ensamblaje en un único espacio de múltiples lugares abiertos y perceptiblemente continuos. Si los espacios puramente productivos ya establecieron esta práctica, la naturaleza del trabajo de oficina ha sido revolucionada por las tecnologías que permiten trabajar en condiciones móviles. (02)

La flexibilidad de los espacios interiores, por lo tanto, perfila la posibilidad de configurar las oficinas como agrupaciones independientes con estructuras de distribución y separación coherentes con la disposición del plano o como un único edificio capaz de diversificar los espacios de trabajo en relación con sus actividades y necesidades, transfiriéndoles una posible variabilidad tipológica: de bloque a red, de celular a placa. (03)

El lugar físico es una condición esencial para estar «en movilidad», transformando, por ejemplo, la oficina en un condensador social, cuya organización hace posible formas mejores y más ricas de colaboración e interacción. (04)

Esto, en última instancia, distingue la oficina de la casa: el mejor rendimiento posible en términos de conectividad y comunidad virtual. Además, en las oficinas hay espacios dedicados a la cultura y al ocio, muy similares a los del hogar, que pueden aumentar la implicación del empleado y promover la lealtad a la empresa.

El tiempo libre es, de hecho, el principal actor en la vida de las personas hoy en día, considerándolo como un tiempo dedicado a su identidad personal individual. El individualismo cada vez más marcado de nuestra sociedad es, de hecho, la unidad básica desde la que proceder para diseñar cualquier tipo de espacio, si se quiere que se corresponda con el «hombre interactivo» contemporáneo.

Así pues, si la Arquitectura quiere convertirse en el motor de la evolución del hombre, tiene que dirigir su mirada procedimental y compositiva al concepto de tiempo, concepto que el mundo virtual y tecnológico contemporáneo ha hecho sincopar: un tiempo instantáneo acortado, que estructura fragmentos y no secuencias, que tiene más que ver con la idea de tiempo libre que con la idea de tiempo estructurado de trabajo, porque en el fragmento encontramos formas de libertad inmediata y absoluta. (05)

Precisamente por esta razón el concepto de tiempo libre tiene mucho que ver con el concepto espacial de «tercer lugar» (Ray Oldenburg), capaz de producir una red de relaciones físico-perceptuales y cultural-creativas capaces de configurar múltiples lugares reales y virtuales.

Esta multiplicidad de espacios es la estructura latente que debe diseñarse para obtener una correspondencia real y no sólo virtual entre el hombre y el lugar físico, entre la experiencia humana (siempre más virtual y libre en términos económicos y de tiempo) y la experiencia del lugar (siempre menos física y más costosa en términos económicos y de tiempo). La arquitectura tiene que pensar en el hombre en constante movimiento y en la red, en términos perceptivos físicos reales y en términos sensoriales intelectuales virtuales.

De este nuevo concepto de arquitectura surgen nuevas dinámicas que se aplican al diseño de los espacios públicos, que sólo pueden sobrevivir como lugares de encuentro, de intercambio y de patrimonio si interceptan y crean una red de relaciones físico-perceptivas y cultural-creativas que puedan configurar múltiples lugares reales y virtuales. (06)

En este sistema de coordenadas el espacio público debe ser capaz de interpretar múltiples identidades (virtuales y reales) para corresponder al mayor número de usuarios y ser concebido como real para todos. Así pues, en un proceso de eterno retorno, la arquitectura debe volver a pensar e investigar sobre el hogar para poder configurar los espacios públicos: aquellos comunes a todos, en los que cada uno lleva su identidad individual y debe desplegarla.

Hoy en día no es posible configurar la ciudad, sin repensar la casa, porque sólo en el interior de la casa, concebida como unidad mínima de vivienda, las personas pueden desplegar su vida, en conexión física con los demás: familiares, parientes o amigos. (07)

La casa, por lo tanto, se convierte en un lugar de excelencia para la experimentación de la arquitectura y de ella pueden surgir las características decisivas capaces de configurar todos los demás espacios privados y públicos, que serán cada vez más lugares de mediación y activación de prácticas sociales mixtas virtuales y reales.

Christian Gasparini
NAT Office

07

Sculpture Atelier House
NAT Office. House

Flexibility and density related to a project for an atelier of a sculptor, that has in case be able to become an house in the future.

Skulpturen-Atelier Haus.
NAT Office. Haus

Flexibilität und Dichte im Zusammenhang mit einem Projekt für ein Atelier eines Bildhauers, das in Zukunft eventuell zu einem Haus werden kann.

Maison de l'atelier de sculpture.
NAT Office. Maison

Flexibilité et densité liées à un projet d'atelier d'un sculpteur, qui pourrait éventuellement devenir une maison dans le futur.

Casa del Taller de Esculturas
NAT Office. Vivienda

La flexibilidad y la densidad relacionadas con un proyecto para un taller de un escultor, que es capaz de convertirse en una casa en el futuro.